THE SPECIAL ONES

Chelsea By The Fans

Edited by Martin Knight and John King

LONDON BOOKS
www.london-books.co.uk

First published in Great Britain in 2006 by
LONDON BOOKS LTD
www.london-books.co.uk

ISBN 0-9551851-0-6

A catalogue record for this book is available from the British Library

Typesetting and layout by Saxon Graphics Ltd, Derby
Printed and bound by Bath Press Ltd, Bath

This book has been typeset in Helvetica Neue and Palatino

Acknowledgements

The publishers would like to thank the following people for their help in producing this book: Paul Liddiard whose idea this was and who organised the polling of the supporters; Chris Steers who collated and made sense of all the questionnaires; David Johnstone who channelled his energy and unbridled enthusiasm for the club into helping with the project; the current and former Chelsea stars who gave their time to be interviewed for the book; Tommy Baldwin for his introduction; Jose Mourinho for his blessing; Gary Bacchus, Nick Brown and Mark Meehan for putting their love of the club into words; cfcuk for the match reports and their support; Simon Greenberg for his co-operation; Pippa Hancock, Thresa Conneely and Gary Staker for their assistance in arranging interviews; Alan Delaprelle for his expert knowledge; Joe Denyer from Gate 17 for general help; and finally, and most importantly, all those Chelsea supporters whose rich, detailed and enthusiastic responses made this book possible. You are Charles Abbott, Richard Abrahams, Alan Adams, Diane Adams, Peter Adams, Big Alan From Airdrie, Carson Airdrie, Peter Alcock, Grant Alderman, Clive Aldridge, Phil Alexander, Garry Allam, David Allen, David Allen, Les Allen, Revd JF Allen, Sarah Allen, Dave Almond, Gregory Altekozalian, Kweku Amonoo-Quyst, Simon Ancell, Steen Hurup Andersen, John Anderson, Paul Anderson, Peter Anderson, Michael Andrews, Christine Angel, John Ansell, John Archer, Miguel Ariza, Daniel Armstrong, Matthew James Armstrong, Neil Armstrong, Robert Armstrong, Andy Ashman, David Ashton, Andy Atkins, Chris Atkins, David Atkins, Tony Atkinson, Cliff Auger, James Auger, John Auger, Gary Michael Austin, Paul Austin, Chris Axon, Steve Azar, FE Bailey, Greg Bailey, Ian Bailey, Mark Bailey, Paul Bailey, Steve Bailey, Barry Baillie, Chris Baker, Dean Baker, Geoff Baker, Ian Baker, Ian Baker, Paul Baker, Vince Balaam, Leigh Baldwin, Tommy Baldwin, Derek Banerji, Darren Banks, Robert Banks, Alan Barber, Andy Barham, Peter Barham, Ian Barker, Simon Barker, David Barnes, Derek D Barnes, Gary Barnes, Roger Barnes, Barnet, Mark Barnett, Richard Barnett, Kevin Barney, Michael Barnfield, Anthony John Barrett, 'Budgie' Barrett, Gary Barrett, John Barry, Paul Barry, Tommy Barwick, Martin Bastick, Steve Bateman, Jack Bates, Clifford Batt, Phil Baxter, Ray Baxter, Steven Bayliss, Paul 'Staines Blues' Beacham, Eddie Beale, Alex Beard, Joey Beard, Neil Beard, Roisin Beard, Robert Beattie, Graham Bell, Thomas Bellas, Chris Benger, Gareth Benger, Jeff Benham, Stephen Benjamin, Alan Bennett, Andy Bennett, Brian J Bennett, Paul Bennett, Stephen Bennett, Gary Benson, John Benson, Ian Bernard, John Berry, Maria Bialkowski, Ray Billinghurst, Danny Binnington, Steve Binnington, Anthony Birch, Robert Birch, Glen Bishop, Rob Bishop, Rodney Bishop, James Black, Jez Black, Graham Blackburn, Gary

Blackmun, Barry Bloomfield, Peter Blumire, Nick Board, Bob The T-Shirt, Chris Body, Robert 'Buddy' Bole, John Bollans, Robert Bond, Peter Bonetti, Elizabeth Booth, Patrick Booth, Kirk Daniel Bowden (Memorial), Paul Bowden, Bob 'Ferret' Bowie, Tom Bowtell, Bozi, Mark Bradshaw, Patrick Brew, Charlie Bridges, Alex Brister, Mick Bromley, Peter Bromley, David Brooks, John Brooks, Charlie Brooks-Watson, Mark Brothers, Marc Brothwell, Chris Brougham, Roy Browes, Alec Steven Brown, Chelsea Brown, Dave Brown, David Brown, Jack Brown, Jo Brown, Michael Brown, Nick Brown, Stephen Brown, Graham Brownett, Paul Bruce, Tony Brumwell, Stan Bryant, Andy Buchan, Bob Buckley, Dean Buckley, Gary Buckley, Andrew Bullock, Chris Burch, Steve Burge, Alan Burgess, Geoff Burgess, Geoffrey Burns, Martyn Burton, Graham Butcher, Colin Butler, Glenn Butler, John Butler, Matthew Butler, Barry Buttigieg, Arnold Bynoe, Kevin Byrne, Willie Byrne, John Caldicott, Jonny Caldicott, David Campbell, Ian Campbell, Graham Canfield, Becky Carle, Lesley Carle, Malcolm Carle, E Charles Carling, Mark Carroll, Peter Carroll, Andy Carter, Gary Carter, Ray Cartwright, Adam Carvel, James Casey, Mitzi Casey, Steve Casey, Mark Caswell, Stephen Cates, Paul WJ Challis, Jeff Chandler, Paul Chandler, Paul 'Chindog' Chandler, Christopher Chapman, S Chapman, Steve Chapman, Julian Chappell, Katherine Charlotte, Joey Steven Cheeseman, James Cherry, Gary Chivers, Richard Church, Micky Churchman, Bill Claridge, Steve Claridge, Alan 'Sniffer' Clark, Alf Clark, Dean Clark, Neil Clark, Nicholas Clark, Robert 'Nobby' Clark, Russell Clark, Andy Clarke, Daniel Clarke, Paul Clarke, Stephen Clarke, Steve Clarke, Stuart Clarke, Richard Clasby, Craig Clayton, Martin Clegg, John Clements, Mark Coden, Steven Coe, Davor Cofek, Patrick A Coffey, Andrew Coleman, Tom Coleman, Ian Coles, Gary Collett, Gary Collingwood, Ray Collins, Steve Collins, Becky Collis, Dog Collis, Lianne Collis, Paul Collis, Louise 'Blulu' Comb, Ian Comfort, Andrew Conn, Paul Connelly, Glen Connett, Michael Conway, Chris Cook, Bob Coole, Dave Cooper, David Cooper, Dean 'Deano' Cooper, Liam Corbett, Abbie Costa, Howard Cottrell, Bob Coulthard, George Courteney, Darren Cox, Graham Cox, Ian Cox, John Cox, Wayne Cox, Chuck Crampton, Daniel Crane, Ollie Crane, Peter Crane, Keith Creser, Neil 'Chalky' Croft, Sean Cross, Simon Cross, Bob Crossman, Andy Crozier, Steve Cumbers, WA Cummins, Steve Curtis, Genna Dance, Ken Dance, Scott Dance, Simon Daniel, Fat Dave (Battersea), Sam Davey, James Davidson, Michael Davidson, Glyn Davies, John Davies, Jon Davies, Keith Davies, Kevin Davies, Paul 'Nobby' Davies, Professor Alan Davies, Robert Davies, Steven Davies, Tony Davies, Daniel Davis, Peter Davis, Stephen A Davis, Mickey Dawes, Steve Dawson, Tim Dawson, David Day, Stuart Day, Michael Delaney, Alan Delaprelle, Rob Dempster, Sarah Denyer, Ian Devine, Marcus Diamond, Mark Dickson, Matt Dimock, Phil Disbrey, Stuart Disbrey, William Disbrey, David 'The Ditch' Ditchfield, Kevin Dodd, Paola Domizio, Fraser Donaldson, Dave Dong, Tony

Acknowledgements

Donovan, Simon Dover, Paul Dow, Doyley, Dennis Doyne, Paul Luca Drake, Charles Drayton, John Drewitt, Issy Droppa, Philip Duffin, Michael Francis Thomas Duke, Clive Duncan, Nigel Dungate, Trevor Dunn, Eugene Dunne, Paul Durie, Hels Durie, Alan Dyer, Gary Easy, Andy Economou, Chris Edmunds, Michael Edwards, Stephen Edwards, Mark Eke, Stuart Eke, Lee Eldridge, Paul 'Eldo' Eldridge, Lindsay Eleftheriou, Mark Ellif, Ian Elliott, Lee Elliott, Frank Elsmere, Andy English, Richard P Errington, Chris Evans, Darren Evans, Dave Evans, Davey Boy Evans, David Evans, Mark Evans, Matt Evans, Paul Evans, Richard Evans, Rob Evans, Roy Evans, David Ewbank, Abbie Ewen, Dennis A Exford, Keith Exford, Nick Exford, Mick Faraday, Rob Farley, Seamus Feeney, Andy Fellowes, Harold Fenn, Clive Fentum, Bruno Fernandez, Christianne Fernee, Dominic Fernee, Jean-Paul Fernee, Andrew Field, Mick Fields, Jay T Finan, Mike Finan, Roy Finch, Vincent Finnan, Tim The Fish, Colin Fisher, Steve Fisher, Paul Fizia, Casey Fleming, Raymond Flood, Dermot Flynn, Kate Fogarty, Mick Fogarty, Danny Ford, Eddie Ford, Janet Ford, John AG Ford, David Foster, Derek Foster, Peter Foulds, Ian Fox, Jason Fox, Paul Francis (Eastleigh), Paul Francis (Kings Lynn), John Francis, Bernie Franczak, Robin K Fraser, Fuzz Freeman, John Gerard Freeman, Ted Freestone, Val Freestone, Gary Frost, Roy Fryer, Andy Fullalove, Graham Fuller, Chelsea Galatola, Jusinda Galatola, Tony Galatola, Mel Garfield, Tim Garvey, Dave Gates, David Gauler, Julia Gauler, Nicholas Gauler, Victoria Gauler, Tony Gavin, Adi Gaylon, Steve Geraghy, Peter Gibbons, Rene Gibson, Angela Giliotti, George Gladwell, Dawn Glascodine, David Gloster, Richard Goddard, Julian Goldstraw, Gary Good, Danny Goodge, Luke Goodge, Peter Goodge, Francis Goodman, David Goodsell, Peter Goodsell, Chris Goodwin, John Goodwin, Jonathan Gordon, Steve Gorman, Grant Goudge, Angie Graham, Del Grant, Robert Grant, David Gray, Gary Gray, John 'Curly' Gray, Charlie Grech, Grace Adrianne Green, John Green, Paul Spencer-Lee Green, Phil Green, Geoff Greensmith, Andy Gregory, Steven Gregory, Colin Gribben, B Griffin, Martin Griffiths, Mervyn Griffiths, Kevin Grimshaw, Paul W Grindrod, Nico Gubbins, John Gurney, Ian Guyster, Bobby Hagley, Clive Hagley, Max Hagley, Scott Hagley, Steve Hagley, Tom Hagley, Andy Hall, Keith Hall, Alice Hamilton, Harry Hamilton, John Patrick L Hamilton, Phil Hamilton, Michael Hamlyn, Paul Hammerton, Gary Hammond, Kenneth Hammond, Terry Hanson, Keith Hardwell, Steve Hardy, Danny Harkins, Denis Harper, Paul Harper, Vaughan Harrett, Eric Harrington, Colin Harris, Mick Harris (Forest Hill), Mick Harris (Hayes), David Harris, Jeff Harris, Trevor Harris, Malcolm K Harris, Peter Harris, Steve 'Hutch' Harrison, Tony Hart, Danny Harvey, John Harvey, Ken Harvey, Scott Harvey, Simon Harvey, Matt 'Farmboy' Haste, Steve Hatfield, Hugo Hawkings, David Hawkins, Jon Hawkins, Brian Hayes, Jim Hayton, Clive Hayward, Eddie Hazlewood, Geoff Head, Nic Hearn, Tom Hearn, Clifford J Hearne, Mike Hearne, Paul Hearne, Ryan Hearne, Chris Heffernen, Thomas

Heffernen, Dave Helsby, Andy Hemingway, Harri Hemmi, David Henderson, Mark Henderson, Kevin Hennessy, James Henson, Clive Hewson, Derek Hibbert, Steve Hickmott, Peter Hicks, John Higgs, Allan 'Hilly' Hill, Stephen Hill, Tom Hills, Colin Hipkin, Brian Hipwood, Martin 'Trig' Hobson, Ron Hockings, Steve Hodder, Kevin Hodges, Andy Hogan, Clifford Hogg, Kim Holdaway, Barry Holland, David Holland, Stuart Holland, AW Holliday, Andrew Holliday, Callum Holmes, Gary Holmes, Janey Holmes, Steve Holmes, David Honey, Dave Hook, Simon Hopkins, Freddie Hopwood, Martin Horne, John Horwood, Anna Hoskin, Dave Hoskin, Jack Hoskin, James Hoskin, Kevin Houghton, Ray Houghton, Paul Howard, Peter Howard, Philip Howard, Nick Howe, Bob 'Howlsie' Howell, Iain Howells, Alec Howlett, Bob Howley, Alan Hudson, Allan Hudson, Mark Hudson, Dominic Hue, Stephen Huggins, Caroline Hughes, Colin Hughes, Keith Hughes, Richard Hughes, John Hugman, Dave 'Trigger' Hull, David Hull, Richard Humphreys, Stephen Hunt, Steve Hunt, Guy Huntington, Joe Hussey, Brian Huxtable, Freddie Huxtable, Hynsey, John Ibberson, Cliff Ince, Steve Inwood, Alexander Irani, Charlie Irani, Ken Ironside, Andy Jackson, Matthew Jackson, Tony Jackson, Daniel James, Peter James, Andy Jankiewicz, Jamie Jankiewicz, Lauren Jankiewicz, Kevin Jaye, Chris Jeeves, Matt Jeffries, Powell Jessavala, Manuel Joachim, PT Joe, Jan Johansen, Alex Johnson, Bill Johnson, Jessica Johnson, Martin Johnson, Paul Johnson, Sandy Johnson, Steve C Johnson, David Jones, Derrick Jones, Graham E Jones, Keith Jones, Kevin Jones, Matthew Jones, Peter Jones, Tony Jones, Tony Jones (PBFL), Martin Jordan, Peter Josiah, Clare Joyner, David Joyner, Howard Judd, Thomas Jukes, Chris Junior, Charlie Kane, Ken Kauder, Alex Kearney, Alan Kelly, Ray Kelly, Gary Kelt, Roy P Kemp, Russ Kemp, Russell Kemp, Michael Kennedy, Ian Kennet, James Kennet, Steve Kent, Ed Keohane, Dave Kerr, Mick Ketteridge, Terry Ketteridge, Salim Khoury, Bob Kiell, Alan Kilpatrick, Johnny Kimber, Anthony King, Danny King, James King, John King, Billy Knight, Joey Knight, Martin Knight, Richard Knight, Terry Knowles, Jonathan Kydd, Billy Lambert, Steve Land, Brian Lane, David Lane, Jerry Lane, Olly Lane, Stuart Langsbury, Nick Last, Phil Lattimore, Peter Law, Terry Law, Steve Lawrence, Paul Leahy, Alan Leary, Derek Lee, Graham Lee, Mark Lenton, Terry Leonard, Tony Leonard, Graham Lever, John Lewis, Matt 'The Bear' Lewis, Robert Lewis, Matt Lewns, Tim Liddiard, Suzanne Light, JD Lilley, Martin Lilley, Joshua Lima, Eddie Lintott, Rosie Littleboy, L Littlejohn, Elaine Lloyd, Graham Lloyd, Kevin Lloyd, Steve Lloyd, Chris Lorton, Margaret Lorton, Jack Love, Martin Love, Joe Lowe, Francis R Lucas, Keith Lucas, Kenny Lucas, Rob Lucas, Thomas W Lucas, Jim Luck, Luffy, Clive Lupton, Ian Lush, Tony David Lyden, Andrew Lyons, Tony Lyons, Chelsea Lauren Mabey, Josie-Leigh Mabey, Dave Mackay, Mick Mackay, Andrew Mackenzie, Les Maclean, Dean Magnus, Thomas Mahon, Ken Maidman, Hank Malik, Simon Malloni, Chris Mallows, Paul Mangan, John Mann, Peter Mann, Clive Mantle,

Acknowledgements

Mike Marlow, Gary Marples, Daniel Marshall, James Marshall, Tricia Marshall, John Marston, Daniel 'Neds' Martin, Eddie Martin, Linda Martin, Michael Martin, Peter Martin, Tom Martin, Bryan Mason, Bob Mason, Brett Mason, Carly Mason, Daniel Mason, George Mason, Jack Mason, John Mason, Sam Mason, Paul Masterson, Joyce Matthews, Steve Matthews, Vince Matthews, Hugh May, Timothy Mayes, Glenn 'Pasty' Maynard, Peter Maynard, Leo McArdle, Gerald McBratney, John McCarthy, Michael McCarthy, Richard McCarthy, John McCormack, Janet McCormack, Ian McCrory, Joe McCrory, Frank McGettigan, Harry McGimpsey, Peter McGimpsey, 'Brixton' Pat McGowan, NM McGregor, Jamie McHugh, Ian McKean, Willie McKee, Kath McKenzie, Neil McKinnon, Andrew Richard McKivett, William McKnight, Les McLean, Des McNamara, Charles McNicholas, Peter Mellins, Alasdair Melrose, Andrew Melrose, Barry Merchant, Kevin Merchant, Peter Merchant, Philip V Mifsud, Ron Miles, Roy Miles, Tony Millard, Warren Millard, Stephen Milledge, David Miller, Eddie Miller, Michael Miller, Tony Miller, Gary Millis, Peter Millis, Craig Mills, John Mills, Keith Mills, Andy Milton, David Miner, Malcolm Minnette, Peter Minshull, Michelle Miskelly, Karl Mitchell, Peter Mitchell, Hugh Money, Fleur Monk, Andrew Montague, David Moore, Roger Moreton, Colin Morgan, Gary Morley, Annie Morrad, Kieran Morrin, Alan Morris, Colin Morris, Paul Morris, Paul David Morris, Peter Morris, Terry Morris, Trevor Morris, Philip Morrison, Nick Morrissey, John Morton, Michael Mosquera, Eddie Mounteney, James Mulholland, Barry Mullins, David Munns, Aaron Munson, Eamonn Murphy, Paul Murphy, Jack Murray, Hazel Murray, Stephen Murray, Andy Myers-Rodwell, Brian Myring, Nikolai Nachamkin, Kev Newman, Graham D Newnham, Paul Newton, Jonny 'Blueboy' Nicholls, Billy Nichols, Daren Charles Nichols, Paul Nichols, Alastair Nicolson, Terence Noe, Rory Norris, Gabs Norton, Noel Norton, Colin Norwood, Brian Nuttgens, Les Obre, Gary O'Brien, Chris O'Connor, John O'Connor, Phil O'Connor, Des O'Flynn, Mark Olden, Jamie Lee Oman, Tony O'Neill, Tom O'Rourke, Barry Osborne, Peter Osgood, Wally Otton, Connor Packham, Keegan Packham, Neville Packham, Colin Paddon, Jason Page, John Palmer, Tommy Palmer, Jack Kyriacos Papasavva, Stephen Parker, David Parkin, Ken Parsell, Steve Parsons, Duncan Partridge, Anthony Passarella, Luke Passarella, John Passmore, Mark Payne, Andrew Pearson, Rob Penfold, Nick Penny, Andy Pentecost, Mike Percival, Carl Perkins, Brian Perroton, Clive Perry, Dave Perry, Ellie Perry, Greg C Perry, Matthew Perry, Mike Perry, Reg Perry, John Petts, Dave 'Chelsea Dave' Phair, Alan Phillips, Gary Phillips, Leon Phillips, Steve Philpot, Steve Piercy, Richard Pigden, Dean Pike, Steve Pilbeam, Jeff Pillinger, Steve Pillings, David Pink, Russell Pitt, Neil Pizzey, Dennis Pogose, Richard Polley, John Porter, Posty, Allan Potter, Keith Potter, Mark Potter, Jan Potts, Graham Poulter, Eleni Povey, Harry Povey, Colin Powell, Rob Powell, Wayne Powell, Patrick Power, Clive Poyser, Nick Poyser,

Michael Price, Thomas Price, Nicholas E Priest, Richard Priestley, Barry Prior, Jackie Prosser, Roger Prudden, Charlie Purslow, Alan 'Percy' Pusey, Bradley Puttock, Danny Puttock, Mark Puttock, Mitchell Puttock, Ricky Puttock, Martin Quantrill, Oliver Quantrill, Carol Quarrington, Graham Quick, Natasha Quick, Stuart Quigg, Martin Quinn, Peter Rand, Peter Rapaport, Joy Raymond-Barker, Robert Rea, Phil Read, Philip Read, Steven Read, Paul 'Oggi' Reader, Rachel D Redwood, Allan Reece, Richard Reed, David Rees, Nigel Rees, David Reeves, John Reeves, Ron Reeves, Brent Reid, John Reidy, Peter Reilly, Mark Reuter, Dave Reynolds, Mark Reynolds, Martin Reynolds, Peter Reynolds, Samuel Rhodes, Stanley R Rhodes, Mark Richards, Leslie Richardson, Michael Richardson, Andy Rider, Philip Riding, Jack Ridout, Jeff Riley, Simon Ringer, David Roberts, Hannah Roberts, Kevin Roberts, Nick Roberts, Nicola Roberts, Paul Roberts, Ron Roberts, Nicholas Robinson, Nick Robinson, Peter Robinson, Steve 'Stomper McBolt' Robinson, Stewart Robinson, Jose Rodriguez, Leigh Rodwell, Greg Rogers, Keith Rogers, N Rogers, Tom Roland, Fred Roll, Rolls, Charles Rose, LJ Rose, Bridget Roser, Paul Roser, David Ross, Jim Ross, Paul Rowe, Martin Ruck, Lee Ruczakiwskyj, David Russell, Ron K Russell, Roscoe Russell, Joe T Ryall, Chris Ryan, Hayley Chelsea Ryan, Mark Ryan, Martin Ryan, Andrew Rye, Nick Ryland, Michael 'Saf' Safroneo, Chris Sales, Mark Sandom, Richard Sapsford, Frank Sarath, Greig Sarath, Bryan Saturley, Nick Saunders, Tony Saunders, Derek Sawyer, Sam Sawyer, John Sayer, Andy Scarr, Richard Schaller, Mark 'Battersea CFC' Scoble, Rob Scrivens, George Scullion, Mark Sealy, Neil 'Sek' Secker, Joe Serra, Kevin Severs, Dave Seviour, Adam Seymour, Dave Seymour, Ian Seymour, David Sharp, Kevin Sharp, Ron Sharp, John Sharpe, Hadleigh Shaw, Philip Shaw, Graham Shean, Michael Sheehan, Patrick Sheehy, Ray Shepherd, Steven Shepherd, Gavin Silsby, Steve Simmonds, Colin Simmons, Mark Simmons, Ian Simpson, Mark Simpson, Rob Sims, Graeme Sindle, Gary Sirett, Brian Skinner, Andrew Smith, Brian Smith, David Smith, Gordon Smith, Ian Smith, John Smith, John E Smith, Lynn Smith, Martin Smith, Michael Smith, N Smith, Neil Smith, Nigel Smith, Pete Smith (Large), Phil Smith, Scott Smith, Stephen P Smith, Trevor Smith, Harry Soames, Dave Sorrell, S Soteriou, Paul Southey, Mark Southon, Paul Southon, Roger Spicer, David Spring, Dennis G Spring, David Springate, Steven Springate, Neil Squires, Paul Squires, Phil Stanhope, John Stapleton, Del Stead, Lacey Stead, Clint Steele, Justin Steele, James Steer, Chris Steers, Mick Steers, Ray Steers, Dave Stevens, Henry Stevens, Kirk Stevens, Renee Stevens, Robert Stevens, Mark Stevenson, James Steward, Danny Stewart, Rick Stewart, Andy Stracey, Neil Stratford, Philip Street, Roger Stringer, Michael Studd, James Sullivan, Mark Sullivan, Callum Summerfield, Leon Summerfield, Dave Suttie, Alex Syme, Caroline Sztaba, Dom Tancock, Daniel Taylor, Ian Taylor, James Taylor, John B Taylor, Mark Taylor, Neil A Taylor, Nick Taylor, Norman Arthur Taylor, Ron Taylor, Cut-Throat Tel, Charlie Tellerman, Michael Terry, Paul

Acknowledgements

Tester, Chris Thomas, Dale Thomas, Gordon Thomas, Mark Thomas, Martin 'Tommy' Thomas, David Thompson, Mark Thompson, Clive Thomson, Niall Thomson, Gary Thordarson, Bob Thorpe, Matthew Thorpe, Ollie Tiley, Chris Till, David Tobin, Pete Tohall, Mike Tomkins, Carol Tonkin, Michael Tooley, Joan Topper, Lloyd Torry, Paul Tosey, Spyros Toumba, James Tovney, Spencer Townsend, Russell 'Raving Iron' Trew, Nick Truby, Sarah Truby, Richard Tucker, Perry Tunbridge, Colin Turner, Ken 'The Cat' Turner, Paul Turner, Ben Twilley, Andrew Twyman JP, Pete Vann, Paul Varela, Dave Vickers, Geoff Vincent, Rick Vincent, Luke Vint, Peter Vint, Alan Vosper, John Wade, Steve Wakeling, Adam Walczak, Bernie Wale, David Walker, Mark Walker, Bill Wallis, Kevin Wallis, John Walsh, Michael Walsh, Martin Walters, David Ward, Nigel Warman, Thomas Warren, Nic Warwick, Richard Waterfield, Alan Waterman, Angela Watford, Chris Watford, Clive Watson, Geoff Watson, Linda Watson, Tom Watson, Peter Watson, Richard Watson, Mark Wattam, Billy Watts, Lee Watts, Neil Watts, Paul Watts, Rob Way, Alan Wayman, Ashley Webb, Gary Webb, Luke Webb, Michael Webb, Pete Webb, Sam Webb, Pete Webster, Robert Webster, Tom Weedon, Peter Welby, Andy Welford, Anthony D Wells, Arthur Wells, Mark Wells, Matthew Wells, Wend Of CFC, Stephen West, Terence West, Alan Westbrook, Dave Westbrook, Sarah Westbrook, Ray Wheals, Mr E Wheeler, Mark Wheeler, Phil Wheeler, Steve Wheeler, Martin Whiffin, Alicia Whitby, Darren White, David White, Martin White, Simon White, Steve 'Chelsea' White, Gary Whitehead, Mark Whittemore, Sean Wickens, Eric Gordon Wicks, Neil Wicks, Stuart Wicks, Bill Wiles, Michael Wilkinson, Alan Williams (London), Alan Williams (Norfolk), Barrie Williams, David Williams, Graham Williams, James Paul Williams, John Williams, Martyn Williams, Paul Williams, Steve Williams, Neil Willoughby, Paul Vernon Wills, Dave Wilson, Gary Wilson, John Wilson, Ian Windass, George Windsor, Kevin Winter, John Wise, Tim Withey, Peter Wonacott, Andrew Wood, Chris Wood, Simon Wood, Stephen Wood, Jack Woodhouse, Sam Woodhouse, James Woods, Ian Woolley, John Woolley, Adrian John Wooton, John Wrench, Johnny Wright, David Wright, Louis Wright, Paul Wright, Paul Wright, Peter Wright, John Wyatt, Mark Wyeth, Nik Yeomans.

Contents

THE CHELSEA DREAM TEAM

Manager: Gianluca Vialli
Goalkeeper: Peter Bonetti
Right back: Ron Harris
Centre half: John Terry
Centre half: Marcel Desailly
Left back: Eddie McCreadie
Right wing: Charlie Cooke
Midfield: Frank Lampard
Midfield: Alan Hudson
Left wing/midfield: Dennis Wise/
   Damien Duff
Forward: Peter Osgood
Forward: Gianfranco Zola

MOST MEMORABLE GAME

1. Liverpool in the FA Cup, 1996-97 –
   2-0 down, won 4-2
2. The 1970 FA Cup final replay vs Leeds
   at Old Trafford
3. FA Cup final vs Middlesbrough, 1997
4. Champions League quarter-final first
   leg vs Barcelona in 1999-2000 –
   won 3-1
5. The 5-0 win at home to Manchester
   United in 1999-2000
6. Bolton at home, 1978-79, 3-0 down
   with fifteen minutes left – won 4-3
7. The 1998 Cup Winners Cup final
   victory vs Stuttgart in Stockholm
8. Cup Winners Cup semi-final second
   leg vs Vicenza, 1997-98 – won 3-1
9. Cup Winners Cup vs Bruges in 1971 –
   won 4-0 after losing the first leg 2-0
10= Beating Bolton 1-0 to prevent
   relegation to Division Three in the
   1982-83 season
10= Cup Winners Cup final replay vs Real
   Madrid in Athens, 1971

MOST MEMORABLE GOAL

1. Roberto Di Matteo versus
   Middlesbrough in the 1997 FA Cup
   final
2. Peter Osgood vs Leeds United in the
   1970 FA Cup final replay
3. Zola's flick vs Norwich in the FA Cup,
   2001-02
4. Zola vs Stuttgart in the 1998 European
   Cup Winners Cup final in Stockholm
5. Zola vs Wimbledon in the 1996-97 FA
   Cup semi-final at Highbury

6. David Webb's header vs Leeds in the
   1970 FA Cup final replay
7. John Spencer vs Austria Memphis in
   the 1994-95 Cup Winners Cup
8. Mark Hughes vs Vicenza in the 1997-
   98 Cup Winners Cup semi-final
   second leg
9. Gustavo Poyet's scissors kick vs
   Sunderland in 1999-2000
10. Clive Walker vs Bolton in 1982-83, to
   keep Chelsea in the Second Division

WORST MEMORY

1. The 4-0 FA Cup final defeat by
   Manchester United, in 1994
2. Relegation in 1987-88, after the play-
   off vs Middlesbrough
3. FA Cup final defeat by Spurs, 1967
4. The 1974-75 relegation, after losing to
   Spurs
5. FA Cup final defeat by Arsenal, 2002
6. Nearly being relegated to Division
   Three, in 1982-83
7. All losses to Arsenal
8. The 1984-85 League Cup semi-final
   second-leg defeat by Sunderland
9. Kanu's hat-trick in the 1999-2000, 3-2
   home defeat to Arsenal
10. The death of Matthew Harding

FAVOURITE SONG

1. Carefree
2. Ten Men Went To Mow
3. Blue Is The Colour
4. Blue Flag
5. Celery
6. His Name Is Tommy Baldwin
7. Blue Day
8. We Will (All) Follow The Chelsea
9. Osgood, Osgood, Born Is The King Of
   Stamford Bridge
10= The Famous Tottenham Hotspur Went
   To Rome To See The Pope
10= Liquidator, Harry J & The All-Stars

BIGGEST RIVALS

1. Arsenal
2. Tottenham
3. Manchester United
4. Leeds United
5. West Ham
6. Fulham

Foreword

The Special Ones grew from a form which asked Chelsea supporters to choose their Dream Team – the eleven players they would most like to see in the same side, irrespective of the era in which they appeared for the club. This questionnaire also included sections headed Most Memorable Game, Most Memorable Goal, Worst Memory, Favourite Song and Biggest Rivals, and what started as a simple Dream Team exercise quickly turned into an outpouring of pent-up feelings and memories from the fans, many of whom appear unable or unwilling to attend games and, in a significant amount of cases, although thrilled with the current success on the pitch, feel disenfranchised from the club they love. We could have filled a book twice this size if we had included everyone's comments and we are sorry if your words did not find their way on to the coming pages. We did our best.

In an effort to reach as broad a sample as possible the forms were mailed to the members of the Chelsea Pitch Owners Club. The aim was to reach, among others, those who are now geographically, physically and financially separated from the club. Conscious that this may have skewed the results in favour of older voters we are indebted to the cfcuk stall opposite Fulham Broadway station which distributed thousands of forms, as well as the people who handed them out around the ground. We sincerely believe we reached a representative cross-section of genuine Chelsea supporters.

However, such a poll can only ever be a snapshot of sentiment at a particular time, and will always be coloured by the freshest memories. If the poll had been taken ten years earlier it is likely that the results would have been quite different. It is an inescapable fact that each year there are less and less people around who watched Vic Woodley between the sticks, or saw Roy Bentley power the team to the 1955 First Division championship. Having said that, the detailed replies and letters received from our senior citizens were among the most evocative, and brought to life some of the names and events from the first half of the last century in a powerful and thought-provoking way.

The voting itself took place in the year leading up to Chelsea winning the league for the second time in the club's history, but the completed forms reflected many decades of achievement. The passing of time allows for measured reflection, and reading and absorbing your comments was a rich and rewarding experience and confirmed the qualities of the average Chelsea fan. In no particular order they appear to be humour, self-deprecation, long memories, a love of individualism and flair, a seething hatred of just a handful of rivals, but an appreciation of the good things in most other teams and clubs and, finally, loyalty.

This last quality was underlined when we invited fans to nominate their worst manager and player. We were surprised by just how many refused to answer this question and replied in uncompromising tone with a simple 'don't agree with this category' or 'they all tried their best'. Considering there could not have been any collusion, the similarity of the responses was both uncanny and touching. For those who are interested, Winston Bogarde won this category as a player, and we don't feel we will offend too many by revealing this fact. Managerially Geoff Hurst (now Sir Geoff) seems to have ruffled not just the players' feathers. John Drewitt spoke for many when he commented: 'Hurst and Gould – the dream ticket. Pathetic. We would have been better off with Morecambe and Wise.'

No fewer than twenty-three respondents sent in Dream Teams that included players such as Bobby Moore, George Best, Paul Gascoigne, Stanley Matthews and so on. They had elected to tell us the names of players they would have liked to have played for Chelsea, regardless of whether they did or not. Others became so carried away telling us about their memories, and best and worst moments following Chelsea, that they forgot to actually fill out their Dream Team nominations altogether.

A few fans used the poll to air ancient grievances. Peter Carroll is still fuming thirty-five years later about being two vouchers short for a 1970 FA Cup final ticket and he sent us the relevant correspondence for our perusal. And another supporter with a long memory was Chris Sales, who nominated as his worst player a poor chap called Mike Pinner who deputised for Peter Bonetti just a few times in the early 1960s, saying 'he had a problem with crosses'. The prize for understatement, though, could go to a Mr Rolls who wrote that 'Robert Fleck was disappointing'.

We asked you to tell us who you considered to be our biggest rivals, or put another way, which team do you hate the most. The results surprised us: Arsenal pipped Tottenham in the venom vote, with Manchester United, Leeds and West Ham comprising the remainder of the top five. This category unleashed an outpouring of emotion like no other. Scores of people listed The Scum. They know who they mean, but we cannot be sure. Mr Paul Hearne decided that Chester were our biggest rivals. We can only trace having played them once. Arsenal were variously referred to as Arsesmell, Arse, Arsescum, Arsenala and Dirty Cheating Arsenal. John Drayton said: 'I cannot fill this in, I am too angry'. Tom Weedon, perhaps worryingly, said 'everyone'.

We are grateful to the current and ex-players who gave their time to recount their memories and answer our questions. Only Marcel Desailly showed a lack of enthusiasm. He agreed on two occasions to be interviewed, at specific times, but then went missing. The rest of the Dream Team were a pleasure to interview and we are especially grateful to Alan Hudson who helped us set up several interviews, and who during a meal on the Kings Road and a drink in the World's End pub was his normal eloquent and amusing self. Peter Osgood provided more good value in one of his watering holes in Hampshire, and has also been very supportive of the book.

We are indebted to Charlie Cooke, who gave up so much of his limited time on a fleeting visit to England and submitted himself to an afternoon of verbal probing from two strangers, while Gianfranco Zola was, as always, charming and humble – a true gentleman. John Terry, Frank Lampard and Damien Duff all managed to find time in their hectic playing schedules. Dennis Wise was a victim of his own versatility, with more votes than many of the other players who qualified for the team, but with these evenly distributed between midfield and the right wing. It would have be unfair not to have included him, so he is interchangeable in those positions.

Ron Harris and Peter Bonetti provided fresh insights into the game both then and now, and were genuinely humbled to have received your votes in the face of such tough competition. Eddie McCreadie, loved as both a Chelsea player and manager, was a coup in many ways, talking after many years of silence from his home in America. Finally, the Dream Team manager Gianluca Vialli floored us with his hospitality and honesty, and along with Eddie is someone who is loved as both a Chelsea player and a Chelsea boss. He remains the most successful manager in the history of the club, and his desire to become a Chelsea legend when he first arrived at Stamford Bridge has been confirmed by all of those who voted for him. Thanks Luca.

To borrow from footballer's parlance, at the end of the day this book belongs to you – the fans. It is based on your choices and your memories. Thank you for writing The Special Ones.

Martin Knight and John King, London, 2006

Chelsea old boys lend Chelsea youth a hand

The Famous CFC

Of all the categories listed it was that of earliest memory which provoked the most detailed and informative replies, with just as many people citing atmosphere and other miscellaneous details as there were those who listed particular games, goals or players as their first lasting impression.

Nobby Davies attended his first game against Wolverhampton Wanderers in 1968 and it is the smell of hot dogs, Juicy Fruit chewing gum and peanuts in their shells sold by vendors around the running track that remains with him. This is a common theme. Tom Watson says his first memory is of just standing in The Shed, no cover, miles away from the pitch and what little view he had being obscured by a parade of three-wheel cars. Many fans recall being lifted as boys and girls and passed down the crowd in The Shed to better viewing positions nearer the front, or being hitched onto adult shoulders or standing on boxes. The atmosphere in The Shed, it seems, did as much to capture the heart of the young football fan as anything that was happening out there on the pitch. From what you say, most of you could not see much anyway.

John Wise sums up the emotions of a ten-year-old boy circa 1971: 'It was like stepping into a benign tidal wave as soon as you burst out of Fulham Broadway station into the dazzling sunlight. You were lifted from the ground by the force of the crowd and carried all the way to The Shed turnstiles. Once inside you could hear the thunder of the fans clapping and stamping and you clambered up those concrete steps barely able to contain your excitement and forced your spindly little body into the legs of the bigger boys and disappeared into the darkness of The Shed. From our ground level vantage point we had entered a world of shiny Dr Marten boots, turned-up Levis and squashed Kia-Ora orange cartons. You wanted to find the middle, the very vortex of The Shed, but you never did. You floated around in this pond of humanity for two glorious hours, each rendition of Knees Up Mother Brown pushing you six feet forward, but somehow you never ended up at the front, and you never saw daylight. Wonderful.'

Literally hundreds of respondents echoed the feelings of Mr Wise and the period of 1967-72 seems to have been a particularly fertile time for converting new Chelsea supporters. Because this period of great success on the field coincided with the first coming of the skinhead youth cult – to many of you the two things are inseparable. Bill Johnson remembers The Shed in full song with thousands of shaved heads bobbing up and down as one; John Drewett recalls ranks of skinheads clapping in urgent unison to Liquidator, by Harry J & The All-Stars, as it was played through the tinny loudspeakers; Barry Hogan was amazed that everybody seemed to have a different colour Fred

17

Perry, Ben Sherman or Brutus shirt; Tony White was disappointed to discover that the fabled Mick Greenaway was a skinhead by nature and not by choice. David Gloster remembers being taken in The Shed by his local hardnut Basher Briggs, and then seeing Bashers everywhere. Willie Byrne tells of that special feeling walking down the Fulham Road – he says he can't describe it adequately, but we know what he means. We certainly do.

Many fans recall being squeezed through turnstiles as children and many attest to not being charged and therefore counted. It seems that the turnstile operators were often local men who believed in helping their community in any way they could and this practice was far more widespread than previously believed. As many suspected, those official crowd figures we read the next day in the Sunday papers were probably at least a few thousand under the real number.

Graham Bell is one of several supporters who remembers with childhood glee the floodlights going out in an evening game against Preston North End. For Tom Coleman it was Terry Venables looking over his shoulder and winking at him when he was taking a throw-in that cemented his relationship with the club. A surprising amount of supporters, including Nick Robinson and Phil Alexander, seem to have been mentally scarred by the treatment dished out by a young Ron Harris to the veteran footballing treasure that was Stanley Matthews on his final visit to London with Stoke City.

Stephen Wood and others were attached to the words 'Chelsea Football Club' whitewashed on the corrugated iron of the old East Stand, and more than twenty correspondents made reference to the small cafe by Fulham Broadway station where they ate their fry-ups before kick-off. Tony Matthews can remember the players joining the fans inside on more than one occasion.

First memories are often very personal. Neil Wicks, for example, was a mascot against Southampton in the early 1980s. Brian Nuttgens and John Stapleton were small boys in the mid-Fifties when they were passed overhead all the way down the terrace and then placed kindly on the dog-track to view the game. For Andrew Twyman, JP, it is his (presumably unsuccessful) trial at the club. Eleni Povey remembers falling in love with Peter Bonetti while Richard Waterfield was slightly disconcerted by David Webb's distinctive features staring out at him from a picture card. Paul Varela delighted in entering The Shed and being passed celery to brandish. Nick Board's debut was watching Chelsea versus Peterborough reserves in 1968, which was hardly a scintillating fixture, but he had gone to see Peter Houseman, specifically because Peter's brother had recently married his auntie.

Another unlikely game that imprinted itself on a supporter's memory was Ken Shellito's testimonial. Chris Edmunds was there and he records the surreal substitution of Alan Birchenall for Jimmy Tarbuck. James Henson revives the excitement of reaching the heights of rebellion by throwing half-eaten hot dogs at Preston players from the West Stand benches when they were taking throw-ins in the 1968-69 season.

Our earliest earliest-memory is probably from E Wheeler, who recalls his first visit to Stamford Bridge in 1928, nearly eighty years ago. Chelsea were in Division Two at the time, knocking on the door of Division One and attracting crowds of 40,000 plus. AW Holliday is one of two correspondents who inform us they were present at the match against Arsenal in 1935, a fixture which attracted Chelsea's highest ever attendance, as 82,905 fans crushed into the ground – a figure that is unlikely to ever be exceeded as long as the club remains on its present site.

Hugh Money evokes the occasion: 'Arsenal were legendary and although there was no TV then we knew all their players from the Saturday morning pictures and our football cards. Their full backs were George Male and Eddie Hapgood, who were also in the England defence, and the forward line of Alex James, Cliff Bastin and Ted Drake was mouth-watering. My father took me and he was openly supporting Arsenal as were nearly 50,000 others. Remember, our average gate at the time was about 30,000. It was 1-1 and not really a great game although to be honest I never saw much such was the crowd. I remember it seemed to take hours afterwards queuing up for a train from Walham Green Underground.'

It is the Second World War, though, that provides a substantial bank of common memories. Eddie Miller offers one of the most evocative of these when he writes about the crowd standing on the Stamford Bridge terraces in 1941 and averting their eyes from the game to watch a British fighter pilot above shoot up a Luftwaffe plane. One can only imagine the applause when the German bomber careered downwards. Perhaps this is why Bomber Harris is such a favourite with modern-day Chelsea fans?

Gordon Smith was lucky enough to be taken to Loftus Road for his first game and witness Chelsea stuff Queens Park Rangers 11-2 in a war-time match. Joe Payne, he remembers, scored four of the goals. Payne is recalled with affection by many of this generation and he entered football's record books when he scored an incredible ten goals for Luton Town in a league match. At Kenilworth Road a lounge is named in his memory.

It is another war-time game that prompts John E Smith's first recollection. Chelsea beat Reading 2-0 and it was so foggy that only one of the goals was visible. A local boy who had designs on nine-year-old John's sister said he would take him to the game only if he could persuade his sister to come along as well. She did, and John began a sixty-year love affair with the club, but does not elaborate on how his sister's relationship developed, if at all.

We can only wonder how many of the 74,496 fans who filed into the Bridge to witness the historical friendly with Moscow Dynamo on November 13th, 1945, are still watching Chelsea. Well, Alan Leary, Gerald McBratney, Joyce Matthews and Ron Miles were among them, while Peter Mills saw the game from the roof of the old East Stand. Poor Ron Reeves was one of the many locked out. This match was chosen by supporters in both the most memorable game and earliest memory categories. The final score was 3-3, with Chelsea's goals coming from Reg Williams, Len Goulden and the legendary Tommy Lawton. Many of those fans would have travelled to Wembley seven months earlier to see Chelsea defeat Millwall in the Wartime Football League South final, and this now barely-remembered match was for older fans, at the time, the first Cup that their team had brought home in living memory.

Stanley Rhodes was hooked when he filed through the turnstiles for the first time on April 5th, 1947, to see Chelsea bamboozle Derby County in a 3-0 win. The Chelsea fans gave warm applause to old boy Vic Woodley, now keeping goal for the Rams, but had no qualms about Tommy Lawton putting two past him and Len Goulden the other. Also in the team that afternoon were Harry Medhurst in goal and Dickie Spence, both who would continue to serve the club long after their playing days were over.

In the 1949-50 season Chelsea enjoyed an FA Cup run that ended in semi-final defeat by Arsenal at White Hart Lane (what a combination) after a replay. Several respondents refer to Roy Bentley giving us a two-goal lead in the first match, only for two fluke Arsenal goals to earn them the replay, a game Arsenal finally won after extra time.

Remarkably, it was a goal scored by Roy Bentley in the sixth-round victory over Manchester United at the Bridge that has stuck in people's minds to such an extent that it nearly made the top ten goals of all time. This is one goal that has really stood the test of time. George Mason describes it: 'Billy Gray deftly back-heeled a ball into the path of Bentley who smashed it from the corner of the penalty area into the back of the net. Jack Crompton, the United keeper, gave up before it left Roy's boot. If only we had TV replays then.'

Understandably, many fans were introduced to the club during the 1950s, the only decade in the 20th century when Chelsea managed to win a league championship. The decade did not start so well, as Gordon Smith remembers. His debut at Stamford Bridge saw Chelsea trounce Bolton 4-0 and therefore avoid relegation from the First Division by 0.44 of a goal. Roy Bentley, Bobby Smith, Ken Armstrong and Bobby Campbell were now all in the side. Things could only get better thought the fans, and slowly but surely they did. It didn't help that at the other end of the table, as champions, Tottenham Hotspur were delighting the country with their fresh push-and-run style of football.

In 1951-52 Chelsea avoided relegation again, finishing 19th, but this time having the cushion of a handful of points. The next season the team fared only slightly better. Few fans have volunteered recollections from these seasons, but in 1953-54 things start to take off. The team finished eighth and centre-forward Roy Bentley was hitting his prime, bagging twenty-one goals.

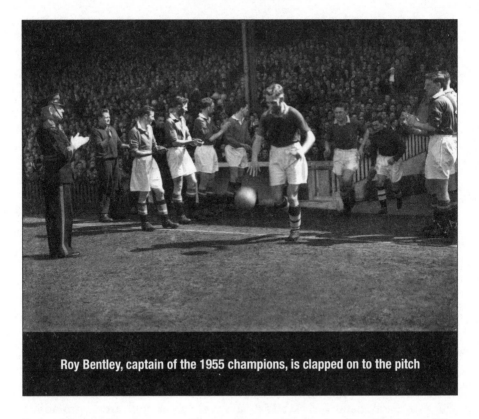

Roy Bentley, captain of the 1955 champions, is clapped on to the pitch

From this era, Bentley more than any other, dominates the affections of the supporters. Other accomplished players, such as Ron Greenwood, Eric Parsons, Frank Blunstone, Peter Sillett and Ken Armstrong, had now established themselves in the team, but most importantly, perhaps, was the fact that Ted Drake had succeeded Billy Birrell as manager.

Ted was a legendary centre-forward with Herbert Chapman's all-conquering Arsenal team of the 1930s and it is possible that a full realisation of his impact on Chelsea's fortunes and history has been lost in the sands of time. Even so, he was still voted sixth best Chelsea manager ever. Supporter John E Smith pays him fitting tribute when he says: 'I place Ted Drake as best manager for changing national perceptions of our club from the old pensioners, who were the butt of music hall jokes, to champions and being taken seriously.'

The historic 1954-55 season therefore provides many first and best memories. FE Bailey is one of many who rated Peter Sillett's penalty against Wolves on April 9th, 1955, as his favourite ever goal. It was almost certainly the goal that won us the championship, he says. Peter McGimpsey treasures being a mascot during that season, as did a certain Michael Greenaway, then a Chelsea-mad kid from nearby Billing Street. Sadly Mick is no longer around to tell us his stories about that season and whether, on a cold afternoon in 1955 when he toddled on to the Stamford Bridge turf, he first felt the urge to release a throaty Zigger Zagger.

Professor Alan Davies recalls seeing Billy Wright and his all-conquering Wolves team in that championship-winning season not because the match was particularly exciting, but because he won a ticket for the FA Cup final in the half-time lucky number programme draw. Of that championship-winning team, an incredible half a century on, Peter Sillett, Roy Bentley, John Harris, Ken Armstrong, Eric Parsons and Frank Blunstone all received votes in our poll.

Sadly, the championship form could not be maintained and in the following two seasons Chelsea finished in the bottom half of the table. We even elected not to compete in a new competition known as the European Cup. Who would pay for all that foreign travel? We have to wait until the beginning of the 1957-58 season to see the imagination of the fans stirred once more, and that was due to the emergence of Jimmy Greaves. His stay was short but extremely sweet, and his impact was such that he is a runner-up for one of the forward positions in our team of all-time Chelsea greats.

Eddie Martyn rates Greavsie's goal on his debut away to Spurs in 1957 as his best ever Chelsea goal. In the Spurs side that day was Tommy Harmer, who a few years later had a brief stint with Chelsea. Despite only nine appearances in a blue shirt he did enough to endear himself to many fans. Michael Terry treasures the only goal Tommy scored for Chelsea as it gave us a 1-0 win over Sunderland at Roker Park and was crucial in securing promotion back to the First Division in 1962-63. Tommy bundled the ball over the line with his torso and the next day the papers dubbed him Tummy Harmer.

Back to Greaves. Perhaps his Chelsea peak was when he scored five goals in the 6-2 home demolition of Wolves in 1958. Many of our contributors cite this game as either their best-ever match or their first memory. This was Wolves, the best team in the country at the time, and Chelsea fans must have believed that a corner had been turned. Greatness surely beckoned. Alas, the very next Saturday they trotted out at White Hart Lane and lost 4-0. Oh to be a Chelsea fan.

Jimmy stayed at the Bridge for four seasons before being lured by lira to foreign parts. Allan Potter and others remember his final game in 1961 against Nottingham Forest. Chelsea won 4-3 and Jimmy bagged each one of our goals and could have scored three more. It was an emotional day for the fans as they knew they were saying goodbye to a man they felt could have become their greatest ever goal scorer if he had stayed. They swarmed on to the pitch and lifted him aloft and chaired him to the tunnel. They would see Jimmy Greaves again, of course, but he would be a Spurs man then, and they would be worrying about his lethal poaching ability rather than celebrating his goals.

Following the departure of Jimmy Greaves and a relegation to Division Two, Ted Drake was sacked from the club he had revitalised and for which he had delivered a league championship. A young, fiery Scot called Tommy Docherty took over and the age of Docherty's Diamonds was upon us.

Richard Humphreys saw a photograph of that 1962-63 squad and found them aesthetically pleasing. He told his grandfather that he had decided to support Chelsea and the more experienced man warned he would never be happy if he did. On the other side of London, in the East End, just a few seasons later, young Grant Goudge was similarly being seduced by this exciting Chelsea side, and walked into Bobby Moore's shop and attempted to buy a Chelsea kit. The looks of astonishment from the shop staff remain with him to this day.

A number of supporters refer to a virtuoso performance by Bobby Tambling in 1966 when he put five goals past Colin Withers in the Aston Villa goal at Villa Park. Some of you were there, while others saw it on the television, remembering it as one of the earliest instances of Chelsea appearing on TV. George Scullion points out that not only did Bobby score five, but he also went off in the 66th minute.

Several specific goals are recalled from this era, some only surviving in the ether of combined memory. Peter Osgood's solo effort and superb finish against Adam Blacklaw of Burnley seems to be the favourite – as Charlie Brooks-Watson remembers, even the Burnley fans clapped. Eddie McCreadie's amazing goal in the victorious League Cup final against Leicester City, recalled by Eddie himself in this book, is still etched on many memories other than his own, and probably that of Gordon Banks as well. Another strike from Bobby Tambling at Anfield, when Chelsea knocked Liverpool out of the FA Cup, is also fondly remembered. Bobby scored many goals for the club and, of course, remains our top ever scorer, and is mentioned time and time again. Gary Millis' earliest memory is of seeing Bobby Tambling with '200 on the back of his shirt'.

Steve Pilbeam summed up Docherty's Diamonds this way: 'That mid-Sixties Chelsea side could have been explosive, but for all sorts of reasons they were broken up before they got in their stride and that was sad. Fans would have been a lot more upset about that if the 1970s glory hadn't come along to make them forget about it. Docherty was at his peak as a manager and the likes of Peter Bonetti, Ken Shellito, Terry Venables, Bobby Tambling, Barry Bridges and a young hick from the sticks called Osgood were a solid nucleus of a championship-winning side.'

Tommy Docherty and Chelsea Football Club parted company in 1967 and Dave Sexton took over as manager. Dave's reserved and methodical personality contrasted greatly with the flamboyant Scotsman, but perhaps The Doc had left some of his spirit in the Fulham Road air because Sexton's Chelsea soon acquired the reputation of a flair-based, cosmopolitan and hard-living side. Quite where urban myth and reality merge nobody can be sure, but the Chelsea team of the late 1960s and early 1970s are remembered as much for their style and extra-curricular activities as for their very substantial achievements on the field.

Such is the well of affection for this era that half of the Dream Team are drawn from the side. Peter Bonetti, Ron Harris, Eddie McCreadie, Alan Hudson, Charlie Cooke and Peter Osgood all feature, and each one of these players provides varying memories for our correspondents.

Charlie Tellerman delighted in seeing Chopper Harris kicking George Best up in the air on his visits to the Bridge. Peter Bonetti saving an Alan Ball penalty in an Everton draw in 1969 enthuses Bernie Franczak, while Steve Holmes spent hours following Peter Osgood around his home town of Windsor, but could not pluck up the courage to approach him and ask for his autograph.

Bryan Mason remembers being saddened by the way the crowd sometimes barracked Peter Houseman and dubbed him 'Mary'. When ten-year-old Joe Hussey asked his father why he was called Mary, the diplomatic reply was that it was cockney rhyming slang for 'Scary'. John Hollins is another player from this era regularly mentioned, and his stunning goal against Arsenal in 1971 has been chosen by several people as their favourite ever.

Many supporters regard the FA Cup final defeat to Spurs as their worst Chelsea memory, but three years later Chelsea's fortunes changed and, predictably, the 1970 FA Cup campaign and victory, and 1971 European Cup Winners Cup triumph in Athens, provide many of your earliest and best memories. A surprising number of former children recount playing afternoon truant from school to attend the Watford FA Cup semi-final in 1970 and more still relish the moment when Ossie hung in the goal net after scoring like a 'delirious monkey'.

The FA Cup final replay against Leeds at Old Trafford in 1970 was a watershed in Chelsea's history. More people mention that their earliest memory was watching the match on TV and being converted to the Chelsea cause than any other specific event. The foundation of today's supporter base was laid down that muddy evening in Manchester, and to underline this a recent national survey of the biggest TV audiences ever had this match in the Top Ten along with the 1969 moon landing, the 1981 Royal Wedding, the 1966 World Cup final and Princess Diana's funeral. No other FA Cup final caught the public imagination in such a way, either before or since. It is no surprise then that the two goals Chelsea scored at Old Trafford – Ossie's equaliser and David Webb's winner – are listed in our top-ten favourites. The match itself remains the second most loved single game in the minds of the supporters until this day.

Although Ian Hutchinson did not make the Dream Team, he figures in the collective Chelsea memory. His bottle, extreme courage and incredible throw-ins have left a lasting mark on many. David Gray votes his comeback game

Bobby Tambling scores against Aston Villa and plants himself in the net of collective Chelsea memory

against Norwich after nearly two years out with injury as his most emotional Chelsea moment. Hutch managed to score twice and the ovation from the crowd was overwhelming. Rob Scrivens says that picking up the paper a few years back and reading of his premature death is his all-time worst Chelsea moment: 'He had an aura of vulnerability yet he was totally committed to Ossie and the others. You never saw much of him after he retired, and I just wonder if he knew how much he meant to us all.'

A number of supporters list Ian's death as their worst Chelsea moment. Others feel the same way about Peter Houseman's tragic car accident and Matthew Harding's demise in a helicopter crash. All three are fondly remembered.

The eventual defeat of Real Madrid in the European Cup Winners Cup final replay is a durable favourite, but many fans treasure memories of the whole experience as much as the actual games. Some of them regard the trip to Athens and the enforced extension of their time in Greece as an experience of Dunkirk proportions. They remember sleeping in doorways and on streets and beaches, going hungry, surviving three days without a penny to their names and not being able to wash and clean their teeth. This, it seems, is the Chelsea fan's idea of a great time. Fat Dave from Battersea says it was the longest he ever went without eating. Johnny Wright says that on his return he had lost his job in Burton's The Tailor and his girlfriend had gone off with his best friend. This is his best Chelsea memory.

The glory years were relatively short-lived and within a couple of seasons of the Cup Winners Cup triumph Chelsea had entered a period of decline. Over the next decade and a half the team were relegated to the Second Division three times, narrowly escaped the drop into the old Third Division, teetered on the edge of financial ruin, witnessed a succession of managers and struggled with a particularly active hooligan element. Conversely, there is no shortage of fans who regard this era as the golden one. 'Cold, damp, dark and dismal Saturday afternoons at a half-empty Stamford Bridge in the early 1980s. Hooked for ever,' muses Mark Reuter.

Steven Davies' first memory is leaving the ground in 1982 after an ignominious 4-1 home defeat to Rotherham United (who had already stuffed Chelsea 6-0 at their place) and a man ruffling his hair and saying 'don't worry son, one day your dad will take you to a proper match'. Vince Matthews relays how the disillusionment with the team was so intense at one point that when a particular full-back had possession of the ball the home crowd burst into The Laughing Policeman song, and then wondered why he wasn't playing well. Different fans pinpoint particular incidents as the beginning of the decline. The League Cup final defeat to Stoke City, the FA Cup loss at lowly Orient and the departure of Peter Osgood and Alan Hudson to Southampton and Stoke City respectively are the perceived pivotal moments.

The dark days on the field coincided with trouble on the terraces up and down the country. The Chelsea fans took pride in the paradoxical situation whereby the worse the team fared the more loyal, vocal and mobile the travelling support became. For a decade or more, with the exception of Manchester United, no other team took more fans away. Often, trouble was not far behind. John Benson tells us his proudest memory as a Chelsea fan was making the Wolverhampton promotion game in 1977, when the Government had attempted to stop Chelsea supporters from travelling. He is fifty-one years old and still owns his You Can't Ban A Chelsea Fan badge. Many others cite the taking of away ends and town centre chases as their best memories.

Glenn 'Patsy' Maynard remarks: 'I now have an eleven-year-old son. He will probably never experience the likes of being chased through the back alleys at Everton, or being confronted by a six-foot, seven-inch chain-wielding madman at Sunderland, and I hope he never does. That was a different era, not necessarily good, but nevertheless it happened and I was glad to be part of those times. Up the Blues.'

The Spurs game at White Hart Lane, when Chelsea were relegated in 1975, is a common theme and along with the 1967 FA Cup final defeat appears to be a key factor in the Chelsea fans' pathological hatred of our North London neighbours. The 1975 match in particular still rankles.

Mark Scoble's christening at Chelsea included being chased at twelve years old around the perimeter of the Stamford Bridge pitch by rabid Newcastle fans with funny voices. The League Cup semi-finals against Sunderland in 1985 prompted over twenty of our correspondents to name the trouble at one or both of these games as their worst Chelsea memory. It has to be said that an equal number thought they were the best of times. But the hooliganism did leave scars, and not all of them mental, on some of our followers. Neil Secker tells of how he was slashed at a game against Walsall, by a Chelsea fan: 'Twenty-six stitches, not nice, ruined my looks but a long time ago now and I still love the Blues.'

There was one vintage year during these dark days, and for the long-suffering fans of the time it is fondly remembered. The 1976-77 season saw the club in serious financial trouble, manager Eddie McCreadie cobbling together a side that included ten, and sometimes eleven, home-grown players. Save The Bridge buckets were rattled outside The Shed, while further collections were held on the trains travelling away. The bond between the supporters and the club has never been stronger.

Peter Bonetti and Ron Harris were still turning out, and David Hay had been bought from Celtic, but the rest of the team consisted of youngsters. Led by Ray Wilkins, Chelsea turned on the style and huge crowds flocked to Stamford Bridge. Wilkins was a revelation, galvanising his team-mates and scoring regularly from midfield, while Steve Finnieston became the first reliable scorer since Peter Osgood. This was the era of the boot boy and punk rock, and the Kings Road was in the news again, albeit minus the expensive fashion and hippy values of the Sixties. Punks and Teds fought on crowded Saturday afternoons, with more than one Chelsea fan joining the fray. Britain was descending into chaos and Anarchy In The UK provided the soundtrack as across the country football specials were burnt out and high streets demolished, the country's youth wrapped up in a teenage rampage unimaginable today.

Eddie McCreadie seemed about to revive the glory days, but having won promotion he left the club after a disagreement with the board, and within two seasons Chelsea were back in the Second Division. The team collapsed. Steve Finnieston was injured and later sold, while Tom Martin remembers crying as a child when Ray Wilkins departed for Manchester United.

This sadness at the loss of a favourite player is a repetitive strand. Freddie Hopwood was one of many junior fans who were inconsolable when Peter Osgood left for Southampton and more recently scores were similarly affected by Zola's final bow. Peter Crane, though, is the only supporter admitting to crying tears of joy, and this was when Robert Fleck left Stamford Bridge.

Apart from that one season, the mid-Seventies to early-Eighties were tough if you were a Chelsea fan, but many stayed loyal. This loyalty is a badge of honour that is still worn today, and when opposing fans sing 'where were you when you were shit?' there are plenty of people around who can hold their heads high. Home gates dipped as low as 6,000, yet thousands would follow the team away. There were also, of course, patches of light and heroes emerged. While these players don't feature in the Dream Team, they remain cult figures who fought for Chelsea when the odds were stacked against us. Mickey Droy is one such example, and he is described as 'a colossus, who gave everything, in every single game,' by John Marston, while others recall his total commitment to the cause and an ability that belied his physical appearance.

Clive Walker was often the sole source of skill during these dark days. A speedy, goal-scoring left-winger, he features in both the top ten most-memorable goals and top ten most-memorable matches. These lists are dominated by more successful eras, which shows the quality of Walker's contribution. When Flasher received the ball anything could happen. At home to Bolton in October 1978 it did. Chelsea were 3-0 down with twenty minutes left when Clive came on as a substitute and demolished the visitors. Chelsea won 4-3.

Jon Hawkins has a tale about this game: 'The winning own goal came from one Sam Allardyce. My Daily Star (a right riveting read) reported that the top Yugoslav coach Miljan Miljanic was at the game with a view to taking the Chelsea manager's job. He was quoted as saying that with a team spirit like that, the club didn't need him. Well, we did – because we got relegated anyway.'

At the end of the 1982-83 season Chelsea faced the same opposition, this time away. The game was crucial, maybe even to the club's existence. Walker scored the only goal of the game and relegation to Division Three was avoided by two points. It is ironic that over twenty years later the Premiership was sewn up against Bolton, managed now by Sam Allardyce. Frank Lampard's two goals and the match itself are no doubt now imprinted on the long-term memory of a whole new generation of Chelsea supporters. It has been a long journey from that narrow escape from relegation to becoming the champions of England. Many of you were there on both occasions.

The close season saw manager John Neal speculating in the transfer market. Many Chelsea fans were bemused as the newspapers reported the arrival of Eddie Niedzwiecki, Joe McLaughlin, Nigel Spackman, Kerry Dixon and Pat Nevin. Who were these players? We soon found out. Neal's judgement was sound and he created a classic side still rated the best ever by many of those who wrote in.

This new-look Chelsea hit the ground running with a 5-0 victory at home to Derby. The support swelled once more as those travelling away at times reached 10,000, and Chelsea finished Second Division champions. Another memorable 5-0 home win came near the end of the season against the hated Leeds United, with Dixon scoring three. The following two seasons saw Chelsea finish sixth in the First Division.

During the darkest days Clive Walker was often the only flash of light

During this period Kerry Dixon emerged as our most significant goal scorer since Peter Osgood. He and his fellow attackers David Speedie and Pat Nevin won the fans over. Many boys and girls, but mainly girls, emerging from their teenage years now have Kerry Dixon to thank for their Christian name. There was a rash of Kerrys for a couple of years in the 1980s, just as Chelsea fans had been naming their pet dogs Chopper in the decade before, and more recently Zola and Vialli.

Kerry Dixon went on to challenge Bobby Tambling's all-time scoring record, and according to Mark Olden his goal against Arsenal in front of a packed Clock End on the first Saturday of the new season in 1984 was his favourite ever Chelsea strike because it signified one thing – Chelsea are back.

Ian McKean, meanwhile, puts this team in context: 'With a crowd brought up on Tambling, Greaves, Osgood and Hudson, it was always going to be hard to step into their shoes, but Dixon, Speedie and wee Pat were the first players really to do this. I never believed that Dixon was in the Osgood class, but with those two little guys working their socks off they raised him a level. I think history has shown they were exactly right for each other because none of them achieved as much once they were separated.'

In 1985, the League Cup tie against Sheffield Wednesday at Hillsborough is recalled by many as their most memorable game. It ended 4-4 and Chelsea prevailed in the replay with goals from Mickey Thomas and David Speedie. The following year the victory in the Full Members Cup final at Wembley over Manchester City is considered by more than a handful as their best ever Chelsea moment. A hat-trick from David Speedie contributed to a 5-4 win. The excitement of this particular game in a now nearly forgotten competition has to be put into the context of the times. George Courteney reminds us that no sooner had we left Wembley than we conceded ten goals and scored none in the next two First Division matches.

The play-offs against Middlesbrough that resulted in Chelsea's relegation again in 1988 still haunt many Chelsea supporters. Only the 1994 FA Cup final defeat to Manchester United received more votes as Chelsea fans' worst ever memory. In 1988-89, though, Chelsea bounced straight back as Second Division champions under Bobby Campbell and in 1989-90 had a stomping season in the First Division, finishing in fifth place and taking revenge on Middlesbrough by beating them in the Full Members Cup final at Wembley. By now new players were establishing themselves, people such as Steve Clarke, Tony Dorigo, Andy Townsend, Graeme La Saux and Dennis Wise. In 1992-93, the first season of the Premiership, Chelsea finished mid-table.

Jeff Riley writes: 'The last game of the season was away to Sheffield United and we all travelled up in fancy dress. Most of us dressed as thick Northerners. Even David Webb, who was caretaker manager, came out on to the pitch in a flat cap. In the close season Glenn Hoddle was appointed player-manager and the era we are currently enjoying had begun. I see that game as the turning point. Webby handing the old era over to the new one.'

Glenn Hoddle's impact as a manager and on the style of football played by Chelsea was immediate, and although the team only finished fourteenth in the Premiership, he took us to Wembley for our first 'real' cup final in years – in the FA Cup against Manchester United. However, the 4-0 defeat proved hard to swallow. Clive Mantle has no doubt that this day was the worst ever since he started to follow Chelsea many years before: 'I never felt as bad as I did that day. Leaving Wembley in the pouring rain, knowing the score line did not tell the story, feeling like death and trying to stop fights breaking out left, right and centre. Horrible.' Enough people felt the same way to make this your overall worst memory.

John Higgs compares the feeling of despair that Saturday afternoon to the sense of loss Chelsea fans felt when they received news of Peter Houseman's tragic death years earlier. Still, because of Manchester United's success else-where, it meant that Chelsea were back in Europe the following season.

The Cup Winners Cup run in 1994-95 provided some rich memories, mainly from the trip to Bruges in the quarter finals. Bill Wiles recounts how he first realised that the local police may have been over-reacting to media speculation when he came out of a local pub an hour before the game and found himself face to face with a water cannon. He concludes it was the best game he didn't see because he spent the next four hours locked in an aircraft hangar with 200 other bemused but angry Englishmen. We fell at the semi-final stage to Real Zaragoza, but the highlight of the campaign without doubt, in the eyes of the people that sent their thoughts to us, was John Spencer's magnificent solo goal in Vienna in an earlier round. This goal and the little man's extraordinary commitment to the club has guaranteed him a place in the hearts of Chelsea fans for many, many years to come. 'Little legs, little man, but what a heart,' says Greig Sarath.

Glenn Hoddle's signing of Ruud Gullit the following season was the signal for Chelsea to step up to another level. Maria Bialkowski comments: 'When Ruud first came it could be embarrassing. His quality was awesome. Remember, this was before the Premiership was flooded with Continental players. Ruud would put a wonderful ball into space but there would be nobody there. His thinking was streets ahead. It took a while for others to raise their game to his standards.'

By 1996-97 the side, now boasting Mark Hughes, Roberto Di Matteo, Gianluca Vialli and Gianfranco Zola, had hit a roll and Ruud had replaced Glenn Hoddle as manager. A return to Wembley was this time victorious with Roberto Di Matteo scoring the fastest FA Cup final goal ever, and this has been chosen as the best all-time Chelsea goal by the fans. The speed and power of the strike will stay with those who saw it forever. The roar was deafening, decades of disappointment finally buried as Eddie Newton made it 2-0 and Chelsea lifted the FA Cup for the second time in their history.

The following year we went all the way in the European Cup Winners Cup, beating Stuttgart 1-0 in the final in Stockholm. Many consider this Chelsea's greatest moment and the Gauler family echoed the views of many when voting Zola's goal from a Dennis Wise chip as their best ever. Zola's flicked goal against Norwich is another much loved strike. In fact, he claims three of the top ten goals, with the FA Cup semi-final effort at Highbury against Wimbledon also chosen.

Strangely, it was the events in Stockholm before and after the actual playing that excited most. The majority of these memories concern bars and alcohol. Dave Wilson was relieved that 'rumours of lager costing eight pounds a pint proved untrue', while N Smith ended up in a campsite on the edge of town, next to a forest. The sight of fifty or more half-naked, overweight men with Chelsea tattoos waiting for two showers proved particularly disturbing, but seeing 20,000 fully-dressed Chelsea fans with their arms stretched out, mim-icking British bombers, humming The Dambusters March, appears to have restored his confidence. These are his worst and best memories.

For Billy Nichols, the highlight of Stockholm occurred immediately after the match. Hearing Born Is The King Of Stamford Bridge being sung outside the ground, he turned and saw Peter Osgood jogging down the street with an ever-growing mob of celebrating fans following in his wake. 'Ossie was there with us. More than a quarter of a century after he scored against Real Madrid he was leading us again. I felt as if a quest had been fulfilled that night, when Wise lifted the Cup, but seeing Ossie celebrating with the boys was the icing on the cake. Pure magic.'

Other fond memories of European travel include a rather great Dennis Wise goal, the 5-0 win against Galatasaray, and for one of our more parsimonious supporters the good value that Slovan Bratislava presented: 'Meals, cabs, bang on it all day and still change from £20.'

Alan Delaprelle, meanwhile, recalls the game in Tromso: 'Walking around town on the morning of the match, we saw Ken Bates in a massive fur coat. A well-known female fan threw a snowball at him. After a meal in a restaurant which had seal, whale and reindeer on its menu, it was on to a match played in a blizzard 200 miles north of the Arctic Circle. The weather didn't stop five of us taking our shirts off when Vialli scored the second. The locals could not believe it. A long session in a bar called The Railway followed (there's no railway line anywhere near Tromso). When we arrived back at our log cabins, we were met by an irate Ron Hockings, who, as a non-drinker, had gone back straight after the match, only to find no staff on duty. They had all gone to the match, and we never saw them again until the morning. One of the lads had forgotten to hide the chalet key in the agreed place, so Ron had found that the only available shelter was in a phone box. His mood wasn't improved by Superman jokes. At the airport, we bumped into Ken Bates, who somehow already knew the phone box story and ribbed Ron about it. The stewardess agreed to make an announcement telling Ron there was a phone call for him, which had the plane in stitches.'

By the time Chelsea went to Stockholm, Gianluca Vialli was manager following the departure of Ruud Gullit. He could not have got off to a better start, taking the Cup Winners Cup and the League Cup in his first season. Another FA Cup win, this time over Aston Villa, marked the most successful period in Chelsea's history and harvested a whole new generation of fans.

The Gullit and Vialli years are remembered as a golden age. Alan continues: 'Despite the relentless success of the current side, and their ability to play world-class football for long periods, the most fluent, entertaining side I have seen was under Ruud Gullit's management.' This era produced many highlights and plenty of trophies, and in hindsight ended after the 2000 FA Cup final. Luca was soon on his way, replaced by Claudio Ranieri.

Andrew Field says: 'I found the Dream Team very hard to do and ended up with a squad of thirty-six and realised I had turned into Claudio Ranieri.' The Tinkerman set about reducing the age of the team, but won no trophies, Jose Mourinho taking over as manager. This followed the earlier departure of Ken Bates as chairman and the arrival of Roman Abramovich.

Smash-and-grab – Di Matteo celebrates the fastest-ever FA Cup final goal

There are mixed feelings about the Ken Bates years and the man himself. Danny writes: 'Bates was good for the club. He picked it up from the wreckage left by the Mears people and put down the foundations for what we have now.' Mike Tomkins says his worst memory is 'Mears selling the ground'. Elsewhere electric fences are mentioned, while Mr Wicks says: 'Ken Bates forced many loyal, working-class Chelsea fans out of the club with his high prices. He wanted yuppies and that's what Chelsea ended up with.'

John Mills cannot forgive Ken for sacking Vialli, and Kieran Morrin feels the same about the fate of Ruud Gullit. Leo McArdle comments: 'If Roman hadn't come along when he did, we'd be in the same boat as Leeds and probably the same division. We were skint and in massive debt.' John Stanley believes that Ken's biggest flaw was his ego: 'As soon as we started to put it together he couldn't cope with the adulation people like Gullit and Vialli were receiving, so he sacked them. He had the hump because the Chelsea fans would not kneel down and pray at his altar.'

The demise of The Shed is still a sore point among scores of our contributors and the Bates Motel remains unloved. 'For me, ripping The Shed down was like ripping our heart out,' says Ian Fox. A number of you call for it to be reconstructed, ignoring present legislation about all-seater stadia. Manuel

Joachim captured the emotions of many: 'Progress is progress, but when The Shed was bulldozed it felt like my Granddad had died or something. Of course I'd carry on going. The family was still there, but an important member had gone forever.' Scott Harvey simply wrote that his worst Chelsea memory was 'losing our Shed'.

Chopper Harris must have filled a basic supporter need, for many of you list instances of aggression and on-field violence as your most treasured moments. Rory Norris remembers the punch Joe McLaughlin landed on a Charlton player for kicking Pat Nevin over anything else that happened at his first match. Charlie Tellerman was bewitched not by an Osgood goal gem or an acrobatic Bonetti save but the sight of George Best being launched sky-wards by you know who. And then there was Joey Jones. So many respond-ents referred to his connection with the crowd. Somebody who shyly lists his name as Shed Boy puts it thus: 'Joey Jones would run out on to the pitch and always acknowledge us with a clenched fist. Other players did that but with him you just knew he was more violent than all of us Shed boys put together.'

Strangely, Vinnie Jones, who arguably was a player in the Harris, Joey Jones and Joe McLaughlin mould, does not seem to inspire the same lasting affection in the hearts of the Chelsea faithful. He gets a mention from Les Maclean, who cites his worst moment as the day we signed him.

One of the most interesting Dream Team submissions comes from Dennis Spring. It reads: Vic Woodley, Danny Winter, John Harris, Ron Saunders, Eddie Hapgood, William Russell, Dick Foss, I MacDonald, Charlie Mitten, Joe Payne and Tommy Walker, with Ted Drake as manager. Sadly, there are few supporters remaining who could qualify Dennis' selections from genuine living memory.

Other unusual submissions include one from Ron Sharp who nominates someone called John Read as our best-ever manager. Ken 'The Cat' Turner, meanwhile, states that his earliest memory is of Chelsea being the 'first club to produce a colour programme'.

In other novel areas, Brixton Pat McGowan names his worst player as 'Wanker McAllister', while Peter Smith adds a category of best drunk and nominates Tommy 'The Sponge' Baldwin.

Remembering far away pubs and clubs is a common theme. The Painted Wagon in Chesterfield crops up several times as it was a popular stopping off point for travelling Chelsea fans for some years. Trips to Pudsey near Leeds are mentioned as is an eventful night on Morecambe Pier. Paul Southon says his worst memory was paying £4 for a pint of piss labelled as lager, though he does not specify where. Yates' in Nottingham was another favourite, as Steve Dawson notes: 'With the highest ratio of women to men in the country the town had a special draw, seeing as we were from Slough where the ratio was reversed.'

There are also more interesting references to food, though oddly no mention of prawn sandwiches or smoked-salmon bagels. The Peanut Man is remembered, on the touchline as previously stated, but also sliding through the packed Shed selling his wares, barking 'peanuts, peanuts'. Martin Clegg says: 'He never lost his balance and when the crowd left at the end of the game broken shells covered the terraces. I bet he's sitting in a big villa somewhere hot right now, next to the swimming pool, watching Chelsea on Sky and laughing his head off. He did good enough business.'

A young Gary Morley recalls the exotic smells of the pre-gentrification years, when police horses fed the Fulham Road with manure and beer fumes filled the afternoon air. Most of all, he savours the memory of the roast chestnuts his father bought him. 'I can taste them now, hear the wail of sirens as the pubs emptied. I stood behind my dad outside The Britannia and watched hundreds of green flight jackets come running down the road as some hapless visitors were chased into the North Stand. I consider myself lucky to have been there, watching the action, but safe behind my old man. I can still taste those chestnuts.' The Tea Bar also made an impression on Gary as a place where 'scruffy men grumbled and sipped milky tea, munching on smelly hot dogs that dripped ketchup on their unpolished shoes'. He does not appear to mourn its loss.

Over the years you have been singing your hearts out, and songs first sung in the Sixties, Seventies and Eighties are still around today. A separate chapter deals with this subject in greater depth, but it is worth listing a few of the songs here. For the record, your ten favourites are Carefree, Ten Men Went To Mow, Blue Is The Colour, Blue Flag, Celery, His Name Is Tommy Baldwin, Blue Day, We Will Follow The Chelsea, Born Is The King Of Stamford Bridge and The Famous Tottenham Hotspur Went To Rome To See The Pope.

A huge range of songs garnered votes and songs expressing hatred towards Tottenham unite many. Matt Evans, Alasdair Melrose and Des O'Flynn between them listed a surprisingly rich repertoire. Other battle hymns were also very popular, especially Where The Mile End's Never Been, Hello Hello We Are The Chelsea Boys and Those Were The Days My Friend.

Other ditties celebrate former terrace personalities – The Man With The Staircase Nose apparently salutes the aforementioned Mr Greenaway, The Bloody Red Baron with doctored lyrics is an ode to another Sixties Shed leader, and When Hicky's Coach Comes Over The Hill is self-explanatory.

People chose songs that express humour as much as they do aggression. Geoff Greensmith lists his favourite as the one that begins 'Hey Pedro, who is this Senor Ossie? I don't know Pablo but I think we find out very soon...' which was released to coincide with the 1970 Mexico World Cup finals and refers to our own Peter Osgood. Geoff used this as his answer-phone message for a period, but found that people kept hanging up. More recently a song aimed at Norwich supporters along the lines of 'we've got Abramovich, you've got a drunken bitch,' captured the collective imagination, while there were more votes for The Robert Fleck Song than there were for the player himself.

Ten Men Went To Mow was voted the second favourite all-time Chelsea song and Mick Greenaway takes credit for this confusing chant and its ritual standing and sitting movements. He claimed that it was first sung on a pre-season tour to Sweden in 1982 when he played a tape of Wally Whyton children's songs he had with him and gradually all the Chelsea fans joined in. Similar grey areas surround the origins of the Zigger Zagger chant that is most closely associated with Mick. Firstly, it was not really a song – 'more like an ejaculation,' says David Spring – and again is totally meaningless. Greenaway liked to say he invented it in the early 1960s to announce to other Chelsea supporters where he and his cohorts were situated in cold and hostile grounds of Northern England so they could achieve safety in numbers. This is probably a romanticised version as a play called Zigger Zagger about Stoke City fans was broadcast on TV around this time and for a while kids in every school playground up and down the country walked around chanting Oi! Oi! Oi!

The celery days are fondly remembered by many. More than one supporter wrote in and told us how they were body-searched by the police on entry to the ground only for the disappointed officer to say 'what, no celery?' Others recall grocery boxes by the feet of the policemen for people to surrender their vegetables into before clicking through the turnstiles. This was a far cry from the removal of Dr Marten high-up boots a decade earlier. James Cherry thought the fans were singing Geoffrey when he first heard the Celery song while, strangely, Chris Wood wrote in to say that he prefers to refer to Carefree as Geoffrey. Meanwhile, Frank Elsmere chose Caffreys, although we assume he means Carefree. Perhaps this was wishful thinking. Or maybe he meant Celery?

Misinterpreting the chants seems to be a trait of the Chelsea follower. Renee Stevens bizarrely believed for some years that when in the 1970s Chelsea was sung repetitively to the tune of Amazing Grace the fans were actually singing 'GLC', as in Greater London Council. But Renee prefers the older songs and she and Joyce Matthews bring a version of a song to our attention that would not have been heard around the terraces for some forty years: 'Here we go, With all our lovely ladies, Strolling down the Fulham Road, To watch the Chelsea aces.'

Other songs that picked up votes but do not make the top ten include SW6 Is Wonderful, We Hate Tottenham, He Stands At The Back Of The Shelf, Boys In Blue Division Two, Knees Up Mother Brown, Maybe It's Because I'm A Londoner, Once There Was A Battle There, We Hate Nottingham Forest, Ooh Altogether, Bertie Mee Said To Bill Shankly, Come On And Cheer Again, Chelsea Are Back, Hello Hello Chelsea Aggro, We All Hate Leeds And Leeds, That's Vialli, When Butch/Wise Goes Up To Lift The FA Cup, Que Sera Sera, Molly Malone and We Are The Chelsea Boot Boys.

Chelsea fans in Stockholm salute Chopper Harris – or is it Bomber?

Gary Webb enjoys Posh Spice Is A Slapper, Nick Brown is partial to We Are Evil, while John Taylor selects the monotonous, continuous Chelsea chant 'because it winds up the opposing fans'. Bryan Mason remembers 'Peter is our goalie, Charlie's on the wing, Chopper is our captain, and Ossie is the King'.

Richard Barnett nominates And The Great Man United Got Battered To Fuck, Boz likes In The Dark, Dark Streets Of Liverpool (Where The Mile End's Never Been) and Tommy Barwick is just one of many admirers of Fuck 'Em All. Simon Dover is particularly attached to North Stand, North Stand Do Your Job while Sean Cross is a fan of We Can See You Sneaking Out. Whether he prefers this to be sung before or after the North Stand have done their work is not specified.

The biggest-rivals question stirred up more emotion than any other, as outlined in the Foreword. Frank Sarath, who first saw Chelsea play in 1944, is one of many who name Arsenal: 'This is how it was when I was a kid, and that is how it is now – and always will be.' Whoever sits next to Paul Barnes in the ground, meanwhile, might like to suggest he seeks some counselling. On his form he has written in large block capitals YOU KNOW WHO IT IS. I AM TOO ANGRY TO WRITE THE NAME.

The rivalry with Arsenal seems to be purely football-related, while the dislike of Tottenham is more connected with events off the pitch. There are no songs specifically targeting Arsenal, the fact they have been chosen as our biggest rivals a reflection perhaps of the progress Chelsea have made in the last few years. Claudio Ranieri challenged Arsenal's dominance, but didn't quite overtake Arsene Wenger. Jose Mourinho has changed all that. In his first season he delivered the Premiership, the League Cup and a second successive Champions League semi-final appearance. The win at home to Barcelona is already etched in the collective Chelsea memory, while the two goals Frank Lampard scored at Bolton will be remembered for decades to come. Where we go now is anyone's guess, but one thing is certain – it won't be boring. Nothing is ever predictable at Chelsea.

Elizabeth Booth sums things up nicely: 'I am now over sixty years old and it has been such an absorbing roller-coaster following Chelsea over the years. I am pleased it still has the spirit of a smaller club and that no chairman, player or manager has ever been bigger than the club itself. I'm very proud to call the Blues my team.'

The Chelsea Dream Team

A personal overview by Tommy Baldwin

I was not surprised to see the final line-up of the Chelsea Dream Team. Indeed, I had duly filled out my own form and my choice closely mirrored the verdict of the majority, the only differences being my inclusion of Ken Shellito, David Webb and Jimmy Greaves. When you have played alongside and against these people it is hard to choose others ahead of them, and I hope I have not been too biased to my era. However, I also nominated Luca Vialli as best manager, and despite these few differences I would not argue with any of the final choices.

Ken Shellito was a class defender whose career was ended prematurely by injury. His solitary cap for England would most definitely have been added to and a long and distinguished Chelsea career beckoned. I'd have had Webby in because he battled for Chelsea like no other. His contribution to the club should not be underestimated. I had to put Jimmy Greaves in because Jimmy was quite simply the best striker I ever saw. I realise that many see him as a Spurs man, but he started at Chelsea and he was brilliant.

What I did find particularly interesting was the relatively low percentages each player took to win their respective categories. This shows the wide range of players who received votes. Only Peter Bonetti took more than half of the available vote for his position, and twice as many as his nearest rival. The Cat was, quite simply, in a class of his own, and served Chelsea for twenty years.

Ron Harris was decisively voted as the preferred right-back with only Dan Petrescu from the other nominations harvesting over ten percent of the vote. Chopper remains indelibly imprinted on the minds of Chelsea fans, and it is odd that the chattering classes and other players and managers sometimes do not share our regard for him. He was the right man for the right time.

In the category of centre-backs, John Terry and Marcel Desailly left the rest far behind. Considering John Terry's tender years and the fact that he has not yet reached his peak, it is quite conceivable that he could become the greatest Chelsea player ever.

I was surprised but heartened to see that Eddie McCreadie was chosen as the Dream Team's left-back. Although I also picked Eddie, I felt that as he has not been around for some time, and has retreated completely from the public eye, the fans' memory of him might have faded. I needn't have worried. It is clear that he still retains a great deal of affection. Many also recall his feat as a manager making good with a young, inexperienced team, and the manner of his departure still rankles.

Charlie Cooke is another who has left these shores and has disappeared from view, but his silky skills will never be forgotten. He managed to get double the vote of Pat Nevin, a fellow Scot, and nearest rival for the right-wing position. Charlie was a special footballer. Very individual, but with a terrific work-rate. The fans loved him and the players loved him, yet somehow, in my opinion, he never received the full recognition he deserved.

Frank Lampard is a clear winner for one of the two central midfield positions, and deservedly so. He was made to be a Chelsea player and the best is yet to come. There were those who worried a little about the price we paid for Super Frank, myself included, but already that seems as cheap as chips. I'll bet money that both Frank and John Terry will lead not only Chelsea, but England, to our greatest successes yet. It's an exciting time.

The other midfield position belongs to Alan Hudson. You could not have made Huddy up if you tried. The kid born across the road from the ground who could play a bit. The boy who forced himself into the first-team at a tender age and the young man whose star shone so brightly that, for a while, it looked like he would eclipse even George Best as the finest, most charismatic footballer of his generation. He was a joy to play with – one of those players who knew what you should do next before you did. He kept us all on our toes.

On the left-wing I voted for Damien Duff, but didn't think he would get in the side, given the short time he has been at Chelsea. He was a great purchase by Mr Ranieri and a far more important cog in the team that won the Premiership than is sometimes realised. I love the way he switches flanks and takes defenders on. He is the best crosser of the ball we've had at the Bridge in many years and again, I think the best is yet to come.

I'm glad to see Dennis Wise made the team. Looking at the votes he pops up all over the place, just like he did on the pitch, and I thought he may have spread himself too thin. Wisey's contribution to the club is massive and we should never forget that he was the energy and sparking dynamo of that great Vialli side. This was a side that not only brought trophies back to the Bridge, but also a little thing called pride. The club should forget all this Stamford The Lion nonsense and substitute Dennis' image on the club badge.

What to say about the two men elected to spearhead this mouth-watering Chelsea Dream Team? Step forward Mr Peter Osgood and Signor Gianfranco Zola. If only we could have seen them together. Little and large. Chalk and cheese. Batman and Robin. These two received nearly sixty percent of the total vote cast for forwards. Only Kerry Dixon and Jimmy Greaves managed to notch up over ten percent and let us not forget the quality of the attackers that have worn Chelsea blue over the years – Bobby Tambling, Mark Hughes, Jimmy Floyd Hasselbaink, Roy Bentley and Ian Hutchinson to name but a handful.

Ossie and Zola regularly jostle for the title of Greatest Chelsea Player Ever in various polls and it is easy to see why. In this game of ours strikers have the advantage of being the guys that finish the moves. Finishing a move means goals, and goals are what the spectators remember. Goals are what are recorded for posterity. Goals are what win games. And Peter and Gianfranco have given us gold nuggets of goals and plenty of them. With these two guys, though, it is not only the goals that have ensured their place in Chelsea hearts, it is their footballing personalities.

Ossie – big and strong. Outspoken. Jocular. He could head the ball like others volleyed it. He could volley the ball like others wanted to. He could jink, swerve and run with the best of them. Even better, he could make history. He was your man for the big occasion. Okay, so he went to Southampton, but everybody knows Ossie is Chelsea. Always was. Always will be.

Zola – slight in build. Modest and humble. Sweet tempered. You just knew that here was a nice man. His ball skills had not been seen at English grounds since the demise of George Best and Stanley Matthews. That real feeling of expectation when he received the ball was a sensation that many thought they'd never have again. Here was a Continental that could never be accused of being mercenary and scoffing at the Premier League crust. He embraced Chelsea and Chelsea embraced him.

How would this Dream Team have fared against the Dream Teams of Arsenal, Manchester United and Liverpool? Who knows? Would Mike Tyson at his peak have beaten Muhammad Ali at his? It is an exercise in fantasy. But fantasies are good. They often sustain us. In my fantasy it is this team who are running around Wembley holding the FA Cup aloft while the likes of Roy Keane, Bobby Charlton, Eric Cantona and Denis Law are slinking off the pitch, heads bowed.

My name is Tommy Baldwin.

When the ball hits the back of the Old Trafford net it's Vialli

Gianluca Vialli

Gianluca Vialli was born on July 9th, 1964, in Italy. In the UK a team of Geordie animals sat at the top of the hit parade with The House Of The Rising Sun, while in the US, New York State was swept by race riots. At home we were dealing with the more genteel Beatles riots. Luca won the European Cup in his last game for Juventus in 1996 and then moved to Chelsea as the vanguard of the Glenn Hoddle/Ruud Gullit revolution. As a Chelsea player and player-manager he won the FA Cup, the League Cup and the European Cup Winners Cup. As manager-only he took the FA Cup again in 2000. He goes down in history as a World Player Of The Year and the manager who has brought the most silverware to Stamford Bridge to date. He also has the dubious honour of having entered mainstream rhyming slang, Gianluca Vialli currently being one of Britain's favourite recreational drugs

Where did you grow up and what is your family background?

I grew up in a place called Cremona, a mid-sized town with about 80,000 inhabitants just an hour away from Milan. My father worked in the construction industry and we were comfortable, but not as extremely rich as some people have claimed. There is no class system in Italy like you have here so it did not matter who you were. I have three brothers and one sister who all still live in Cremona and now, as you can guess, I have many, many nephews and nieces. My childhood was a happy one.

Which football team did you support as a child and who were your heroes?

Inter Milan. My heroes were Roberto Boninsegna and Sandro Mazzola. They were great players, but I loved the whole team. I didn't really get to watch them at the ground when I was a boy because my father was not a football fan, so you could say I was a supporter from the armchair watching the television. Instead I went to Cremonese almost every week. They played in what you would call the Third Division, but they got promoted and finally when I played for them in 1984 they made the Serie A. Sadly they went down to the Fourth Division, but are back in the Second Division now. You know how it is, like in England, some small clubs can go up, down, up. I still look for their results today and also those of Inter Milan. By Sunday night I am up to date with what is happening with those clubs. I love Inter still because I feel for them not having won the championship in twelve years and Mancini, their manager, is a very dear friend of mine. My job now is working for Sky Italy and I have to keep close tabs on what is happening in Serie A. I commute to watch Serie A matches, although more recently I am concentrating on the Champions League. That is good because Italian league matches can be crazy and not always pleasant places to be.

Do you still look out for Chelsea results too?

Oh come on! You are playing? I have two season tickets. Very expensive season tickets as well.

How did you become a professional footballer?

We didn't play football at school like you do here. In Italy it is different. We played football at the oratory. In order to encourage children to practice Catholicism and learn about Christ they packed some football in to get the boys to turn up. You go there at three o'clock, you play till four, do religion for half an hour and then carry on with the football until 7pm. They made it very inviting by providing good pitches and equipment. So that is where I learnt to play football and also with my friends at the courtyard at my house.

When I was twelve or thirteen years old I entered a team for a year and then I went to Cremonese and started to play in a professional structure about a year later. I finally debuted for the first team when I was sixteen years of age. I never thought I was a brilliant player and did not as a young boy have a burning desire to be a footballer. When people started telling me I was good and that I could make it as a professional then I started to think. Later when I saw that the heroes and superstars were men just like you and me, and had started the same way, I realised that if I really worked and wanted it, I could be.

Cremonese had a good academy and they broke their young players in very early because they wanted to establish them quickly and sell them on. They were a poor club and that is how they survived. That was good for me as my career got started quickly. If I had been at Juventus, for instance, they go out and buy superstars and I would have had to wait much longer to become established. My first game was Parma away. I came on with twenty minutes to go and caused a few problems for the opposition and I was brought down blatantly, but no penalty was given. It was obvious to anybody it was a penalty. Perhaps the game was meant to finish 0-0, if you know what I mean? There was match-fixing in Italian football in those days.

How did your career then develop?

I stayed with Cremonese for about four years. When I made my debut we were in the Second Division and then we were promoted. I played for them in the First Division for three years before I was transferred to Sampdoria. The club was fantastic. An excellent chairman and managing director and an all-round good set-up. Most of the players were roughly my age so it was like

44

being back at school, except now we had plenty of money and pretty girls chasing us instead of us chasing them. We were living in a city by the sea and the weather was always pleasant. I had eight wonderful years and I look back at that time as among the best years of my life. While I was there I got the first of my caps for Italy. The peak of my time with the club was when we made the European Cup final at Wembley against Barcelona. We lost, but it was a real achievement. Soon after, I joined Juventus and with them I did manage to win the European Cup, after four years, and it was the day after that final win that I signed for Chelsea.

When did you first become aware of Chelsea Football Club?
When I was nine years old, my friend who lived next door had a father who travelled to London on business. He came back with some football scarves and one was Arsenal and one was Chelsea. That was the first time Chelsea registered with me. Later, when I was at Sampdoria, another friend came to London and went to the Chelsea shop and came back with some Chelsea bomber jackets. I wore mine now and then and once a photographer took a picture of me with it on. Many years later when I came to Chelsea I desperately looked for the picture so I could say to the Chelsea fans 'hey, look, I was supporting Chelsea many years ago', but I never could find that photo.

What were your impressions of Chelsea when you first arrived?
To be honest, when I took my first look at the facilities I was not very impressed. They took me to the Harlington training ground and after Juventus, where they have doctors, dentists, chiropodists, everything, well, I thought 'not good'. Of course, the training ground at Cobham now is out of this world. Chelsea have absolutely everything imaginable and so they should. If you want to build a world-class side you have to have world-class facilities. It is simple. Back at Harlington I could not complain though – because the medical examinations were not very thorough they did not pick up a knee injury I had. I was worried they would find it and send me home on a plane. So, yes, there was a bit of culture shock, but I had to understand that Italy was one thing and England another. I had to make the best of what was here and get on with it.

As far as coming to Chelsea though, it was what I wanted to do. I could have stayed in Italy or I could have gone to Glasgow Rangers, or even France or Spain, but I wanted to come to Chelsea to broaden my career and broaden my life. It was not about money at all. Actually, I made up my mind I wanted to come to England firstly, then London, and then Chelsea. When you look at the London clubs and you are thinking about where to live, about your family and your lifestyle, there is really no competition. Of course, people such as Glenn Hoddle and Ruud Gullit were also influencing factors, but it was the area that drew me to Chelsea most.

What do you remember about your first game for Chelsea?

My first official game was at Southampton at the old Dell. I did not play very well. In my defence my hamstring was not right, but still, I was not very good. I did hit the post with a scissors kick, but other than that there is very little to remember. My first official game at home was against Middlesbrough, I think. It was 1-0 and Ravanelli played for them. We had played together only a few months before in the European Cup Final that I mentioned. It was an evening match and I played a bit better. Then we played Coventry and I scored. Things slowly became better. This is one reason I love the Chelsea fans so much. They were always patient and never got on my back at all. They loved me and started to sing about me before I had done anything to deserve it, so I can never forget them. I do not think other fans are like that.

Is it true that Ruud Gullit made you stop smoking when you came here?

No (*laughing*), it is not true. Smoking would be my choice and Ruud Gullit could not tell me to stop doing this. It is funny, but in Italy players smoke. Players smoke in the dressing room at half-time. But in England players do not smoke. If you smoked your career would be finished. Yet it is okay to drink gallons of beer. In Italy players do not drink beer. Countries are different. When I realised that my smoking was offending people I stopped (*smiles and glances towards a packet of Marlboro on the table*). I still have one now and then. Why not? I enjoy it and I like cigarettes. You must enjoy life a little. If you do not do anything because you want to live a long, long time, you will wake up one day dead and will have done nothing. No, definitely Ruud Gullit did not tell me to stop smoking.

Do you not get on with Ruud Gullit?

Maybe Ruud does not get on with me. After he was sacked and I became manager he did not speak to me again. I suppose he thought I was disloyal, but I do not think that is true. We always had a professional relationship.

What is your most memorable match as a player and as a manager?

As a player it has to be the European Cup Winners Cup final in Stockholm. Wasn't that a marvellous night? And as a manager it would have to be the League Cup final when we beat Middlesbrough in 1998, because it was my first final as a manager.

What is your most memorable goal at Chelsea?

A goal I scored at Tromso in Norway.

Who was your most difficult opponent?

Martin Keown of Arsenal.

What do you regard as your biggest regret in your career?
I don't regret much. I have made mistakes, but I have learned from them and then they become positive things, so then you should not regret them. If I had to pick something I would say that I wish I had played better in the 1990 World Cup for Italy, when we finished third. I should have done better.

Do you have a favourite terrace song?
I think the Frank Leboeuf song is very nice. It always made me smile: 'He is here, he is there, he is every fucking where... Frank Leboeuf, Frank Leboeuf.' You say he didn't like that song? Why not? I didn't know that. I like it very much. And, naturally, I liked that song that goes 'When the ball hits the back of the Old Trafford net, it is Vialli.' That one is very pleasing. The Chelsea supporters are brilliant with me, as I said, and they stuck by me at the beginning. To hear them singing my name made me feel even stronger in my desire to become a Chelsea legend. When I walk around, even now, people stop me and tell me the nicest things. That is why I love living in London. I was lucky to have been at Chelsea when we were moving into a successful period and we all had a great time – the players, the managers and the supporters. We can all look back on this time and smile.

What do you think of the Dream Team, voted for by the fans?
You cannot say this is the best team ever, and you cannot say I am the best manager, because clearly I am not. Jose Mourinho is by far a better manager than I am. He has won the Premiership and I did not. He will win much, much more. I think a Dream Team is a vote by the fans on who they like best rather than who is the best. And, as you have told me, these votes have been cast over more than a season. I think if you started today then Mourinho would get nearly all the votes for manager. But, of course, I am very pleased that the fans made this vote. For everyone who reads this and voted for me I would like to say thank you. It really is a great compliment, but it does not mean I am the best manager. I did not see all these players in the Dream Team so I cannot say he should be in, or he should not be in the team, but someone like Dennis Wise is a very important part of Chelsea's history. I must say I am surprised that Ruud Gullit is not in there. Ruud was a really wonderful player. He was absolute world-class, even if he was past his best when he came to us.

When you were manager you sent John Terry out on loan. Why did you do this, and would you have sold him?
No, certainly not. I would never have sold him. I sent him out to Nottingham Forest on loan because the manager, David Platt, was my friend and I trusted him. I knew he would develop John and look after him. I think it was the right thing for him at the right point in his career. It is difficult for me to

47

prove now, but before I was sacked, and perhaps this was one of the reasons I was sacked, I was not happy with Frank Leboeuf and I was about to try out Marcel Desailly and John Terry together at the back. But I did not get the opportunity.

Is it right you tried to sign Paolo Di Canio?

Yes, that is true. It was again shortly before I was sacked. I think Paolo could have been excellent for Chelsea and at the time we needed a player who could play with both his right and left foot, and someone who played with his heart. A couple of years earlier I had tried to sign Atillio Lombardo as I felt he was right for Chelsea at the time and he could play on the right wing, left wing and as a second striker, but both moves were turned down by the board. It was a bit annoying because if we signed a bad player it was my fault, and if we didn't sign a good player it was my fault as well. I was the manager, but really I was the coach because important decisions on signings and sales were taken away from me.

How did you feel when you were sacked?

I was shocked and disappointed more than anything. I went to the club one day for a meeting thinking they wanted to renew my contract. We were four matches into the season, we had already won the Charity Shield, and we had lost one, drawn two and won one. I did not think it was a too poor start to the season. They told me then that I was sacked. I don't know the reason. They gave me some reasons, but I do not believe they were the real ones. I walked out that day and went home and thought about it and the next day I went back in to to see Ken Bates and I told him that I thought he was making a mistake, that instead of sacking me he should be sacking somebody else, but sadly he did not listen.

Looking back I guess they decided it was time for a change and you have the choice of changing five or six players or changing the manager. The manager, in this case, was a cheaper option. Ironically, four months later they changed six players. Actually, I would like to use this interview to set the record straight about a couple of things as I have never really tried to put my side of the story over. Maybe now it is fine to do it. You see, I never wanted to sell Emerson Thome and I never wanted to sign Winston Bogarde – both moves were organised over my head and against my advice. I liked Thome. He was an ideal player to be part of a squad, but the club wanted to sell him and sign Bogarde, who was available on a free transfer. I said no, Thome is good for us and Bogarde is not needed.

I was in Cremona and Colin Hutchinson phoned and said the club had sold Thome to Sunderland and signed Bogarde. I was very upset and when I found out what Bogarde was earning in a year was almost what was paid for Thome I felt angry. It did not make financial sense either. When Bogarde became a burden to Chelsea later and the papers would talk about the money being wasted on his wages it made me mad that certain people implied he was my signing. That was unfair and untrue. In life there are people who admit their mistakes and learn from them and I hope I am one of those, but there are also those who will not and will seek to blame others.

It is a strange notion that you can be a football manager yet not decide which players go and which players come.
I agree. But to be fair, a manager has a lot to do these days, especially at a big club, so if the managing director or chairman is going to negotiate with a player then that is a help, and if it is a player you know, that helps remove you from any difficulties, though the board and the manager should be in broad agreement on the players they will try to sign. Colin Hutchinson also stopped me signing Di Canio, which made the relationship more difficult, and this was a few weeks before I was sacked. I think it was a case of me or him.

What do you think about the decisions that Claudio Ranieri and Jose Mourinho have taken since your departure?
I wouldn't have done things the same as Claudio, although he brought some great players to the club, but I cannot say that Jose has a put a foot wrong. What he has achieved in such a short time is nothing short of amazing and all this about how it is easy because he has a lot of money to spend is not really true. To make a great team requires much more than a large cheque book.

Would you like to get back into football management?
Very much. I would like to manage in England again rather than Italy. In Italy I think being manager is too stressful, whereas in this country it can be enjoyable. I would like to manage a Premiership club for about five years, do a good job and enjoy my work, and then concentrate on my family. After all, I have been in football totally for many years and I need to spend time close to my family, as they are the most important thing.

I learnt a lot from managing Watford. I cannot pretend that things did not work out because there was no money – there was. I did not spend the money particularly wisely. We paid the players too much – that was not my fault – and when the ITV Digital collapse happened we were in a bad way financially. If I remember right, there were eleven directors, and although they were lovely people and so enthusiastic, it made getting decisions made difficult and progress in changing the set-up was very slow.

Obviously cut-backs had to be made and when they wanted me to get rid of certain members of staff I was not happy, and I had to go. It was a valuable education, although if I do return I feel that my value would be in the Premiership. Some managers are not cut out for the lower divisions and vice versa. If there is a next time I will give it my everything and you might as well do this on the big stage if you can. I am confident I can bring success to a club. One good thing that came out of managing Watford was that I had a good time. I was never unhappy with the work, and I also met Elton John.

What are your big passions outside of football?
Golf. I absolutely love golf. I play often. I sometimes play with Franco Zola and he is now the best out of the old Chelsea players, while Dennis Wise is the worst. I love going to the cinema and I love reading books. I do not want to name favourites because that would then exclude so many. My passion is really life, and I do try to make myself happy and the people around me happy. I love where I live and feel just as at home among the people of Chelsea and this part of London as I do back in Italy. I am so grateful I came to Chelsea. I really am.

What are your ambitions for the future?
Firstly, to be a good husband to my wife and to be a good father to my children. Secondly, I have set up a charitable foundation and I get pleasure from raising money for that. It is called Fondazione Vialli E Mauro Per La Ricerco E Lo Sport, which translates as The Vialli And Mouro Foundation For Research And Sport. Thirdly to do my job for Sky Italy to the best of my ability and as I said earlier to manage again. Finally, to be happy and have a good time.

The Cat – a mere kitten at the time

Peter Bonetti

Peter 'The Cat' Bonetti was born on September 27th, 1941. Britain was at war with Germany and the hit song of the time was White Cliffs Of Dover by Vera Lynn. Those children who were not evacuated were being taken by their parents to see the new Disney film Dumbo. He made 729 appearances in the Chelsea goal between 1959 and 1979, and in one season managed twenty-one clean sheets. Peter won the FA Cup, the League Cup and the European Cup Winners Cup with Chelsea, and at one time held the record for most appearances for a single club by a goalkeeper. He played for England on seven occasions, appearing on the winning side six times and keeping five clean sheets. Pele once said of The Cat: 'The three greatest goalkeepers I have ever seen are Gordon Banks, Lev Yashin and Peter Bonetti'

Where did you grow up and what is your family background?
I was born in Deodar Road, Putney, so I suppose I can claim to be a local lad, like Huddy, who fulfilled his dream and managed to play for his local team. However, my father was a hotel manager, and when I was seven years of age we moved down to Worthing on the south coast with his work, so my association with the Chelsea/Fulham/Putney area ended. For a few years anyway. I came along in 1941 at the height of enemy bombing of London during the Second World War. Perhaps that gave me a grounding for catching things flying through the air. Who knows?

What team did you support as a child and who were your heroes?
I supported Manchester United. No real reason. I can't remember why. It happens doesn't it, when you're a kid? I picked them, but wasn't fanatical or anything like that. There was no football on the TV in those days and all we kids were interested in really was playing. That was what was most important. I can't remember hero-worshipping any players.

What were your feelings about Chelsea at this time?
I never really thought about Chelsea when I was a kid. As I say, I was too busy playing. I remember them winning the First Division Championship, but there was nothing like the fuss you get today.

How did you become a professional footballer?
I started to flower as a footballer down in Worthing. I was an outfield player until I was nine years of age, but nothing too special, even though I loved

playing. One day my games master says to me 'Bonetti, go in goal'. I'm glad he did, because I knew straight away that I had a natural ability and soon so did others. I quickly moved through school teams to better sides in Brighton and then I played for Sussex. Because of the family connection with the Chelsea area, my mum wrote to Ted Drake, legendary manager of Chelsea Football Club, and to our delight he invited me up for a trial. I passed and signed for the club in 1959.

What was your first professional game and what are your memories of that game?
My first team debut was on April 2, 1960, against Manchester City in front of 34,000 fans. It was a wonderful occasion. I kept a clean sheet and we put three past City. Our goals came from Jimmy Greaves, Frank Blunstone and Johnny Brooks. City had a good side at the time, with the great Bert Trautmann keeping goal for them and a scary young goal poacher up front by the name of Denis Law.

The following week we stuffed Arsenal 4-1 at Highbury, but I was quickly returned to this planet when I conceded a Bobby Smith hat-trick in a 3-1 home defeat to Spurs. I thought that might cost me my place in the team, but thankfully it did not.

What were your first impressions of Chelsea when you came to the club?
When I first got signed I spent very little time at Stamford Bridge. None of us boys did. We did our training over at Welsh Harp – miles away from the Kings Road. Miles away from anywhere. We were assigned to the ground once a week for special duties that would be helping the groundsman or the kitman or something similar. It was so different then – it's hard to imagine now – but if we saw one of the senior players like Frank Blunstone or Reg Matthews you wouldn't dream of addressing them first, and if they spoke to us it would be 'yes Mr Matthews', 'no Mr Blunstone'. Mind you, society was different then altogether.

What are your thoughts about the Dream Team and are there other players you would have included?
Number one – I am enormously flattered to have been selected by the fans. It really is an honour and extremely touching after all these years. I can't stress that enough. It makes you feel wanted and valued. I would just like to thank everyone for thinking of me and remembering.

Number two – I hate filling out dream teams and rarely do it. It's like when someone says Stanley Matthews was a better player than George Best. It is almost irrelevant. Different players, different positions, different teams and different eras.

Having said that, I would not argue with the verdict of the Chelsea fans, except in one position – the goalkeeper. And no, this is not a case of false modesty. I really believe that our current goalkeeper Petr Cech is, or soon will be, the best goalkeeper in the world, and possibly the best keeper ever. He is truly stupendous. I can't take my eyes off him. Sad, as it is for me to say, I am convinced that if you took this poll again next season, he would garner more votes than yours truly, and it would be completely justified. Chelsea are blessed with a player of this rare calibre, and I believe he is still a long way from his peak.

You know, people sometimes say to me that us old boys must feel a bit threatened by the success of the current team. Feel that they will take, or have taken, away some of our kudos. Absolutely not. I can't speak for anybody else, but I can honestly say that I am delighted and thrilled at the success of the current Chelsea team.

Who is the best manager you have ever played under?
This is a hard one to answer. I only really played for Chelsea and England. At Chelsea I played under Ted Drake, Tommy Doc, Dave Sexton, Ron Suart, Eddie McCreadie, Ken Shellito, Danny Blanchflower and Geoff Hurst. My best years as a player were with Dave Sexton and I think he brought the best out in me. Chelsea enjoyed a golden period under him and I rate him highly as a coach and as a man. I still see Dave now, when I pick him up and take him to games. He's well and enjoying the game he loves. He gave football and Chelsea a great deal.

What is your most memorable game as a Chelsea player?
There have been many. There have been games where I know I played exceptionally well, but they have no historical significance and tend to get forgotten, so I suppose you have to look at the two finals against Leeds. Marvellous, swashbuckling affairs both of them, and of course we prevailed. I think the proof of the pudding of those games, especially the replay, is that so many non-Chelsea and Leeds fans remember them and talk about it still. You don't get that from neutrals about other finals.

What is your most memorable save?
Again, the most memorable saves are the historically important, or were televised and dramatically acrobatic. I know what my best ever save was because only I know how hard it was to get to that ball. It was against CSKA Sofia at the Bridge in an early round of our successful European Cup Winners Cup campaign. I had to arch my back and hook back a rocket shot that was about to rip the net open. I was really proud of that and seeing that we won only 1-0 it was pivotal because we went on to lift that trophy as some of you know.

What is your favourite terrace song?
No doubt about it – Blue Is The Colour. Of course, I sang on the original and appearing on Top of the Pops was a real thrill, but it's a lovely, atmospheric song and when The Shed sang that at full pelt it almost knocked me forward in my goal. Lets face it, no football team song before or since comes anywhere close.

Which team do you dislike the most and why?
I never really disliked a team. They were just eleven guys like ourselves after all, but there were grounds I didn't like to go to. Millwall springs to mind. We didn't go there very often, but when we did it was always threatening and hostile. It was unsettling and more so for a goalkeeper who had no choice but to have his back to the mob that were aiming missiles at him. I didn't like it at all.

What is your worst Chelsea memory?
There were ups and downs in my career at Chelsea, but I loved the club and I loved playing. Maybe time has coloured my thinking, but it was all so good, I can't pin down any particular event as my worst memory. I hated being injured because it stopped me playing, and I hated losing because it spoiled the playing. That's the best answer I can give you.

Who was your most difficult opponent?
I wasn't frightened of any player due to their physicality, or because there was a jinx or anything like that. I just took them as they came. However, as a goalkeeper, I had to be wary about the big centre-forwards who had command in the air. They were dangerous and during my time there were two in particular who could not be touched for their aerial power. Funny enough, they were both called Davies – Ron Davies at Southampton and Wyn Davies of Newcastle United – although they were not related. I still have nightmares about the day Ron Davies put four past me in a league game at Stamford Bridge. To make it worse, Martin Chivers scored another two. A bit later on, Joe Jordan presented similar problems.

Which young player do you tip for future success?
I'm scouting for Manchester City at the minute and I get to see some really exciting prospects. There's one or two I am sure are destined for bigger things, but I would be failing in my duty to my employer to name them here, just for somebody else to come along and pick them up.

What did you dislike most about being a professional footballer?
The end. The day I had to finally put those gloves away for the last time. That was very hard.

What do you regard as the biggest mistake you have made in your career?

I can't say I made any huge career mistakes but my biggest playing mistake was the goal I conceded against West Germany in the World Cup finals in Mexico in 1970. I'm talking about the first goal from Franz Beckenbauer that I misjudged and it went under me. I take full responsibility for that, but not for the other two goals that caused England to lose 3-2 in extra time to the Germans. The second goal was a fluke and the third a defensive error. However, I am always associated with that game and sometimes blamed for England not retaining the World Cup. I thought that was harsh. We all make mistakes, but my misfortune was making my mistake at such an important juncture in such an important match.

What ambitions do you have for the future?

Undoubtedly to stay in the game. It's what I know. It's what I do. I want to stay involved for as long as I can.

What is your big passion outside of football?

I love travelling. There's so much to see in this world and I never tire of seeing new places and meeting new people. My wife Kay and son Scott went to Mauritius in 2002 and we fell in love with the place. I also enjoy watching my eleven-year old son playing football. He's a striker and developing very well.

Favourite book, film, album?

I'm not a massive reader, but I do enjoy football autobiographies. I read most of them. They stir the memories and bring it all back. My favourite films remain the old ones: The Magnificent Seven and West Side Story still do it for me. I like all sorts of music and can't say I have one favourite album or artist. There's plenty I don't like. How long have we got?

If there was one thing about this country you could change, what would it be?

The weather. It is the main thing that lets this country down. Sunshine is so important as it enhances everything. When the sun comes out and rests on you, everything lifts. The power of the sun and negative power of being deprived of it is much underrated.

What is your view of English goalkeepers today?

Contrary to popular opinion I believe we have some very good English goal-keepers around, with some even better ones coming through. I like the young boy at Liverpool, Chris Kirkland, as well as Paul Robinson and David James. If only Petr Cech was English. He's the one to aspire to.

What is the story behind your move to the Mull Of Kintyre?

It has become a bit of an urban myth that one. Like there was just me on this desolate island with a postbag and no letters. When I retired from football (or did football retire from me?), I was upset and to get away from it all and clear my head I took on a guest house on the Isle of Mull, a Scottish Island in the Hebrides. Anyway, the island postman retired and they asked if anyone wanted to do the job. I had time on my hands and wanted to maintain my fitness so I said 'I'll do it'.

I had a small van to do the round around the island, but a lot of the roads were impenetrable or just not there, so I ended up running people's mail in and the customers said they'd never had their letters so promptly. The place was so sparsely populated it reminded me of playing at Craven Cottage. I loved it there and it certainly helped me take stock of my life, but when my kids reached secondary school age it was time to come back to the mainland.

What have you been doing since you left Chelsea?

I had a season in America with the St Louis Stars. They're into nicknames out there and seemed more excited about the fact I was called The Cat than anything I had achieved in the game. After the Postman Pete episode, I came home and decided to get back into the game. I rang my friend Bob Wilson and asked his advice. He thought I would find work as a goalkeeping coach, but warned me it would be difficult to make a full time living at it. I rang Chelsea, where John Neal was manager, and he kindly invited me down. I worked with Steve Francis and Eddie Niedzwiecki, and John was very pleased with the work I did with them and he offered me a job. I have been pretty fully occupied ever since. I was goalkeeping coach at Manchester City until recently and am still scouting for them. I'm always on the look out for work and feel I have a lot to offer.

Who gave you your nickname The Cat?

It was a guy called Ron Tindall. He played up front with Jimmy Greaves before moving to West Ham United. He just started calling me it and I don't really know why. I'll ask him when I see him, but I think he's out in Australia these days. I hope it was a reference to my goalkeeping agility, but you can never be sure. I did have a habit of crawling past him on all fours and rubbing my fur against his shins. Whatever, the name stuck and I love it. I regard it as the greatest compliment.

Recently, I have been made welcome at Chelsea again and it is the greatest feeling, I'm telling you, to be back. The love and affection that is still there has astounded me. I really feel like I've come home. I was walking in to the ground the other week and I heard a man say to his son, or maybe it was granddad to his grandson: 'That's the Cat, that is.' I felt great.

Chopper – not arguing with a referee

Ron Harris

Ron Harris was born on November 13th, 1944, as the Allies closed in on Germany towards the end of the Second World War. He made 795 appearances for Chelsea, a club record, and a great deal of those were as team captain. Ron won the League Cup in 1965, the FA Cup in 1970 and the European Cup Winners Cup in 1971. His reputation as a tough defender led to the nickname Chopper, but his peers and those who watched him over the years will testify that there was a lot more to his game. Stanley Matthews, no less, said of Ron: 'He could really play and on the ball was as assured and stylish as the best defenders of the day'

Where did you grow up and what is your family background?

I was born in Hackney, East London. My father was an Arsenal supporter. He was good with figures and a book-keeper by trade, but he loved football and spent hours with me and my brother Allan, in our back yard playing with a ball.

What team did you support as a child and who were your heroes?

Because of Dad, me and Allan both supported the Arsenal and we went every week. First team one week, reserves the next. They had a fella on the right wing called Arthur Milton and I really liked him. There was also Wally Barnes, a great full back, Jimmy Logie, George Swindin and Cliff Holton.

What were your feelings about Chelsea?

No, never crossed my radar. Had no interest in them. Never thought about them. Don't remember them.

How did you become a professional footballer?

Like I said, me and Allan played football all the time. All the time. And we got to playing for a junior side in Hackney called Craven Park and we were beating everyone and winning everything. I was only eight years old and we were playing kids of eleven and twelve. Looking back on it I think that toughened me up. If you're eight and the kids you are playing are eleven unless you toughen up they'll have you for breakfast. There was a buzz when Craven Park played and people were saying 'the Harris brothers are playing' and things like that. Funnily enough, I played inside-right in those days and right up until I went to Chelsea when Dick Foss, the trainer in those days, moved me to left-half. I played for the district as a kid, I always remember, and I was inside-right and an ugly kid called Rodney Marsh was inside left.

In those days there were scouts all over the place and they'd get to hear about anyone that was half-good and Chelsea, who had a great 'juniors' system, picked up my brother Allan and he signed professional. It was sort of just accepted that I'd follow him. I signed on as a ball boy first, and got 7s 6d every home game, and then became an apprentice, and so on. Ted Drake signed me as an apprentice, but he soon moved on and Tommy Docherty took over. Tom was the first manager I had a relationship with.

What was your first professional game and what are your memories of that game?

I was captain of the England youth side that won the World Cup in November 1961. There were some great players in that side: Tommy Smith, Len Badger and Bernard Shaw (Sheffield United boys), John Sissons, Jon Sammels and Graham French. Also, Chelsea won the Youth Cup two years on the spin and I was in the side that second year. We beat Everton. It was after one of those games that Tommy Doc came up to me and said 'congratulations son'.

My first-team debut was against Sheffield Wednesday in 1962, at the Bridge, and we won 1-0. I was eager to please and Tommy said to me that I must make myself known, make whoever I was marking know I was there. So I did. The guy who felt my presence was a good pro called John Fantham, and I took him out of the game. Not literally, but I isolated him and basically it was nine against nine on the rest of the field. After the game Tommy said 'well done' and I think that set the tone for the future. Fantham was Wednesday's threat and I did a job. I'm sure he played for England.

If what I did pleased the boss then I'd carry on. If a team had a particular threat like Greaves at Spurs, or Best at Man U, my job was to make them safe. I think Greaves only scored one goal against me in twenty-odd years. I was like a dog. I followed them every bloody where. That's why some of those guys didn't like me. It was nothing to do with chopping or clattering, it was just that I wouldn't leave them alone. My game was making sure they did not have a game. Don Megson, Gary Megson's dad, was in that Wednesday side that first day, by the way, as were Tony Kay and Peter Swan, who later did some bird over a match-fixing scandal.

What were your first impressions of Chelsea when you came to the club?

To be honest with you, my first impressions were that Chelsea were not a big club like Arsenal or Spurs. They'd won the Championship a few years before, but that was sort of forgotten. Not by Chelsea fans, of course, but by almost everyone else. They were not a glamour club. They were... Chelsea. It didn't really change until 1970 I think. Even though we won the League Cup and played in the FA Cup final against Spurs, I don't think we were really on the map and taken seriously until we done Leeds, and for a few years after. A lot of the support we have now stems from then. People who were kids in 1970 and watched that bloody replay on the telly and became Chelsea fans.

What are your thoughts about the Dream Team and are there other players you would have included?

I wouldn't really argue with the team. You're not far wrong. Am I captain? I hope so. John Terry will agree to that, I'm sure. I'll have a word with him when I see him. Some people might argue that Petr Cech should be there instead of Peter Bonetti – he is certainly special – but we've had one season of him and we had The Cat for nearly a quarter of a century. I hope it won't, but anything could happen. Cech could move on after a couple of years.

Those who remember him will tell you that Ken Shellito was a superb player, but injury cut him off in his prime. If he had gone the distance I think he'd be in there. Perhaps I'd have myself playing alongside the centre-half and Ken at full back. Can't argue with Frank Lampard, Charlie Cooke and Alan Hudson in midfield. Great players those three. Imagine them together! And up front I love Zola. I miss him down here at Stamford Bridge, but Ossie was without any argument the most gifted player I ever played with. He was a genius.

Who is the best manager you have ever played under?

I have a great respect for Tommy Docherty and will always be grateful for the opportunity he gave me. He was a fantastic motivator of players, but I also admire and respect Dave Sexton. He was a different sort of man from Tommy, but just as good in his way. I can't name one over the other.

Geoff Hurst was the worst manager I played under, but that's another story. I'm fond of Danny Blanchflower because he played me in midfield and gave me a new lease of life. I really enjoyed it while it lasted.

Tommy could get up to some stunts. In some ways he was more game than the players, so I suppose it was hard for him when he had to bollock us. I remember the Blackpool business when he sent eight players home because they went out on the piss. I was the captain at the time and although I went to this fateful party I was back by midnight. Others made a night of it. In the morning we came down to breakfast at the hotel and Tommy was standing there and he just handed train tickets out to those who were guilty. We ended up playing reserves and St John's ambulance men and things and we got stuffed. We were as close to winning the Championship that year as we had been for ages and that defeat blew our hopes. Tommy had to make a stand but maybe he could have handled it differently. Easy to say that with hindsight.

Going back to Danny Blanchflower, I remember being up at Middlesbrough and we got stuffed 7-2. It was a terrible time. We were already about fourteen points adrift and we were going down. Ossie made his comeback that day and scored, but even he couldn't save us. On the coach on the way back Danny sat next to me and says: 'Look Ron, you're thirty-five years old and I'm going to give a couple of the boys a run-out now, I hope you don't mind.' I said fair enough, but of course I minded. Nobody likes being told they're on the way out, do they?

Anyway, he says he wants to play a lad called Mickey Nutton and another called John Sitton, who had both come through the youth system. So I think I'm not playing in the next few games and I went out on the Friday night a few weeks later, went to a do and stayed up all night and drank fourteen Irish coffees. I'm not a big drinker, but I do like Irish coffee. Chris Matthews, who was secretary at Chelsea at the time, rang me in the morning to tell me I was playing. She knew the state I was in because she was with me the night before. Then Danny rang. I didn't say too much in case I slurred. You've guessed the end of this story – I played and was man of the match.

What is your most memorable game as a Chelsea player?

The highlight of my career was lifting the FA Cup up at Old Trafford. No doubt about it. That was a great day. It really meant something to beat Leeds United. They were good and they knew it, and we beat them fair and square and did it in style. Especially after having lost in the Cup final three years earlier to Spurs it was great. I suppose it would have been better if it had been at Wembley and we could have climbed the steps, but you can't have everything. There was some Chelsea mob at Old Trafford that day, so it was almost the same. And coming home with the Cup and driving around Fulham, that was so special.

The Cup Winners Cup was fantastic too, especially when we drove back from Heathrow and the fans were lining the road all the way back into Chelsea. We felt like The Beatles that day. That final went to a replay too and we thought we'd won – they even brought the Cup out on to the running track ready to present it to us and then Madrid scored in the final second. That was a real downer. But we got it in the replay. The fans were brilliant, staying out for the replay. Nobody had money in those days and employers were still allowed to sack people, so they made some sacrifices. I can remember Mickey Greenaway out there rallying them all with his Zigger Zagger. Great days. Years later I went to a few of his parties, and was very sad when I heard he died.

The Chelsea fans were better away from home because at the Bridge they were so far away from us, what with the running track around the edge. I know The Shed was special to the fans, but you were in it. We weren't. Away, though, Chelsea turned up in their hordes and more often than not made more noise than the home teams, and at the smaller grounds you were right on top of us. That was a real boost.

Another thing I loved was the training games we played on the concrete outside the old Shed end. They were memorable games, mark my words. You used to get more people turn up and watch them than you did reserve games. We'd split up into two teams. We had white shirts and blue shirts, and Dave Sexton had them printed up with The Goodies printed on one set, and The Baddies on the other. The Goodies were Peter Bonetti, Dave Sexton, Johnny Hollins and Peter Houseman – all that lot – and The Baddies were Ossie, Alan Hudson, Webby, me and a few others. They were the most competitive games you've ever seen. Stupid really, because we didn't care if we injured each other. Poor old Johnny Boyle carries a broken nose to this day where Ossie put one on him.

What is your most memorable goal?
My first in front of the Chelsea fans. I had to wait until 1964 before I scored at home, but the wait was worth it. I scored against the best goalkeeper in the land, Gordon Banks, and that was when he had two good eyes. He was playing for Leicester City at the time and we beat them 1-0 at the Bridge. Frank Blunstone cut the ball back to me and I thumped it home. I scored fourteen goals for Chelsea and some of them were put past the best – Pat Jennings and Peter Shilton and Banksy.

What is your favourite terrace song?
Blue Is The Colour is special because I sang on it. Mimed actually. No seriously, most football pop songs are shit aren't they? But Blue is the Colour and You'll Never Walk Alone are the only two I reckon that can really lift teams. I mean, I hate You'll Never Walk Alone because it did affect you. It made Liverpool play better and I used to think when they were beating us up there and The Kop were singing that song, 'why don't you shut up'. I had twenty years of Liverpool beating us at Anfield and that bloody song. It worked for them.

I love the banter at matches more than the songs. Football fans can be so sharp and I wonder who makes these things up. I was at Fulham when Mohammed Al-Fayed came in and sat down near Roman Abramovich. The Chelsea fans started chanting 'You've only got a corner shop' to Al-Fayed. Great stuff.

Which team do you dislike the most, and why?
People always say Leeds because of the antics they got up to, and I suppose there is a lot of truth in that. You heard things about Don Revie and you didn't like what you heard, but the teams I didn't like were Tottenham and Arsenal. I saw them more as my rivals.

What is your worst Chelsea memory?
It's bad to lose in an FA Cup final, but at least you've got there. Personally, I

think it's more gutting to lose a semi-final and we did that two years on the trot. The one that sticks in my throat is the second one, when we were beaten by Sheffield Wednesday. We were such favourites nobody dreamt we could lose, but we did. I was captain and the tie was played up at Villa Park in front of 60,000 people. They done us 2-0 and we didn't play well. The only consolation was they got beat by Everton in the final.

Who was your most difficult opponent?
The two that used to give me the most problems were both Jocks. Denis Law was one, and he was slippery and artful, and the other one was a big lad who played for Aston Villa and Burnley called Andy Lochhead. He'd give as good as he got, Lochhead. He was a big, strong, old-fashioned centre-forward. I had a lot of respect for him.

Which young player do you tip for future success?
Although John Terry is established now I tip him for more and more success. He could reach Bobby Moore stature. He really could. I remember talking to Dave Sexton a few years ago and he told me about John and predicted great things for him. Dave has always been a shrewd judge. Then I think John came under the influence of some people who weren't good for him, though we won't mention any names. And I said to John that he had a golden opportunity and that he mustn't waste it, that he had to stop himself being led astray. I let him know that Dave Sexton, who was part of the England set up, had been looking at him. I don't know if he took any notice of me, because I expect a few people would have been saying the same thing to him at the time, but I saw him the other day at a do for Ossie at Langham's and he came up to me and said 'I owe you Ron, you did me a favour'. He'll tell you that himself.

What did you dislike most about being a professional footballer?
Very little. If you push me on it I suppose travelling home from Carlisle when you've lost 1-0 in a League Cup tie wasn't a barrel of laughs.

What do you regard as the biggest mistake you made in your career?
It depends if you mean my footballing career or my business career. I don't think I made many in football, but I made a couple of bad ones in business. Trusting the wrong people, that type of thing. In football, I suppose I should have stayed at Chelsea, if I could have, when my playing career ended. Instead I went to Brentford as a coach. Perhaps if I'd stayed at Chelsea I could have ended up looking after the youth side or something along those lines. I would have loved to have done that, but Geoff Hurst was manager at the time and I didn't like him and he didn't like me, so it wasn't going to happen. You've just got to get on with things in life, haven't you?

Who would have won a fight between you and Norman Hunter?
That's a bit of a stupid question, isn't it? I thought you were doing a sensible book. I'll tell you something now, and you might not believe it, but I've never had a fight in my life. I mean a proper fight with fists. I'm not saying I couldn't have a fight, I'm just saying I've never had one, and I hope I never will.

Did anyone scare you, either in terms of aggression or skill?
Nobody frightened me. Names didn't mean anything to me. I got kicked just as much as the next man. People forget that. I just got on with it.

Do you get angry being called a dirty player, when many Chelsea fans would call you hard but fair?
I'll throw the question back to you. Was I a dirty player? I was at a dinner the other day, up in Wales, and a couple of Jack the Lads were full of drink and started getting lippy. One of them shouts 'Oi Harris, all you ever did was kick people'. I collared them in the corner afterwards, when they never had the crowd around them, and said: 'Listen to me a minute son. I played football at the highest level for twenty-one years. I served under seven managers. I must have had something better than the ability to just kick people. Don't you think?'

What did they say?
They agreed.

Who gave you the nickname Chopper, and why did this end up replacing Buller?
Mickey Greenaway and the boys gave me the name Chopper, because I chopped people down I suppose. I remember hearing them shout 'get stuck in Chopper' and things like that, and it just spread. Before I knew it even the milkman was calling me Chopper. I soon got used to it and I preferred it to Buller. Peter Osgood gave me that one because he reckoned I'd come in to training each morning and come out with a load of bullshit, which was a bit rich coming from him.

What is your big passion outside of football?
I enjoy watching rugby. The internationals are great. Rugby is a good old-fashioned, honest game and I have to be truthful and tell you that if football is on the telly, and rugby is on the other side, then I'll watch the rugby. Unless, of course, it's Chelsea playing.

Favourite book, film, album?
I never read a book. I had a book out last year and I never read that. I don't even read the newspaper, except the sports pages. I don't really watch films

either. The last time I went to the cinema was when somebody dragged me along to see Titanic. No, I didn't cry. Tell a lie, a friend took me to see Bridget Jones Diary or whatever they call it and I slept through the whole thing. So Titanic was the last film I saw. Music? My favourite musician is myself. I love karaoke and can do Elvis – Always On My Mind. Why are you laughing? I've made number three in the charts. I bet you ain't. They can't take that away from me.

Do you have a favourite country or place you like to visit?
Australia was nice. I went there with Chelsea. We also did Barbados about three years running. Tommy Docherty knew how to pick a holiday.

If there was one thing about this country you could change, what would it be?
I've never voted and I never will. I don't think it makes any difference. The Government, whoever they are, is a big con. They bullshit all the time and what they give with one hand they take away with the other. I just want to live to a good age and enjoy my three wonderful grandchildren.

What have you been doing since you stopped playing football and what is your ambition for the future?
A long, long time ago I was a millionaire, and that was before a house with four windows and a door with the right postcode was enough to make you minted. I came out of football and bought a golf club for £330,000 and sold it for £1.8m twenty years back. Sadly, I trusted people, and got fleeced. There are people who have nice houses in the country bought with my money and I was not advised well. A thing called capital gains tax tripped me up – big time. I lost a lot. My ambition is to get back there and I think I will.

After Brentford and the golf club episode, I recovered and bought a small holiday complex in Warminster, down in Wiltshire. I still live there now, but I sold the holiday park about three years back and I now concentrate on the after-dinner and corporate hospitality circuit. I've formed a business called Chopper Harris Promotions and it's going well. I am really enjoying myself. It is nice to be back here at Chelsea and to be welcome. The club now involves us old players in events and they've even got a Ron Harris Suite dining area.

I'm glad it's happened this way because under Bates you never knew whether you were coming or going. One minute he wanted you around and you were invited to functions and to speak, and then the next we were treated like parasites. It was all very confusing. In the end I just walked away for a few years. Did you know Bates sued me once? I said something in the press he didn't like and he set the lawyers on me. I think they were called Ruck & Ruck or something. Very appropriate. I think it cost me £1100.

What are the key differences between the modern game and when you were playing?

The honesty has gone. The game is full of cheats. I'm sorry to say that, but it's true. They're at it all the time and each season the barriers are pushed a bit further. How can we allow a group of players to surround a referee and physically jostle him, shout and bawl at him? And then there's all the stuff that happens off the ball. They should set up a panel and use the technology we have and discipline people for incidents the camera has picked up and the referee hasn't. Referees have to put up with so much shit it is unbelievable. Referees are under such pressure, but they should feel able to send off nine players on one side if necessary. The balance of power has shifted. People don't like the way the game is going, but there is nobody strong enough to stand up to the players, the television companies, the clubs, the managers, or whoever it may be.

I am glad I played when I did, I really am. I know there is lots more money swishing around nowadays, and of course, I would have loved a slice of that, but we played honestly and we all had a healthy respect for one another – for the refs, for the managers, and for the fans. I'm proud of that.

John Terry – charms his women and drinks his beer

John Terry

John Terry was born on December 7th, 1980. Fittingly, a record by Abba called SuperTrouper was top of the pops. He made his Chelsea debut in 1998 and in 2004 succeeded Marcel Desailly as captain. In 2005 he led the club to the Premiership title and a League Cup victory over Liverpool, his season crowned when he was voted the Professional Footballers Association Player Of The Year. He has firmly established himself at the heart of the England defence and is widely tipped to become the country's next captain

Where did you grow up and what is your family background?

I grew up in Essex, in a little town called Barking, on the Thames View Estate. My mum and dad split up when I was fifteen or sixteen years old. I have a brother Paul, who is eighteen months older than me. He's just had a great season at Yeovil Town. They took the Second Division championship and they've only been in the league five minutes. I'm delighted for him. Two championship medals in the Terry family in one year can't be bad. My brother is married to Paul Konchesky's sister. They met through me. This was when Paul was still at Charlton. We played in the same district side and now they're married with two lovely kids. Obviously his dad wants the boy to play for Yeovil and has got him a sweet little kit, but his uncle bought him the Charlton strip. To put the cat among the pigeons I have arranged for Richard Millham, the Megastore Manager, to send him down the new Chelsea kit.

What team did you support as a child and who were your heroes?

It's got to be Man United I'm afraid. Sorry to say it, but that's how I was. My dad and granddad were both big Man U fans and I followed suit. I loved Bryan Robson and Eric Cantona, and thought they were great players. They had skill but were strong as well, and both of them scored goals. My dad was a big Ray Wilkins fan. But let's be clear, I'm Chelsea through and through now. I was only a kid when I followed Man United. I love this club.

What were your feelings about Chelsea at this time?

I spent a year in between Chelsea and Man United, deciding which one to sign for, but deep down I knew all along. Every summer I went up to Man United and had two weeks of training, but throughout the season I was at Chelsea. We had a trainer at Chelsea called Bob Orsborn who was brilliant. He's still here now and I get on really well with him, and he was the main reason I signed for Chelsea. The training was brilliant, so enjoyable. I just fell in love with the club and we had a great bunch of lads who I stayed with for about six years after that.

How did you become a professional footballer? Did you follow your brother?

In a way, I suppose, with my brother being older, and seeing him progress must have had an influence, but my dad was there for me from the start. He had a chance to become a professional when he was younger, had the opportunity to sign for West Ham as well as a couple of other clubs, but he decided against it in the end. He met my mum, thankfully, and my brother and myself were born, so he didn't take that path. But you know, when my brother and myself were born he drummed football into us right from when we were babies. There are pictures of us with a size five football in hospital, soon after we were born, and it's almost bigger than us. Since I can remember I always dreamt of becoming a professional footballer.

Bobby Moore grew up on the Thames View Estate, and he was a big hero for us. Everyone knew where his mum lived and I often used to go and look at the house. I ended up playing for Senrab as a boy, and they produced a few players over the years, people like Ray Wilkins, Jermain Defoe, Ledley King and Paul Konchesky. It all started with my dad, though, and people say that we are similar.

Does your heart go out to your brother as he is in a lower league?

No. I mean, growing up with my brother I saw how things went for him, and he was at Charlton for a couple of years and did two years YTS and then got turned down when it came to turning professional. I remember seeing him for those two or three weeks after, you know, sobbing his heart out, so I knew how much it meant to him. Seeing that disappointment was terrible. Then, when I had my chance of a YTS, my brother and Dad said 'you've got two years and it goes so quickly, don't waste it and make sure you go and try your hardest'. And I did that. I worked so hard in my first year at Chelsea as a YTS and then I was given a professional contract. Yeovil have a good side, a good stadium and a good manager, and my brother is playing football and doing well. They might not be in a lower league for long either. Look at what Wigan Athletic have achieved.

What were your first impressions of Chelsea when you came here?

I fell in love with the club straight away. I remember coming to one game and then driving home in the car and Dad said to me 'you love it, don't you?' and I said, 'Dad, I do, I think I want to sign for Chelsea'. As I said, he was Man United and he kept saying to me 'just wait and see, get a feel for Man United and don't go jumping into anything'. That was the right advice at the time, to consider my options, but my heart was set on Chelsea. I waited a year and made my decision, but all along I knew I was going to choose Chelsea.

What was your first professional game and what are your memories?

My first professional game came when I was seventeen years old, against Aston Villa in the Cup. We beat them 4-1 and Wisey got sent off. I was on the pitch for about two minutes, having come on as a substitute for Dan Petrescu. He wasn't too happy about being brought off. He walked straight down the tunnel and didn't even bother to shake my hand, which at the time was disappointing as it was my debut. So I was on the pitch for two minutes and Wisey got sent off and what with all the commotion my debut was sort of taken out the limelight. The papers the next day were full of Wisey's sending off and nobody seemed to notice I had played my first game for Chelsea. Nobody except me and my family.

The whole experience was very vivid. I walked out on to the pitch and felt like the proudest man ever. To have worked so hard to get to where I had dreamt of being as a boy, to be standing out on the pitch at Stamford Bridge meant an awful lot to me. That memory will stay with me for the rest of my life. My full debut was against Oldham and we won 2-0. Tore Andre Flo got injured that day.

What do you think of the Chelsea Dream Team?

The honest truth is that I can't believe it. I am shocked and gobsmacked that the fans have voted me in there with the likes of Zola and Peter Osgood. I really am touched they rate me in the top eleven Chelsea players of all time, and I would like to thank everyone who voted for me. I've always had a great relationship with the fans and I think it stems from the time when I was one of the few young English players coming into a side dominated by foreign stars. The fans know that with me they will always get two hundred percent, and that even if I have a bad game I always give my utmost, and I want to stay at Chelsea Football Club for the rest of my career. But that team looks pretty special, doesn't it?

Who is the best manager you've ever played under?

Jose Mourinho, without a doubt. He is the best manager by a long way. He has great self-belief and this is passed on to the players. I have a lot of respect for Claudio Ranieri. He was very good. I had a little spell with Luca Vialli and he was great, but you know, Jose is the best I have worked under so far. They call him The Special One, and that is quite an accurate description.

What is your most memorable game?

Winning the Carling Cup against Liverpool was special as it was the first Cup victory for me and most of the other lads. Although the Charlton match itself last season wasn't particularly memorable, the celebrations before and after were, as that was the game where we received our champions medals. The victories against Barcelona and Bayern Munich in the 2005 Champions

League were fantastic games. We knew we'd played in big matches those evenings, and we did well against top-quality opposition.

How disappointing was the 2002 FA Cup final?
It was very disappointing to lose to Arsenal like that, but it made me hungrier to succeed next time. I think it's important to have a plan in the FA Cup. To get my chance and then see things go wrong, from the moment I woke up really, was a massive letdown. But we are like a big family at Chelsea, and want to win as many trophies as we can, and that defeat made everyone much more hungry for success. It wasn't just me. The thing is to keep going and do better next time. We know the big one for all the fans now is the Champions League and that's the one we want to bring home.

What is your most memorable goal?
The one I scored against Fulham in the FA Cup semi-final meant a lot, as it put us through to the final, but the winning goal against Barcelona in the 2005 season was pretty special. If I had to choose, though, it would be the goal against Barcelona.

Which team do you dislike the most and why?
Tottenham. It's part of the culture here, hating Tottenham. I don't know why or when it started, but it has rubbed off on me.

What is your worst Chelsea memory?
Three really. Losing to Liverpool in the Champions League, losing to Arsenal in the FA Cup final, and the Monaco fiasco. Monaco still hurts today, so that must have been horrendous. If I had to choose the worst out of those three it would have to be losing to Liverpool.

Who is your most difficult opponent?
Thierry Henry at Arsenal. He's got everything – pace, great touch, and he is a great finisher. He is the most difficult forward to mark, and you really have to be on top of your game when you are up against him. There are some pretty useful players about, but Henry stands out for me.

Which young player do you tip for future success?
At Chelsea I would say Robert Huth. I don't think of him as a young player, but he is, and he is going to be a legend.

What do you dislike most about being a professional footballer?
Did anyone say the training? Not me, I love the training. There is nothing I dislike. I love every minute of being a professional footballer. It has to be the best job in the world.

What is the biggest mistake you've made in your career?

I was disappointed with the situation that happened with the night-club incident. That was a big strain, going to court and everything. Doing stupid things is all part of growing up, but nevertheless, I should have known better. People say famous footballers are targeted unfairly, but I don't really agree with that. If you want to keep out of the papers, then keep your nose clean. That's the bottom line.

How did it feel becoming the Chelsea captain at such a relatively young age?

I was vice captain to Marcel Desailly and Franco Zola, but I didn't expect it to come so soon. Jose Mourinho arrived at the club and decided to make me captain and naturally I was over the moon. He told me on the way to America. Hopefully I can stay captain for a long time. I don't think I was too young. My dad's hero Ray Wilkins, he captained Chelsea when he was in his teens, didn't he? That was before my time, but I don't think age matters too much. People have mentioned me as a future England captain, and obviously I would love to do that job for my country, if the opportunity arose, but even to be an England regular is a huge honour.

Do you have a favourite book, film and album?

I'm not a great reader, but I thought Tony Adams' autobiography was a class book. I admire Tony Adams and watched him a lot as a kid. I think I learnt a great deal from him, seeing how he played the game. He was strong and determined and a great leader. Music-wise, I like old-school R&B. Usher, that kind of thing. I don't see many films.

Do you have a favourite country or place that you like to visit?

I've been to Dubai for the last four years. Just a bit of sun with the girlfriend. Ten years ago nobody really knew about Dubai over here, but it seems to me they are building out there at a rate of knots. It really is a fantastic place. A chance to unwind and soak up the sun.

If there was one thing about this country you could change, what would it be?

There are a lot of things wrong with this country and we all know it, but the problem is we have allowed a situation to develop where you can no longer voice opinions. I'm not going to stick my neck out here. I'm a footballer. There are people we pay and elect to speak out. It's just a shame they don't.

What do you think you'll do when you retire?

I'd still want that everyday involvement with football. Hopefully I can help Chelsea in some way. Maybe I will be manager one day. You never know.

Eddie McCreadie – attending a fancy dress party as a Gestapo agent

Eddie McCreadie

Eddie McCreadie was born on April 15th, 1940. Adolf Hitler had just invaded Denmark and Norway. Whispering Grass was the popular song of the day. He was signed from East Stirling by Tommy Docherty in 1962 and went on to make 410 appearances for Chelsea over the next twelve years, including the 1965 League Cup victory, the 1967 FA Cup final defeat, and the 1970 FA Cup and 1971 European Cup Winners Cup triumphs. He was capped by Scotland on more than twenty occasions. In 1975 he became Chelsea manager and, against the odds, took a team of youngsters out of the Second Division and back into the First. Sadly, a contractual dispute led to Eddie resigning and he subsequently emigrated to America, his talents and potential lost to the British game

Where did you grow up and what is your family background?

I was born and raised in what could only be called the slums of Glasgow in Scotland, the youngest of a family of two older brothers, Jim and Jack, and my older sister Esther. It was a very difficult upbringing. There were many days we didn't have very much to eat and the memories are still with me to this day. My mother's love for us, her willingness to sacrifice to put us first everyday of her life until she died, at the cost of her own dignity at times, and finding a way to feed and clothe us, was awe-inspiring. And yet, as poor as we were, I don't remember having an unhappy childhood. We weren't alone. Everyone around us was poor also.

What team did you support as a child and who were your heroes?

Partick Thistle was my team. I shall always remember the yellow and amber stripes when the players would enter the field prior to kick-off, and how the colours would complement the beautiful green grass of the Firhill pitch. I never missed a game on a Saturday. Firhill was only a half-hour walk from where we lived. I would go by myself if no one would take me. I was between eight and eleven years of age then, and as I was pretty small I would invaria-bly find a broken fence to get in or I would ask some grown-ups if they would lift me up and drop me over. Somehow I always managed to get in without paying. This was handy, as I had no money.

I loved playing football, but wasn't aware at that time if I was any good or not. But like most boys I would dream that one day I might play for my favourite team.

I brag to friends sometimes that I can still name every player in that team, even today. But my favourite player was their right-winger, Johnny McKenzie.

He was fast, skilful and looked so graceful as he raced past most full-backs. He also represented Scotland on a couple of occasions. He was, for sure, my hero and I just loved watching him play.

Two, perhaps interesting, very brief stories about Partick Thistle and Johnny McKenzie. Years later, after signing with East Stirling, a Scottish Second Division Club, I began to draw the attention of several clubs, including Rangers and Celtic, the big clubs, but no Partick Thistle. Although I was delighted and excited to be the focus of such wonderful clubs, I was, however, hoping that Partick Thistle might come in for me. They never did. Six months after Tommy Docherty flew up from London and had no problem persuading me to sign for Chelsea, in 1962, it was brought to my attention that Partick Thistle had indeed sent their scout to watch me play – and his report to the club was that he didn't think I was good enough. Talk about unrequited love.

Many years later in my career, and some years after Johnny McKenzie had retired, I was invited to the Scottish Sports Writers Dinner in Glasgow, since I was a member and then current full-back of our national team. During a break in festivities I needed to pay a visit to the restroom. As I was washing my hands I glanced in the mirror to see a gentleman who smiled at me and looked vaguely familiar.

'I hope I'm not bothering you,' he said, 'but I'm a huge fan of yours, Eddie. I have watched many of your games with Chelsea and Scotland and I think you are just great.' My mouth fell open. 'I know who you are,' I stammered out. 'You are Johnny McKenzie and you aren't going to believe this, but you are my hero.' Now it was his turn for his mouth to fall open. 'Are you serious, Eddie?' he said to me in disbelief. I proceeded to explain my side to him. He listened in total surprise and was so humble I can't remember in my whole life ever being paid such a wonderful compliment.

What was your first game and what are your memories of that game?
Signing with Chelsea immediately gave me a confidence in myself that I hadn't felt before. I had seen many of their famous players on television – Terry Venables, Bobby Tambling, Peter Bonetti, Barry Bridges, and so on – but when I stopped to think about that it knocked my confidence back a bit. I wondered if I could really hold my own in such exalted company. I had no idea at this time if I could possibly be as good as they were. But I was prepared to play in the reserves for a couple of seasons in the hope I might get a chance in the first team. There was one thing I was sure of, I was going to work as hard as I could and listen to everything that the coaches were going to teach me.

I arrived in time for pre-season prior to the club's debut in the Second Division, after being relegated. The training was something I hadn't experienced before. Apart from the tactical side, which was way above anything I had ever been taught, the hardest thing was the training. Wow. It was so demanding, but I soon became accustomed to it. I also found that I was a better athlete than I had given myself credit for. To my genuine surprise, instead of starting in the reserves I was immediately chosen at left back in the first team for our first game away at Rotherham.

I was obviously very nervous before the game started and when we entered the field I was suddenly aware that I was indeed representing Chelsea. Now I really was nervous. Then, as the game began, I realised the most incredible thing – it was easy. So really easy. As a full-back, when you receive the ball from your team mates at any other level, the passes are not always accurate, and you end up stretching most of the time to get it under control, before passing it on to another player. But now I was receiving passes where the ball would just swoosh perfectly across the turf to my feet, and I didn't have to move. And again, at lower levels, your next job is to pass it on to begin your team's build-up, and you can end up looking a fool when everyone is hiding and nobody wants the ball. This was so different and new. I had stepped up several levels. When I received these passes I would look up, and lo and behold, there were three and sometimes four Chelsea players at different angles looking to take the ball off me and take responsibility.

I realised very quickly that this was indeed the Big League and the Chelsea players, my new team-mates, my new friends, made me understand very quickly what 'world class' meant. We won that game against Rotherham 1-0 and Bobby Tambling scored. We also went straight back up that season. I remember settling in very quickly in the team and stayed there for twelve seasons. Playing with such wonderful players made my job so much easier. I have always felt humble, honoured and grateful to have played with so many great players.

What was your first impression of Chelsea?
It was like a different world. It was the leap from economy class to first. Everything was done for the players in order that we only had to concentrate on winning games. First class travel, first class hotels and they even dressed us in club suits. We had the best equipment and the best coaches. I loved it. I thrived on the respect the club had for our players and the enormous respect and pride everyone had for our club. The sense of history and tradition at Chelsea was immense even then. To this very day I feel thankful and proud to have been chosen to play for such a wonderful club and to be a small part of its wonderful history.

What are your thoughts about the Dream Team and would you have chosen any other players?
First of all, to be included and selected by Chelsea fans for the Dream Team is perhaps the most complimentary honour I have ever received next to

representing my country. I have lived in the United States these last twenty-seven years and I must admit to not keeping up with all the football back home on a regular basis. But I do on occasion watch Chelsea games and it makes me very happy that they are doing so well. I have and always will have great affection for my club and its wonderful fans. Considering the quality of players that have played for our club over the last hundred years, and surely not forgetting the outstanding quality of this present team, this is indeed a great honour. It looks like a very impressive team and one that might win a 'few' games. I can't help smiling when I look at that back four of Ron Harris, John Terry, Marcel Desailly and myself, and know it would not be a welcoming place for the opposing forwards.

Who was the best manager you played under?
I was signed by Tommy Docherty and given my first opportunity by him and for that I shall always be grateful. He was a considerable influence on my career and helped me in many ways to accomplish what I eventually achieved. My other manager was Dave Sexton who was, I thought, a wonderful person and a great coach. I don't remember ever entering a game for him, where I didn't feel his trust that I would accomplish what he wanted from me. They were both also instrumental in any success I may have had as a coach. I am thankful to them both.

What is your most memorable game?
Our FA Cup final series against Leeds in 1969-70 season, for sure. It was a great achievement against a great team. One or two players don't make a team, but I felt then, and I still do to this day, that we desperately missed my dearest friend, Alan Hudson, who was injured and missed both games. With no disrespect to anyone, I believe his leadership and mastery in midfield was sorely missed by us all, and if he had been able to play we would not have needed a second game.

What is your most memorable goal?
Again there is no doubt in my mind. It was the one I got past the great Gordon Banks. He was a superb goalkeeper and only he could have kept our own Peter Bonetti out of that England team. When Chelsea played Leicester City in the 1965 League Cup Final, I remember Barry Bridges was injured and the Doc told me before the game that he was going to play me at centre forward in his place, and did I have any problem with that? 'Are you kidding?' I thought to myself, but instead found myself saying 'none at all, let's go for it.'

It was a rainy, muddy pitch. I picked up a throw from Peter Bonetti just outside our own box and saw a gap between Graham Cross and his other centre back – two headhunters for sure. I hit the ball between them both on the half-way line and ran as fast as I could. Gordon came out to the edge of the box to meet me, and even though I was exhausted I managed to lunge at the ball one last time and knock it past him. It literally trickled over the goal line. The funniest thing is that if Gordon had stayed on his line he could have thrown his cap on it and saved it.

What is your favourite terrace song?
It has to be Blue Is The Colour. I have been told the supporters still sing it today. That is amazing.

Which team did you dislike the most?
As much as I admired their ability as a team and the quality of their individual players, Leeds United lost my respect by the way they intimidated most sides with the wilful endeavours of some players to go over the top of the ball in order to hurt opponents. I was always rather proud of my team mates that they never backed down to them.

What is your worst Chelsea memory?
Misjudging the bounce of the ball in the muddy conditions on the goal line in the 1970 FA Cup final at Wembley, which gave the dreaded Leeds United their first goal. Thank God we won the replay. I could have gone down in Chelsea history for all the wrong reasons. Such is the lot of a professional footballer. You're always on a knife-edge poised between triumph and disaster.

Who was your most difficult opponent?
I had the privilege of playing against the best wingers in the world at both club and international level, and the answer to that question, after careful thought, would have to be George Best. I never kept count of how many times we played against each other, but it was often. I got the impression early on in our duels that perhaps I wasn't one of George's favourite people. I feel sure he didn't appreciate the physical part of my game and he let me know that verbally on several occasions.

It may be of some surprise to him if he could read these words today, but I was one of his biggest fans and admired him greatly. I thought he was the greatest player I had ever seen. I played my first game against him at Old Trafford when I believe he was only seventeen or eighteen years old. I always regretted what I thought his opinion of me was, and we never talked socially over those ten years. I would rather have been his friend, but this was perhaps the most competitive football in the world. He was George Best and I had a job to do.

Our story, however, had an interesting and happy ending for me, and I truly hope for George too. Many years later, George had moved to the States and was playing for Fort Lauderdale in Florida. I had also moved there and was continuing my coaching career with the Memphis Rogues in the North American Soccer League. I was in my office on the afternoon we were due to play Fort Lauderdale in the evening, when my secretary called and told me that a Mr George Best was in the reception area and would like to see me. I got up from my desk in order to meet him as he came through my office door and he looked great, was tanned and had a wonderful smile on his face as we warmly shook hands.

'How wonderful to see you, George,' I said to him, 'and how kind of you to come and visit me.' I was totally surprised. We chatted for a while and he was, as I knew he would be, a wonderful, friendly and charming man, and I immediately liked him. With a smile on my face, I suggested to him that I had always believed that I wasn't one of his favourite people, and with a smile on his he replied 'I hated your guts, as I knew that every time I had to play against you I was going to get some'.

I decided to ask him a favour. 'George, we are going to a gathering place after the game tonight, where our fans come to meet me and my players. I was wondering if I could impose on you. My players, and especially my American players, would love to meet you, and if you could spend five minutes with them I know they would be thrilled.' He immediately replied 'tell me where, Eddie, and I will be there.'

True to his word, he showed up, but instead of spending five minutes he stayed and talked to my players for a couple of hours. Again I was very impressed. I thought he was a gentleman of considerable class. I still remember how much I enjoyed our short time together and have often thought that if we had not been adversaries over those years, I believe we may have become close friends. I liked him a lot. Thanks for the memories, George.

What is your biggest passion outside of football?
About six years ago, my wife Linda and I built a house on the farm where she was born. We have beautiful views of the mountains and countryside and we enjoy entertaining our friends and my family when they visit from Scotland. I have become a fairly accomplished cook and am able on occasions to make five or six different entrées for thirty or forty people when they visit us for dinner. I enjoy cooking a lot. I also enjoy playing golf several times a week, as I am now retired. And, of course, on occasions I sit down and watch Chelsea play on TV. I still have great memories of my career there, and the wonderful reception I always received from our fans.

Do you have a favourite film, piece of music or book?
This may come as a considerable surprise to many people who know me, and those who knew of me, but the Bible is my favourite book. I was baptised three years ago and this was the greatest thing I have ever done. I am a Christian now and attend church and Sunday school classes on a regular

basis with my wife. This is a complete change to the life I led in the past, but for the very first time in my life I am at last finding peace of mind, and truly have never been happier. I owe all of it to our Lord Jesus Christ.

In conclusion, I would like to say thank you again to our fans for this wonderful honour. Not so long ago Alan Hudson made the journey out here to visit me and to see him made me well up. I am so pleased he has battled back from his horrific accident. I'd been out of touch for many years and once when we chatted I asked him 'Alan, do they remember me down at the Bridge?' Huddy gave me his don't be so silly look and it is wonderful to be remembered. It surely makes me feel very proud but also very humble. Thank you.

Charlie Cooke – Chelsea and Scotland

Charlie Cooke

Charlie Cooke was born on October 14th, 1942. The Second World War was at its midway point and Field Marshall Montgomery was about to triumph at El Alamein. White Christmas by Bing Crosby was a hit for the first time. Charlie moved to Chelsea from Dundee in 1966 and during two spells at the club he made 373 appearances, scoring thirty goals. He was a member of the sides that won the FA Cup in 1970 and the European Cup Winners Cup in 1971, and was capped on sixteen occasions by Scotland. Tommy Docherty has gone on record as saying that Charlie was the best player he ever signed

Where did you grow up and what is your family background?

I grew up in Greenock on the River Clyde, twenty miles down river from Glasgow. My mother was a housewife and my father a shipyard engineer. I was actually born in St Monance, Fife, where we were evacuated to during the Blitz in the Second World War. When we returned to Gibbshill all that remained of the street behind Cedar Crescent where we lived was bombed-out rubble.

The Clyde was the town's lifeblood then. Dumbarton Rock and its shipyards on the other bank stood guard to the upper reaches of the river and down below us on our side were all the shipyards from Port Glasgow to Greenock down towards Gourock. British Rail car ferries chuntered to and from Gourock Pier, where we used to fish, to Dunoon and Rothesay. There'd be the occasional cargo ship, or tanker or even a fleet of warships anchored out in the Firth. And less frequently we might spot, or think we had spotted, one of the American nuclear subs from the Gaerloch on the Firth where they were stationed under a much disputed Anglo-American treaty.

Greenock brings back lots of memories. The Tate & Lyle sugar refinery on Dumfrochar Road looked massive to us as kids and we used to joke that the burn alongside it that took the factory run-off had water rats as big as Shetland ponies. I remember many times as a teenager riding the top-deck front seat of the red bus with its picture window view to go train or play at Parklea fields in Port Glasgow.

We'd pass the yards along the river near five o'clock when the workers were pouring out the gates in their dungarees and into our bus, the lines of double deckers waiting for them. My father worked in the yards three nights and a Sunday overtime when things were good. Today they're all gone, including my dad, God rest his soul.

What team did you support as a child and who were your heroes?

Greenock Morton was our team. They played at Cappielow Park. The crowds were bigger than today. There were probably a couple of thousand regulars but it seemed like a lot more. Our goalkeeper Jimmy Cowan played for Scotland and I remember other names like Johnny Divers, Davie Cupples, Tommy Orr and Jimmy White. I remember getting lifted over the turnstile and everything being so crowded and noisy and exciting. Afterwards we'd queue up for the standing-room-only buses home, then get the rest of the day's football scores in the Saturday evening Sporting Green or Pink, and take fish and chips home to the family.

What were your feelings about Chelsea at this time?

Scottish football was all we really knew. We would read the scores from England, but English football seemed like another universe. England were the auld enemy and didn't bear thinking much about except praying to beat them at Home International time. The only other team it would have been possible to support being a Protestant boy from Greenock was Rangers. But they were another world away, even if they were only twenty miles up river. Morton was our team and the only real choice.

How did you become a professional footballer?

I developed my ability in the streets and the parks. That's where we always played. I'd seen the Hungarians and Puskas beat England 6-3 at Wembley on Pathe News at the local cinema and it was so unbelievable to see 'the unbeatable' England lose at home. Embarrassment for the auld enemy and pure joy for us.

The Hungarians had put together some great results the previous year and the world was mesmerised by them and their new system of playing with a withdrawn centre-forward, in their case, Hideguti. But the player I wanted to see was their captain Puskas – their left-footed sergeant major from the Hungarian army who'd been scoring a bunch of goals. I watched him line up in the centre circle just before the kick-off. He juggled the ball a couple of times then kicked it high in the air and as it dropped stopped it dead on his left foot. No doubt I exaggerated what he did in my own mind, but I thought it was the greatest thing I'd ever seen.

So because of Puskas I started to juggle. I'd juggle in the backyard or wherever I could. Now you can't be that loony and practice that much without some improvement. I got pretty good and was made the Greenock School captain when I first went there. I believe everything in my career came about because of juggling. I got fantastic satisfaction beating my previous record. I could tell you each day what my records were for any combination of feet, head, thigh – you name it.

Then in High School I started playing for a local club team Port Glasgow

Rovers. Unfortunately the gym teacher at Greenock High School wasn't happy. Local youth clubs had been poaching high-school players and the schools had suffered when scheduling conflicts arose, so they made it a rule that you couldn't play both. The rule of course made no sense to us boys who would've played three times on a Saturday and again on Sunday if allowed. The outcome was I was banned from playing school football from then on. Later, I learned that I had been pencilled in for a Scottish schoolboys trial. I didn't like the gym teacher at all and would have liked him even less if I had known this at the time.

When I was fifteen and still at Greenock I moved on from the Rovers to a semi-pro side – Renfrew Juniors. They were run by Donald McNeil, a well-known personality in Scottish junior football famed for spotting young talent and moving them on to pro clubs. I used to take the bus there twice a week to practice and on Saturday afternoons to play. The team had journeyman players in their mid and late twenties finishing their junior careers, maybe a couple of older ex-pros finishing up altogether and us schoolboy wannabes. Remember, I was a slip of a lad playing and training with these pros, grown men with years of experience behind them, and I did well, making the team immediately as an inside forward.

I even began taking the penalty kicks. This might seem bizarre that the smallest and youngest player on the team was taking the penalties. But at the time I was juggling and practising so much and growing so confident that I thought nothing of it.

I wasn't at Renfrew long when Bobby Calder, the Aberdeen head scout, unbeknown to me came down to see me play. He visited my parents the following week and I agreed and signed provisional forms. I earned 12/6d a week on the provisional contract and was delighted. Today, and maybe even then, this was a pittance, but to me still in school it was fantastic. I was chuffed about getting paid enough to have beers on Saturday nights and go to Cragburn the local dance hall in Gourock with my mates. But above all I had signed pro forms. My dream was coming true.

About a week later I was in the locker room after a home game when in comes Donald with this well-dressed man. They walk past the old pros and right up to me and Donald says: 'This is Mr Jim Smith, the head scout for Rangers.' I was stunned. We shook hands and Mr Smith asked if I'd like to visit Ibrox and have a look around and maybe talk with the manager. Now this was big. Ibrox. The 'Gers. It didn't get better than that. So what did I do? I didn't ask him to talk to my agent who of course didn't exist, or ask how I might escape from the provisional contract with the Dons. I just looked at him and said: 'Sorry sir, but I've already met with Mr Calder and promised to go to Aberdeen.' And that's where it was left. In less time than it takes to walk the tunnel at Stamford Bridge the dream of a lifetime had come and gone.

What was your first professional game and what are your memories?
I went to Aberdeen and was in the first-team as a sixteen-year-old, but the game I remember best was during the provisional period. I was still at school and living at home and Aberdeen wanted to give me a game with the reserves to decide whether they would take me on full-time or not. So I played for the reserves against Clyde reserves. George Herd, who was a Scottish international inside-forward was playing that day, coming back from injury, and I thought it was fantastic just to be on the same pitch as him. I remember it was a beautiful sunny day and we drew 1-1. I did pretty well and signed shortly after. But playing that game, awe-struck by George Herd's every move and doing pretty good myself and thinking yes maybe I can handle this, was a great moment.

What were your first impressions of Chelsea when you came to the club?
In my fourth season at Aberdeen I was chosen Player Of The Year. The club had sold off key players – skipper George Kinnel, George Mulhall and Doug Fraser to English clubs and had replaced them with youngsters with no experience. Our results were suffering and rightly or wrongly I felt let down and asked away. The result was that I was transferred to Dundee for a Scottish record fee of £44,000.

I was at Dundee a year and a bit and was voted Player Of The Year again and in an ironic twist I met with Tommy Docherty in Edinburgh the next day and signed for Chelsea. This time the fee was £ 72,000 and a game the following season at Dundee, a record between British clubs at the time. I always had fun claiming it was the record as the game put it over the £72,000 paid the previous year by Spurs to Dundee for Alan Gilzean, who apparently was the player I had been purchased to replace.

This never made sense to me as we were totally different players in different positions with different styles and abilities. But that was the Dundee spin when fan favourite Gilly left.

A point here about the Player Of The Year awards. There's a lot of things in my career I feel pretty good about, but the Player of the Year awards I am most proud of all. One at Aberdeen, one at Dundee and three at Chelsea was a pretty good haul I think. In fact I share the record at three with Zola at Chelsea and that's what I'm proudest and happiest of all about in my career.

But back to Chelsea. From Edinburgh we flew to London to join the Chelsea party flying out to Barcelona for the Fairs Cup match. It's been said often that I was bought to replace Terry Venables, but I truly didn't know anything about it. I knew the club had some great results and were being tipped to be the new Busby Babes. Tommy Doc's 'babes' had developed a hard-working, fast-paced style with lots of success and were being tipped as the team for the future.

Charlie Cooke

What are your thoughts about the Dream Team and are there other players you would have included?

I think it's a terrific team and I'm proud to be included. The back three of Peter Bonetti, Eddie Mac and Buller is like old times. Catty was the model pro. By far the best goalkeeper I ever played with. He was often just about unbeatable, especially away from home in some of the toughest grounds. He surely has to be among the best keepers of all time. Eddie and Buller were tough-as-teak pros who never let anything go past them easily. Same thing in training I can tell you from painful experience. What a great foundation for the defence. Terry and Desailly are the perfect combination of youth and experience down the middle with plenty of power in the air for set pieces at either end. And I think I'd add Webby for defensive cover and some attacking umph at set plays when needed.

Wisey would be biting ankles and be just the man to fill in the gaps in mid-field and drive on his team mates. If for any reason Wisey wasn't available Johnny Hollins could slot in there very nicely too. Frank Lampard would get lots of chances to show off his power shooting and score some more fantastic goals. Huddy. What can we say? Mr Smoothie. Always getting himself out of trouble with silky control and brilliant bursts of speed that you never thought he had. Keeping everyone around him in the game with pinpoint passes delivered in that elegant unhurried style of his. Osgood and Zola. What a dream combination. Ossie gliding past opponents and slotting in superb solo goals from the edge of the box. Or shouldering defenders in the air at set pieces and crashing in near-post headers. And Gianfranco. Zorro I like to think of him, moving at lightening speed, beating defenders at will with his quickness and touch and finishing his runs off with rifle shot accuracy. Yes, I think this team could win a few games okay.

Who is the best manager you have ever played under?

That's an unfair question, but if I must choose I'd go for Tommy Docherty and Dave Sexton. Tommy was larger than life. Tough, boisterous and a laugh a minute with rapier-fast repartee. Dave was quiet, contemplative and unassuming, and couldn't have been more different to Tommy if he tried. But both knew their stuff and not surprisingly appealed to different groups of personalities in the team. I'd say that both succeeded and suffered because of their personalities. Tommy could rouse his teams to battle okay and was a terrific manager for someone like me and those others who enjoyed his banter. But his joking personality and painful straight talking sometimes could also be divisive and he had clashes with Terry Venables, George Graham and Barry Bridges before I arrived and they were all soon to be gone, followed not so much later by Tommy himself.

Dave's determination and soccer savvy was a key part of our successful Cup runs, but he was maybe too pensive and reserved when it might have served him better to blow the occasional gasket and get everybody's undivided attention. He was a canny strategist and field general, but I don't think he was ever able to really get to grips with some of the strong personalities, and his ongoing hassles with Ossie and Huddy and the club's financial troubles took everyone's eye off the ball. His signings of players like Tommy Baldwin, David Webb, John Dempsey and Ian Hutchinson and his grooming of Alan Hudson were inspired. They all arrived just at the right time and played key roles in the team's successes. The bottom line is we had some great cup runs from 1966 through to 1972, in quarter-finals, semis or finals almost every season.

I must also mention Eddie McCreadie who did such a great job against all the odds in bringing on the youngsters in the Butch Wilkins era, when I returned to the Bridge from Crystal Palace. If the company-car, parting-of-the-ways story is true I think that ranks as one of the dumbest, penny-pinching decisions a Chelsea board ever made.

What is your most memorable game as a Chelsea player?
It has to be the FA Cup final replay against Leeds. The first draw at Wembley was tough and all our players were tired and angry we had played so poorly. What most folks couldn't appreciate was the terrible condition of Wembley that year. After a horse show and heavy rains the previous week the famous turf was ankle deep and the ball would hardly bounce. That's why Jack Charlton scored his headed goal. The ball didn't bounce on the dead turf as Eddie Mac expected, and as he swung to clear it the ball rolled under his boot and over the goal line.

The Old Trafford pitch in the replay was better, but it was a rough game with some pretty wild tackling from both teams. Leeds were on a roll in the league and playing some great possession stuff and taking some of the best teams in the country to the cleaners. But they were also infamous for their referee baiting and griping, and their all-around gamesmanship didn't endear them to many. We had an ongoing feud with them and the replay was knee deep in the bad blood that existed between us.

The keys to the replay win I thought, apart from Ossie's and Webby's goals, was Dave putting Buller at full-back against Eddie Gray, thereby stopping him playing like he had done at Wembley where he killed us down our right flank, and Peter Bonetti continuing to play after he was hurt early and limping through to the end. Catty was so important to us. With The Cat in goal we always knew we had a chance to keep things close, no matter how much pressure we were under.

What is your most memorable goal?
That goal Ossie scored at Old Trafford against Leeds in the replay stands out. I saw it recently and it reminded me what a nice goal it was. As I did a

takeover with Ian Hutchinson and was running with the ball in the middle of the field I saw Ossie out of the corner of my eye. I figured he might have a chance if I could get it in there slowly enough beyond Jack Charlton and the other defenders. I knew it would have to be a sort of feathered, floating cross laid out in front of him if Ossie was to have time to get to it. As I put it in I remember thinking 'that's a nice ball'. I saw Ossie moving to it and knew he was going to get there. It was a beautiful cross and a great finish. Forty years later I think I'm prouder of it now than I was at the time.

What is your favourite terrace song?
There's an awful lot of them, aren't there? The Shed was where all the energy and noise came from. I've always loved their humour and spontaneity. They were in great form again yesterday at the Bridge against Charlton, although there were a couple of songs I don't think we should repeat. I'm showing my age maybe, but Blue Is The Colour never fails to get me going.

What is your worst Chelsea memory?
Two games stick in my craw. The 1967 FA Cup final loss against Tottenham and the 1972 League Cup final loss to Stoke City. We just never turned up for the Spurs game. They were the better team on the day and easily deserved the win. Coming so early in my first year with Chelsea, and even with some folks saying I had played well, I was sick at how poorly we played. The same can probably be said about the Stoke game although I think we have to look at ourselves in that one.

Stoke hadn't been going any great guns in the league beforehand and I think we were cocky and over-confident and paid the price. It was ironic that George Eastham, the oldest player on the field, scored the winner for Stoke. It was no more than we deserved.

Who was your most difficult opponent?
Eddie McCreadie and Ronnie Harris in practice. Seriously. I've still got the lumps to prove it. But we had tough times against Tommy Smith of Liverpool. Forget all the hard man talk. Smithy was all that and a lot more. I've got no idea what he was like off the field, but he was one of the toughest, most accomplished defenders and best team leaders I ever faced.

Which young player do you tip for future success?
I like Joe Cole. Maybe it's that he plays a bit like I did, working the ball and taking opponents on. But I think it's difficult to stand out as a midfielder these days as there are so many highly-skilled, hard-working players in that position. Scoring goals and carrying a scoring threat is what differentiates the best from the rest and Joe gets through plenty of work and still has the skills, speed and strength to get goals. He's one for the future for me.

What did you dislike most about being a professional footballer?

I think it was the emotional roller-coaster ride you take with every game you play. The anticipation and preparation for the game was fine and playing was what you lived for, but the post-game emotions can be tough to handle, especially when you've lost a big one, or even a small thing, no matter how well you may feel you've played yourself. Losing always sucks and there's no easy way to deal with it.

What do you regard as the biggest mistake you made in your career?

Apart from all the zillions there's one major one I would change if I could. This was believing the press when I was a young pro at Aberdeen and basically becoming what everyone expected of me. As a youngster I was a ball-playing inside-forward who scored goals. Not unlike Joe Cole and Frank Lampard at Chelsea if I can make that comparison. But my ball-playing skills were the things that caught the eye of the press at Aberdeen and they started dubbing me as the 'schemer' and the 'playmaker' and the 'engine'. I was too inexperienced to see what believing this would do to my game and began to think of myself that way.

Before I knew it I was paying less attention to scoring and more to making goals for others. So my game changed from being a fairly prolific scorer in my first two or three years at Aberdeen, to scoring four or five a season for the rest of my career. In hindsight that was a disaster. I was still a very good striker of the ball. Of course, things didn't go that badly after in my career, but I do view that as a mistake.

What ambitions do you have for the future?

I am a director of Coerver Coaching and want to grow our business even further throughout America. We have licensees in forty-one states who run player camps and coaching clinics. Alf Galustian, the international director of Coerver, and I produce soccer-training videos and books and due wholly to Alf's efforts Coerver is now firmly established in Japan, Australia, New Zealand, Singapore and South Africa and is a growing presence in Europe.

It's a technical programme. We train boys and girls of seven to seventeen years of age in individual and small-group skills and encourage them to express themselves. We believe that it's the players and their abilities and not the team systems that are most important. That given two similar systems, as is the case in most pro leagues around the world, it's the players' individual qualities that make the difference. Hardly radical I grant you, but it's surprising how many clubs and coaches don't apply this simple idea in practice.

As for the game in America it's going gangbusters and I think you'd have to have been in a coma for the last ten years not to know it. The US women have already been World Champions and the US men are ranked eleventh in FIFA's world rankings and coming on stronger every year. They are my dark horse to win the World Cup in Germany. If you disagree I'll be very happy to take 200-1 against them winning in Germany.

You played at international level when Scotland had a very good side, didn't you?

I don't know about us being a very good side. Our record at qualifying for the World Cup wasn't great. There again only twenty-four teams went through then I believe and qualification was much tougher. That said I played for Scotland sixteen times, and think of it all as a bit of a mess really. I played in two parts, with a big gap in between. Stage One ended after we had been out partying in Belgium before a game and got caught returning in the early hours to the hotel. There was a big fuss and it made the back page of the tabloids and Bobby Brown the manager later featured it in his exposé of his four years at the SFA when he was sacked. There were several of us out that night, but the others played in Scotland and got a free pass. No names, no pack drill. I was the Anglo and was made ringleader of the whole disaster, which was crazy as I was a relative outsider to the Rangers and Celtic contingents who made up the core of the squad. But there it was in the tabloids and I didn't see a Scottish team sheet again for years. I understood it though, as there was still resentment of Anglo-based players in those days. The Rangers and Celtic players knew the local journalists and SFA members and had the weight of the Old Firm behind them so they could do as they pleased.

Why has the Scottish team declined so much?

You said that, not me, although I thought the appointment of Bertie Vogts was bizarre. Whoever thought that up needs their heads examined. But I've been away from Scottish football for many years and it would be stupid of me to say I know, but my experiences over the last twenty years in the US tell me a couple of things. The weather in Scotland is iffy at best. In Aberdeen where I played for four years it's brutal. It's not conducive to playing football unless you're into mud wrestling and frostbite. Scottish summers are usually pleasant, but they're unpredictable and it's usually the time when pro clubs shut down and youth football follows suit. The bottom line is there are no truly long periods for youngsters to play in really good conditions.

This isn't that much different to many other parts of the world. But one of the reasons football is growing so fast and successfully in the US is that they have lots of indoor facilities where kids and adults can play during any part of the year. Indoor winter leagues are huge. In Cincinnati where I live there are more than a dozen indoor soccer arenas not counting multi-sports facilities at local schools and colleges. In the fall and winter they're always packed with youth leagues who go outdoors in the spring and summer. So kids in the US can play all year long in competitive leagues if they choose. I don't think that's the case in Scotland, although I'm happy to be corrected.

What is your big passion outside of football?
I think my life is still tied up in football. I'm passionate about Coerver Coaching and get lots of satisfaction seeing the business grow and how it can do good things for its students. It doesn't matter if they don't go on and become professionals or just play for the fun of it because they'll learn good habits and terrific soccer skills and life lessons and have fun doing it. Coerver is great for the students' self-esteem. Take a child who's maybe not fast but who pays attention and applies himself. He develops excellent ball skills to make up for his lack of pace and becomes an important playmaker or maybe just an efficient cog in his team at whatever level the team plays at. That child can feel good about himself and his game. He can be proud of what he's achieved and carry the lessons he's learned about discipline and perseverance and the importance of good coaching and learning proper techniques into every other part of his life. Sounds a bit corny maybe, but it's why we're so passionate about Coerver Coaching.

Favourite book, film, album?
I'm not much of a buff about any of them, but I liked Paul Newman in Hombre. I've never been a big music person but I enjoyed the Phantom of The Opera CD after we saw Sarah Brightman and Michael Crawford starring in the show in New York. I enjoy 'How To...' books that tell you how to change your life for the better in three easy lessons or less.

Do you have a favourite country or place you like to visit?
I love the sun in Southern California. My wife is from there so we still go quite a bit. Of course, I went to California in the late Seventies when I joined the LA Aztecs in the old NASL and know the place pretty well. There's not much better in life than a warm sun, good company and a California sea breeze.

How did you find it coming over and going back to Chelsea for the final game of the season versus Charlton?
It was a lot more fun than I expected. Coming from so far back in the club's history you sometimes wonder if people will know of you, or even care. But the fans were terrific. They haven't changed and I must have signed more autographs yesterday than I have in years. Mind you, when they're telling you they used to watch you when they were kids and went to the Bridge with their dads it definitely makes you laugh. It was good to see Johnny Hollins and Ossie again and catch up on news about our old team-mates. We've all gone our separate ways and it's disappointing sometimes how out of touch we get. But just hearing how everyone is holding up and doing well helps immensely.

The Bridge looked great. The stands looked better and brighter than ever and the grass greener and lusher than I think I've ever seen it at the end of a season. My guest appearance for the game on Sky Sports with Holly was terrific fun. We had the studio's front row seats along with my son Chas and Tommy Baldwin's son Sam, with the trophy alongside for most of the match, and watching the team's post-game celebrations was icing on the cake. It was an occasion when words were truly inadequate and a trip of a lifetime that Chas and I won't soon forget.

The club is a slick operation nowadays for sure and there seems to be a push to embrace the club's history and if I'm a part of that – I'm honoured. It's such an important part of my life and even after all the years and all the times I've done it, coming off the Fulham Road and walking into the Shed End entrance still gives me a great feeling. Like coming home and seeing old friends and family. And in many ways it is.

Super Frank – chim chiminey, chim chiminey, chim chim cheroo

Frank Lampard

Frank Lampard was born on June 20th, 1978. Liverpool had just retained the European Cup, Argentina had beaten Holland to win the World Cup, and John Travolta and Olivia Newton-John were number one in the charts with You're The One That I Want. Frank's father, Frank senior, was a defender for West Ham and England, and young Frank started his career at Upton Park. He was Claudio Ranieri's first English signing, moving to Chelsea in June 2001 for £11m. His career has blossomed at Stamford Bridge and he was pivotal in powering Chelsea to the Premiership title. A goal-scoring midfielder, he is an England regular and his contribution to the game was acknowledged in 2005 when he won both the Football Writers Player Of The Year and Barclays Player Of The Year awards

Where did you grow up and what is your family background?

I grew up in Romford, Essex. I have got two older sisters and we are a really close family.

What team did you support as a child and who were your heroes?

West Ham, obviously, because my dad played for them, and I grew up knowing no different really. It would not have gone down well if I had come out saying I wanted to support Arsenal or Spurs, would it? I watched Dad play for West Ham as a kid, and in terms of heroes, Dad would've been first of all, and then Frank McAvennie and Tony Cottee. I can remember the 1985-86 season even though I was very young, because the Hammers finished third – their best ever League position – and Frank and Tony bagged loads of goals between them. You get certain perks when your dad is a professional footballer, though there are some bad things about it as well. When I was a kid I used to go to West Ham and be behind the scenes, visit the training ground and see the players. As a boy, those are the things you love.

At school the other kids knew Dad was a famous footballer, but it was no massive deal. I got a bit of attention for it, but you know what it's like at school, you don't go around saying 'I'm Frank Lampard's son'. Mind you, with my name I suppose that was pretty obvious. My cousin Jamie was in the same boat being the son of Harry Redknapp, and we were and still are great mates. He's a top man, Jamie. Our Mums are sisters, so that is the connection. Harry was great for me. I owe him a lot and hold him in high regard. It could have been difficult, because when I got going at Upton Park the management team consisted of my uncle and my father. Harry gave me my big chance and

I will always be grateful for that, and he also taught me a lot of good habits. I have to say he is a big part of where I am today.

What were your feelings about Chelsea when you were a West Ham fan?

It was neither here nor there. To be fair, I think in football you usually have an enemy and I didn't like Tottenham, and that was a natural thing, and I didn't like Arsenal either. Chelsea was a team I didn't hate. They weren't my team, obviously, but once they got into the Ruud Gullit and Glenn Hoddle era, and began bringing in a few players from overseas, and started to play some silky football, I sat up and noticed. Like the rest of the country, I suppose. I remember seeing Jody (Morris) come through the ranks at Chelsea, because at that time I was just coming through over at Upton Park as well. I think he was the youngest player to play in the Premiership at that time, and when he made his debut I remember watching that with real interest because I sort of knew him.

How did you become a professional footballer? Was it written in stone because of your father?

Yes, sort of, but luckily there must have been some basic ability to work on. I think my family and Dad actually pushed me in that direction, as he made me do training after school, probably at times when I didn't want to. He pushed and pushed. I'm glad he did that, although I soon got the hunger myself. I've got decent school exam results and all that. I did all right academically. Mum and Dad wanted me to do well and have something to fall back on, which was the right thing, and I appreciated it, but football was what was really important to me.

What was your first professional game and what are your memories?

I came on as a substitute against Coventry City. Gordon Strachan was coming on at the same time as me and he was something like thirty-eight, and was just finishing his career as I was starting. I just remember standing on the line with him and thinking that Gordon and my dad would have played against one another. I came on for about fifteen minutes and got a good reception from the West Ham fans. I think it was one of the last good receptions I got from them.

What was your first impression of Chelsea when you came to the club?

Fantastic really. I came and saw the club because I knew I was signing the next summer. I had a couple of options but, once I had a look around, behind the scenes and that, saw the stadium, I really started to think about Chelsea properly. I was overwhelmed. It was a real step up from West Ham. I'm not saying that disrespectfully to West Ham, I just felt that Chelsea were massive and that they had the facilities and the ambition. Just to feel that ambition was special, whereas at West Ham we always seemed as though we were playing to stay up. Here at Chelsea it felt like the club wanted to do something big. That's the thing that attracted me, and of course, it was still in London, which was also important.

What do you think of the Dream Team chosen by the fans?
It is one of the biggest honours I've ever had. I have been at Chelsea for four years and to know I'm in there with the likes of Peter Osgood, Peter Bonetti, Ron Harris and all those legends is fantastic. I think it's a massive compliment, when I just think straight away of people such as Ruud Gullit in terms of midfield players. The Chelsea fans voting for me ahead of so many great players is one of the highest compliments I could hope to receive.

You have really come on since you joined Chelsea. Would you agree?
Yes, I think I have. Watching games from three years ago on Chelsea TV brings home to me how much I have improved. I dominate games more now. When I first arrived, and joined up with all the big name players, people like Gianfranco Zola, maybe I didn't feel I had the stature to dominate games. Perhaps I didn't have it in me to quite dictate like I do now. Today, I look at myself and realise my body has changed. I am a lot stronger.

You seem better going forward and shooting than you were when you first came here. Have you had to work on that?
I have always worked on shooting since my West Ham days, because I've always wanted to score goals. I have that mentality where I think like a striker sometimes. I come off after a game and I've played well, but if I've missed a couple of chances to score it will give me the hump. My dad put it to me that if you practice hard in the week, then come the weekend you will get lucky and strike a good one. So I practice all week to make sure that one flies in on Saturday.

Who is the best manager you've played under?
It has to be Jose Mourinho. What he has done in such a short space of time is an incredible feat. I've got to mention Harry Redknapp again as well, because he was the first one who got me out there, and I will never forget that it was Claudio Ranieri that bought me. He's a great fella and made some shrewd buys that look better and better as the seasons roll by.

Do you think Claudio was too nice?
I wouldn't say he was too nice. I think he was a great man and he could be strong, but the only thing I didn't wholeheartedly support was his changing

the team a lot. I think that disrupted us at times. He was a good manager, and I think he was a great man. He had the faith in me to spend eleven million quid, which is a lot of money. Him and Ken Bates really believed in me when they signed me from West Ham. Ken was the one who had to unzip the purse.

Since I've been working with Jose Mourinho, it's like a step up to another level tactically. The way he speaks to the players, the way we train, makes him the most complete manager by far that I've played under.

What is your most memorable game as a Chelsea player?
My most memorable would be Arsenal in the Champions League. That, for me, was everything. In the week building up to it, I kept getting Arsenal fans coming up to me in London saying 'you'll never beat the Gunners' and all that rubbish, and it did my nut in because we really wanted to beat them. We had never beaten them since I arrived and for some time before as well. That night we played brilliantly and that celebration at the end was special. We went over there and really did the business.

We were in the ground for forty minutes afterwards, singing and celebrating
It was brilliant, wasn't it? For me, that's my top game. The League Cup final against Liverpool is up there with it and, of course, the game and the goals I scored against Bolton when we took the Premiership were also special, but that Arsenal night was unbelievable for me. The nice thing is that there are so many of these great games coming along now. Both the Barcelona games in the Champions League were amazing, and Bayern Munich was top.

How did you feel about losing in the 2002 FA Cup final?
I was gutted. It was a hard one for me as it was my first Cup final. I enjoyed the day massively, and I had always wanted to get to the final. It is a special thing for any English kid, an ambition for any player, but we didn't quite get it together as a team, although personally I thought I did all right and played well against Patrick Vieira.

Jimmy (Floyd Hasselbaink) was struggling and it was really disappointing, but those sort of things come one at a time, and maybe it makes our success now even sweeter. You know how it feels to lose, and you don't take winning for granted.

What is your most memorable goal?
A few stick in my mind. One was the Champions League goal against Arsenal in the 2-1 away win. It wasn't a great goal, but the celebration and the fact we went on to win that game was what makes it so memorable. The other one was against Lazio at home, again in the Champions League. That was my

first real taste of a big Champions League night and I had hit the bar already, then I scored that goal towards the top corner. That night and that goal were both massive for me.

My second goal in the first leg against Bayern Munich in 2004–05 was particularly satisfying, but my most memorable goals were the two I scored at the Reebok Stadium versus Bolton. They were so crucial, giving us the Premiership title.

What is your favourite terrace song?

At the risk of sounding self-centred I have to say that little number called Super Frank goes down well. You are aware of the crowd singing during the game, but it's the pre-match songs that you notice more. When you're warming up, it's quieter, but once you start playing you are concentrating more. Maybe you have a shot and the game stops, and you'll hear the crowd then.

That song, though, was great for me. It seemed to come from nowhere at the start of my second season at Stamford Bridge. The first season went okay, and I started to play better, but the second season started well and then all of a sudden the fans started to sing Super Frank and it felt brilliant. It gave me a real boost and it still does, every time I hear it now. Ask any player and they'll tell you that the feeling they get when the crowd start singing their name is great. It really does help you.

Which team do you dislike most and why?

West Ham. They treat me to this day as not much, but do you know what? The treatment doesn't bother me because I'm Chelsea now and I enjoy the fact they're bothered about where I'm playing. As a player there I took a lot of stick, and I'm not talking about on a Saturday. I took stick in the street, and my family took stick, and I was having a bad time, which as a kid coming through, you do.

I came through when I was about eighteen or nineteen years old at West Ham, and they'd say I was only playing because of my old man. As a kid, that sort of stuff is very hard to take. I was a teenager and I had grown, old men digging me out. I will never forget that.

When people dig me out now they say, 'you kissed the badge when you played for West Ham four years ago', but for me, it's like falling in love with a woman and then you split up. Does that mean you can't fall in love with someone else? I know it sounds bad, but when I came through at Upton Park I loved West Ham, and I loved West Ham as a kid, but the way they treated me, and the way they treat me to this day, leaves me cold. I earned that club eleven million quid and I had four good years there, and now I am a Chelsea player. There's no comparison to the way I am treated here, so why shouldn't I be in love with Chelsea?

What is your worst Chelsea memory?
Losing to Liverpool in the Champions League semi-final was a hard one, but I suppose because we did so well in the Premiership and the League Cup it was an easier pill to swallow. The Monaco semi-final the year before was really gutting, and we all felt the horror of that. I scored a goal – what a buzz. It was such a bad game to lose and we just should've won it, after being 2-0 up. Things happened in the away game, changes were made, and we just should never have lost that match. We were better than Monaco and should have reached the final. We had a great chance to win the Champions League that year. We all want to win the Premiership, but the Champions League is massive as well. We'll get there in the end, I am sure of that.

Who is your most difficult opponent?
I would say Steve Gerrard or Patrick Vieira. I like those sort of players because they do everything. You can play against attacking midfielders, or defensive midfielders, but those two are a bit of both. They are strong and can get forward, then get back and defend as well. I couldn't call it between those two. I think they are both world class.

What did you say to Steven Gerrard after the League Cup final? 'See you next season' or something wasn't it?
No, that was a joke to the press, because they were asking me. I just said 'good luck' and 'unlucky' – that sort of stuff, the normal kind of thing you say when you've just beaten a mate. I play with Steve in the England midfield remember, and I know him pretty well. He is a great player, like I said.

Which young player do you tip for future success at Chelsea?
Huthy (Robert Huth), without a doubt. The problem is, I don't see him as a kid. He's so strong and is capable of playing against anyone – it's just unfortunate for him that we have three world-class centre halves in front of him. It's hard to comment on the younger lads in the youth team because we don't train with them, so it's hard to pick one out. I don't see them enough.

What do you dislike the most about being a professional footballer?
It's probably the press, when they start going into your private life. That's the worst thing. Like today, for instance, my house is in the paper. I have got a new house and it's in the paper. I mean, who wants to know where I live? Why should they know? You can't say who's out there reading these things. As well as that, I've got a steady relationship and I'm settled down, and they still like to drag things up from five years ago, when I was single. Why is it the press always want a bad story? I don't understand that side of the relationship. Do they really believe the English people only want to read the bad stuff? I don't believe that is true.

What do you regard as the biggest mistake you have made in your career?

The September 11th incident. That was another thing that was blown up out of all proportion. We were never purposely disrespectful to anyone. Our only mistake, and it was a mistake, was being naive and going out. The game we were scheduled to play that night had been called off and we went for a drink during the day. If I could go back and change things, then I wouldn't have gone out. We received a lot of bad press and had to take the stick we got on the chin.

What ambitions do you have for the future?

The 2004-2005 season was marvellous and I look forward to a few more like that. I want to play in the World Cup in 2006, and just carry on with England, be a regular and try to win something. Being in the position we're in at Chelsea, we have the capability to win everything. And that's what I want to do. I want Chelsea to have a monopoly on winning things for the next five or six years. I want us to dominate.

I would love to stay at the club for the rest of my career. I just love playing here. I have settled, not just with the club, but in the area as well. I will stay in this area for the rest of my life and will come back and watch Chelsea when I finish. I've never been happier in my football and in my life. My dad loves me being here too and he gets the hump when we're playing West Ham and people say 'who do you want to win?' and that, and there's no contest. He's with his boy. That's the way he has always been. He loves my success and is very happy. I think he gets more pleasure watching me and seeing what I have achieved than he did when he played himself.

What is your big passion outside of football?

My girlfriend and my dogs. I have two dogs, a male bulldog and a French mastiff bitch. I spend a lot of time with my girlfriend. I don't get involved in the golf and all that kind of stuff. I have quite a relaxed life outside of football. I like spending time indoors, or with the dogs at the park. That sort of thing.

Favourite book, film, music?

I read the football autobiographies, but the best one I've read? Any of them I suppose. I like them all. I saw The Football Factory and enjoyed that, especially the banter. I watched it the other night as it goes. I've seen it before, but I watched it again the other night. But I'm not massively into music and films to be honest. I listen to the radio and watch TV. I like Eastenders. I think it is very funny. I don't know if it's meant to be or not, but it makes me laugh. My girlfriend is Spanish and she loves it, so we watch Eastenders together, and I'm always flicking to Sky Sports as well.

Do you have a place you like to visit outside of England?

My favourite place to visit is America. Last year we travelled around a bit and went to New York and Los Angeles. LA is good for a few days, but you have to be careful as you can lose a few quid there. I enjoyed Santa Monica. They like the Brits and it's a nice place to switch off and relax. You can get away from the whole football thing over in the US.

If there was one thing about this country you could change, what would it be?

There are a lot of things I'd change. I'll talk about something in London. Traffic wardens – get rid of them. Get rid of the congestion charge. Bus lanes – we should be allowed to drive in bus lanes. All that sort of stuff really. We should be allowed to speed a little bit. No, I'm only joking. I could go on a lot stronger, but that'll do.

What's it like being an England regular?

It's brilliant. I was in the squad for a long time and it's great being involved, but it's horrible travelling all over Europe and the world and being on the bench. Once you start playing, you feel a real part of it, playing in a big competition as a regular was unbelievable.

Your appearance record for Chelsea is admirable. Don't you ever get tired?

I have patches. I can remember feeling a bit tired over Christmas this year, in a couple of games, but I came through. I like to feel I can battle through those sort of periods.

Going back to the League Cup final, did you feel that the difference between Chelsea and Liverpool was the fitness of the players?

A lot of people have said that and I think they are right. Liverpool were cramping up and everything, and it was one of the reasons we won. The other difference was we played better. To be honest with you, at half time I thought we were going to get beaten. We were better than them, but I was thinking 'where's the goal coming from?' Once it was 1-1, I don't think any of us thought we would lose. That was it then, and our fitness was great. If you feel fit that gives you a head start straight away.

Tell us about your friendship with Alan Hudson and how that came about?

Through my dad mainly. Alan's boy was at West Ham as a youth team player, and was a couple of years younger than me. Huddy knew Dad and we went from there. Alan used to come over and watch the youth games and he played a big part in me coming to Chelsea. He talked to Dad and spoke really well about the club and urged him to get me to come here. I've spoken to him a few times since then and often see him around. I respect him greatly, although I never saw him play, which is the only down side. Everyone tells me about Alan and I wish I'd had a chance to watch him. All I've ever seen are videos and there are not many around sadly. I'm thrilled to be playing alongside him in this Dream Team. It's a shame it's not real.

Would you like to stay in football once you pack in the playing side?
I think so, but I don't like to think about it all ending. Not just yet. I had a patch where I thought I wouldn't stay in the game when I retire, would just want to get out and watch football as a spectator, but now I think I wouldn't mind being a manager or something similar. If I was to stay involved, though, I'd want to be the main man. I wouldn't want to be a coach behind the scenes. I think I'd want to manage more than be just a coach. Still, that's for the future. I'm focusing on the present. We want to keep the Premiership title and win the Champions League. That's what's on my mind right now.

Huddy – walking the walk. The original Chelsea boy

Alan Hudson

Alan Hudson was born on June 21st, 1951, a two-minute walk away from Stamford Bridge. Newcastle had just defeated Blackpool in the FA Cup final and the Government was attempting to snap Britain out of the post-war blues by launching the Festival Of Britain. Alan made his debut for Chelsea in 1969 and went on to make 189 appearances and score fourteen goals in two spells at the club. He played in the 1971 European Cup Winners Cup triumph, but missed the 1970 FA Cup final through injury. In 1974 he was transferred to Stoke City where he transformed a mediocre First Division club. During his stay he was capped twice for England. While at Arsenal he featured in the 1978 FA Cup final against Ipswich. After Alan's England debut versus West Germany in 1975, Franz Beckenbauer said: 'This is the finest international debut I have ever seen.' In December 1997 Alan was nearly killed in a road accident. He emerged from a coma in March 1998

Where did you grow up and what is your family background?

My mum was Florence Mason, a Chelsea girl, and my dad was Bill Hudson, from Fulham. I don't have a clue how they met, though it must have been very bloody funny. I was born in a prefab in Upcerne Road, just up the road from Stamford Bridge, and grew up in the area. I'm probably the most local boy to ever have played for the club. My early life revolved around football really. I used to finish school and play in the playground, before going round my nan's and having some beans on toast or something, and then I'd be back outside playing football again. I went to Park View School and there was a teacher there, Mr Robertson, who encouraged us to play. I don't think he was even a sports teacher, but he was a big football man. We used to put our coats down and use them for goal posts, and spent most our time in this fenced playground across from where I lived. We called it The Cage, and it was our Wembley.

What team did you support as a child and who were your heroes?

I supported Fulham because of my father and his family. I can't remember the first game I went to at Craven Cottage, but most of my memories as a kid are of standing behind the goal at the Hammersmith End. Johnny Haynes was my big hero and I vaguely remember seeing him at Fulham, though he was coming to the end of his tether when I started going. I'd mainly seen him on films before that. That Fulham side was full of comedians. The only person at the club who wasn't funny was Tommy Trinder and he really was a comedian. You could do a Derek and Clive type sketch on that team that would last for days. If you couldn't tell a gag, you were out. I saw Jimmy Hill play for them, which was very unfortunate, but he fitted into the Fulham team well. How he went on to do what he did I will never know.

While I can't remember the first time I saw Fulham play, I do remember the first time I went to Wembley. Crook Town were playing Hounslow in the Amateur Cup final and I went along with Bubbles, who was Johnny Haynes's right hand man around this area. Billy Digweed and Johnny Fennell were both playing for Hounslow and I sat on the benches near the halfway line. It made a big impression on me and when I went home I told my dad all about it and he said I'd be going back one day, but as a player, and not for the Amateur Cup either. He was always saying things like that to encourage me with my football, helping to build up my confidence.

What were your feelings about Chelsea at this time?
To be honest, Chelsea never really entered my head. Once I was at the club I used to play for the youth team and go over and see Fulham play afterwards in my Chelsea jacket. There was no real rivalry between the clubs in those days. We all used to meet up on the Monday morning in the cafe and there would be a load of banter going back and forward, half of us Chelsea and the other half Fulham. The area was different to now and a lot of local people used to see Chelsea one week and Fulham the next. I think that was great. It was very different to the way things are today, how big rivalries have built up. I can remember the last time I went in the The Shed, when I was about fifteen. It was against Leeds and they were throwing coins around. I never went in there again.

As a born-and-bred Fulham lad, how have Chelsea Football Club and the area around the ground changed since you were young?
The whole area has changed out of all recognition. The club is very cosmopolitan now and most of the local community around the ground has gone as well. It's a crying shame, but there's nothing you can do about it.

How did you become a professional footballer?
My father took me to Fulham to see if they were interested in me, but they said I was too small. He told them 'he will fucking grow you know, he's only twelve' and took me down the Bridge instead. I can remember not wanting to go to Chelsea and I didn't want to go to the London trials either. If it wasn't for my old man I wouldn't have become a professional footballer. I was happy enough playing in The Cage, but after joining Chelsea I progressed through the ranks and eventually made it into the first team.

What was your first professional game and what are your memories of that game?
My debut was against Southampton as a substitute, I think, at the Dell in 1969. Maybe I played the whole game. We lost 5-0 and it could have been 25-0. My

biggest memory is of running around in circles. This was when they had people like Ron Davies and Micky Channon in their side, so they had some useful players, even though Bill Shankly called them the Ale House Brawlers. I only played because some of the first-team players were drunk on the Friday lunchtime. Peter Osgood, Tommy Baldwin, Johnny Boyle and Charlie Cooke were caught in Barbarella's, so they were dropped and I was given a chance. John Dempsey made his debut on the same day, having just arrived from Fulham. I had the feeling after that first game that I would never play for Chelsea again.

The first big game I remember was against Spurs at White Hart Lane. Jimmy Greaves was playing. That was an experience. I would be lying if I could tell you the first game I played at Stamford Bridge, but I think it was against Crystal Palace.

What were your first impressions of Chelsea when you came to the club?

I went there when I was about thirteen and we used to train behind the goals, on Tuesday and Thursday nights. After a few weeks I didn't want to go any more. I didn't like trials, tests, all that sort of thing. I don't think you find the best players that way. It's like having exams in school doesn't prove who is the most gifted child. That's why Tommy Docherty was so good, when he brought Ossie into the Chelsea team. He didn't just bring him in for one match, but gave him six games to prove himself, and this was at the expense of Barry Bridges who was an established player and very popular with the fans. You have to show faith in new talent and Ossie quickly won the fans over. Suddenly everyone was mad about him and hardly remembered Bridges.

What are your thoughts about the Dream Team and are there other players you would have included?

I would agree with Catty in goal, Eddie at left-back, John Terry in the middle of defence, Young Frank and myself in midfield, Charlie and Ossie up front, but there are some other players I would include. I would like to have got Gary Locke in there. I think that if that early Seventies team had stayed together and Locke was surrounded by those sort of players he would definitely have played for England. He also had a bad injury later which set him back, and then he ended up playing in a team that wasn't very good. Gary Locke was a class player.

I would play Colin Pates in the middle of the defence with John Terry. Pates is another one, like Gary Locke, who was very gifted and deserved to play in a better side. I trained with Pates for a while and he was a terrific footballer who reminded me a lot of Peter Simpson at Arsenal. He had a great left foot, great composure, and I told him he should play on Saturday like he did in training. His passing and movement were great and defensively he was outstanding, but he told me he wasn't allowed to play his natural game, that he had to get the ball up to Speedie and Dixon as quick as possible. This was making him look a bad player because that sort of game was foreign to him. This was when John Neal was manager, and after him John Hollins.

I didn't really know Zola, so while he was a fantastic footballer, I would put Jimmy Greaves in there with Ossie. Some of the younger fans might not remember him from his playing days at Chelsea, but he was a terrific player, a born goalscorer. He was very fast and had an eye for goal like no other. On the left I would have Mickey Thomas. Mickey has been a great player at every club he's been with, and he always had a good relationship with the fans. He is a real character and you could see the fans reacting to this. I can remember being at Shrewsbury when Chelsea played up there in the Eighties and I was reporting on the match. Chelsea had all their mob behind the goal and when Mickey came out they mentioned his name on the tannoy and everyone went mad. Joey Jones was a similar sort of character who the fans loved. As for the substitute, well, I would go for Marvin Hinton. He was a very gifted footballer, very composed and elegant.

I don't think Frank Lampard is too similar to me and I feel we would complement each other really well. He loves being in possession and getting on the end of things. We're both good at getting up and down the field, and you can see how hard he trains by the amount of work he puts in.

Who is the best manager you ever played under?

Tommy Docherty was the best Chelsea manager and I really believe that if he hadn't fallen out with Terry Venables and George Graham, Chelsea would have won the league during his time in charge. The best ever manager I played under was Tony Waddington at Stoke. He was great for my game and allowed me to develop as a footballer. He was like a second father to me.

What is your most memorable game?

Beating Real Madrid in the Cup Winners Cup final in 1971. The first game on the Wednesday night was a 1-1 draw, so we stayed on in Athens and played them again on the Friday. They had a midfield player called Pirri, who was something special, but when he came out for the second game he had a cast on his hand and I think that affected his performance. Seeing that cast was a boost for us and we went on to win the Cup with goals from John Dempsey and Ossie.

The Chelsea fans were amazing over there in Greece. They had tickets to go home after the first match, but many of them stayed on for the replay. It was incredible. This was a time when there weren't the same connections or money floating about as today. Some of those Chelsea fans are supposed to still be over there, sitting on the beach. Like Japanese soldiers who don't know the war has ended. They didn't bother coming home. In those days, specially being a local lad, I knew a lot of the fans, all that Zigger Zagger mob who would often be in the next compartment on the train coming back from a game up north, so there wasn't as big a gap between the players and fans as there is these days.

My outstanding memory of that time is sitting on the bottom of my bed at the hotel and watching the sun come up after being out celebrating with the other lads. I had been playing professional football for a couple of seasons, had only missed out on the FA Cup victory against Leeds because of injury, and here I was having just won the Cup Winners Cup against the legendary Real Madrid. That really was amazing.

What is your most memorable goal?
My first goal for Chelsea was against Derby, a volley past Les Green, but my best goal was at Coventry, when I picked up the ball on the edge of our box and ran through the lot of them before putting it in the net. I scored two of those in four weeks, with the next one against Sheffield Wednesday at the Bridge.

What is your favourite terrace song?
It's funny, but when you're out there playing you don't really listen to the crowd too much, maybe look around if they sing your name, but one of the things about Stamford Bridge when I was playing was how far the fans were from the pitch. There was the dog track going right round the field and you could look at the fans but not really see who was there. I really noticed this when I moved to Stoke because suddenly I was so close to the spectators every week. One song the Stoke fans used to sing said that I walked on water. I liked that one. It made me feel very buoyant.

If that Chelsea team I played in had the Stamford Bridge of today, I am sure we would have won the league. That old ground was a big hindrance for us. Really, we did very well to have as good as a home record as we did. That's why Stan Bowles did so well at QPR, the fact that the crowd was right on top of the players, urging them on all the time. That sort of support was great for someone like Stan.

Which team did you dislike the most, and why?
Leeds. Their manager taught them they had to win at all costs. They were a fantastic football team, but they were arrogant. There's that fine line and they went over it. It was just the way they were. It's like their old players now. For them everything revolves around Don Revie and Leeds United. They had horrible ways. Even Mick Jones, what he did to Catty at Old Trafford in the replay was diabolical really, and he was their mildest player. Then we had the Sprake incident with Johnny Boyle in the semi-final when Hateley scored, in 1967 at Villa Park. Leeds were just nasty. We got on with just about every other team except Leeds.

What is your worst Chelsea memory?

Getting married, in the Kings Arms. As far as football goes, the last goal at Leyton Orient when we got knocked out of the FA Cup in 1972. The goals given away by Ronnie Harris and Webby were like schoolboy errors, and that allowed Orient to come back from 2-0 down to win 3-2. We would have played Arsenal in the next round and we began to struggle after that defeat. We had won the FA Cup and the Cup Winners Cup in the two previous seasons and had a very good side. Losing to Orient was a big blow and things went wrong after that.

We lost against Atvidaberg, when Johnny Hollins missed a penalty. We would have gone on to win the Cup Winners Cup if we'd beaten them, and then we lost to Stoke in the League Cup final. That led to the break-up of the team and it all started at Orient. I think Dave Sexton used those games as an excuse to have a go at us. It was okay having a drink when we were winning the FA Cup and Cup Winners Cup, but suddenly everything changed.

Who was your most difficult opponent?

My second wife was a tough nut. In football it was Alan Ball. You couldn't get near him. People talk about the hard men like Tommy Smith and Norman Hunter and Peter Storey, but I'd rather play against them every week than Alan Ball. He was the best one-touch player I have ever seen. You just couldn't get near him. You think you're going to close him down and he knocks it off and is gone. Fantastic. In a way he doesn't get the respect he deserves today, which could be because of his record as a manager, but playing one-touch is one of the most skilful things you can do in football. The nearest contemporary player to Ball is probably Paul Scholes when he is on song. Billy Bremner and Johnny Giles would hold onto the ball so you had a chance to have a go at them, but Alan Ball was special.

Which young player do you tip for future success?

There's a young kid I saw the other night playing for QPR, Lee Cooke, who scored the first goal for them. He looks pretty good. Another outstanding young player is Darren Fletcher at Man United. I think he is going to be a great player. It's hard, though, because a lot of players who should make it don't. Mickey Fillery at Chelsea had fantastic ability and could have gone on to play for England. Maybe he didn't have the desire. Sometimes the game comes too easy for people. The same is true of Dale Jasper. He had a great future, but was playing centre half when he was a midfielder. He couldn't get a look in. I rated him very highly and tried to get him to move to Stoke when I was there the second time. I spoke to Dale's dad, but he said he didn't want to leave London. Then Dale ended up at Crewe.

Joe Cole worried me for a while. It was looking like he might not fulfil his talent, but it seems that Jose has done great things with him and Joe has really flowered. He is a great kid. In terms of what Chelsea have achieved recently, he is up there with Frank and John Terry.

What did you dislike most about being a professional footballer?
Friday nights. I never went out on a Friday night when we played at home, and I don't watch TV so I used to just sit in an armchair making paper aeroplanes and throwing them around the room.

What do you regard as the biggest mistake you made in your career?
I should have got the manager's job at Stoke when I was there second time around. I should have gone and seen the manager Bill Asprey, who'd just had a heart attack, and told him I would take over the day-to-day stuff so he could take it easy, but I never did. That was a big mistake. Otherwise, I don't have a lot of regrets. I don't regret leaving Chelsea as I got to play under Tony Waddington. I wouldn't have become the player I did if I hadn't moved to Stoke. I was given lots of responsibility there, something that wasn't going to happen under Dave Sexton.

You could write ten books on Sexton. You just don't sell your best players and then when things go wrong sack the manager. How many thousands went to see Peter Osgood play on a Saturday? You have to talk to the players as well as the manager, and I said this to Brian Mears. I have been told that a lot of Chelsea fans gave up on the club after Ossie and I left.

What ambitions do you have for the future?
My future is in writing, and I want to do as well as I can. The Working Man's Ballet is due to be released again soon, and The Tinker And Talisman was published last year. I write a column for the Stoke Evening Sentinel and used to write one for The Sporting Life, but they closed it down. The paper, not the column.

What is your big passion outside of football?
Socialising. Being out with nice people and having a laugh is one of the greatest cures. It is very healthy to socialise. Betty Shine told me that when I was in hospital recovering from my accident. I had a problem in my groin and she told me that it wouldn't get better if I was miserable. You've got to be happy. I have a wide circle of friends. People I have known in the area since I was in short trousers, people I know from playing for Chelsea and Stoke, when I was also in short trousers, and people I have met along the way. People I have met today. We're all human beings and we're all interesting and have things to offer each other.

Do you have a favourite book, film, album?
The best book I've read was Steve McQueen's life story. That was amazing. Two of my favourite films are The Godfather and Ben Hur. I like Phil Collins and his music, while Frank Sinatra is a big favourite of mine. There's not many who can hold a candle to Frank Sinatra.

Do you have a favourite country or place you like to visit?

I would like to go back to Seattle one day, and also Tampa Bay in Florida. I haven't been abroad since I had the accident, but the United States has a lot of good memories for me. When I played out there I had a great time. We were young British men who were used to the rain and the mud, and suddenly we were out there in the sun, able to extend our careers and playing good, entertaining football.

If there was one thing about this country you could change, what would it be?

Let's just say that Guy Fawkes fucked it up.

Do you think individual skill is returning to the English game, and if so which Chelsea players most excite you?

The coaching has become a lot better, thanks to the foreign managers who have come into the English game. Foreign players coming here has also helped a great deal. I think our game would have been totally on its knees if it wasn't for this firm coming in. The likes of Klinsmann, Ginola, Di Canio, Zola. It's not so much what the fans think, but when you go into work everyday and you're training with these people it improves your game. When people say it's a bad thing having the foreigners here they're wrong. It improves the kids. Helps bring them through. If English kids are good enough they'll get a game.

I was watching young Frank Lampard when he was at West Ham and, to tell you the truth, I can't believe how well he has turned out. He was always a good player, but his game has improved so much by moving to Chelsea and playing with quality. It was the same with Dennis Wise, and Tony Adams at Arsenal as well.

Arjen Robben is the player who excites me most at the moment, but young Frank wouldn't be far behind. If you look at his stats and percentages it's unbelievable how many shots Frank gets in. When he hits a bad one he is really angry with himself, as he is always looking to score goals. If you can get ten or twelve goals a season from midfield that's worth a lot to your team. Robben is a real talent, just runs at the heart of teams and rips them apart. That's unusual. Damien Duff does great as well, playing on the right.

What are the key differences between the modern game and when you were playing?

The most obvious differences are the ball and the pitch. We never had such luxuries. Look at the pitches when we played Watford in the FA Cup semi-final at White Hart Lane in 1970, and the final against Leeds at Wembley, and I can't see Dennis Bergkamp relishing that. They were in terrible condition and they didn't suit skilful football at all. The pitches now are great and this makes for better football. The ball is lighter as well. It flies and bends and everything. Those changes would have suited my game. I wish I was nineteen again and playing with a modern ball, on a perfect pitch.

What are the strengths and weaknesses of the current Chelsea team?
There is a strong sense of unity, thanks to Mourinho, and the defence is very good with John Terry. He is a terrific player. People like young Frank can work and score goals while Robben and Duff up front are quick to take people on. Every part of the team seems very strong at the moment. The weaknesses we have yet to discover, if they have any.

Chelsea have a big squad, but if you could choose a new player, who would you advise the manager to buy?
I said a while ago that Jose should buy Jermain Defoe and I think he would score bundles of goals for Chelsea. He's just their type of player. He's quick, and would fit in, especially with Robben and Duff who both take on people. I like Gudjohnsen, who is a very good footballer, but he doesn't have Defoe's nose for goal.

Several Chelsea players are fixtures in the England squad these days. Apart from Peter Bonetti, Ossie, John Hollins and yourself, are there any other Chelsea players from the early Seventies team who should have played for England?
Not really. Charlie Cooke and Eddie McCreadie both played regularly for Scotland, and John Dempsey for the Republic Of Ireland, but among those four names mentioned we didn't win a lot of caps. That was very much down to the managers England had at the time, and this attitude affected a lot of other talented English footballers.

Catty was a fantastic goalkeeper and was unlucky he was around at the same time as Gordon Banks. I think he only played for England seven or eight times and was unfairly blamed for the game in Mexico when Germany beat us 3-2. Ossie and myself weren't the sort of players those England managers seemed to want. There were a lot of personality clashes between the more individual players and the England managers of the time.

Don Revie took over as England boss and all of a sudden Trevor Cherry and Paul Madeley were playing. They weren't bad players, but they weren't England players. You're never going to win the World Cup with people like that. In my case, if Tony Waddington had been manager of England I would have won 110 caps for England, no doubt. Tony Currie would have been in the same range as well. So you've just got to get lucky, like anything in life. I've had my good luck and I've had my bad luck. What is it someone said? You've got to treat those two impostors the same? That's what I do.

Dennis Wise – he will fight fight fight for Chelsea

Dennis Wise

Dennis Wise was born on December 16th, 1966. A children's TV series from America about four young musicians was causing a stir. By the time baby Dennis left hospital MonkeeMania had exploded. He broke into football with Wimbledon and came to symbolise the Crazy Gang personality of the club. But they weren't just crazy, and proved it by beating the mighty Liverpool in the 1988 FA Cup final. Dennis came to Chelsea in the 1990-91 season and became one of the greatest ever Chelsea captains, bridging the old and new eras. His drive and talent were as pivotal as anyone's in bringing the good times back to Stamford Bridge, with the FA Cup arriving in 1997, the European Cup Winners Cup and League Cup in 1998, and the FA Cup again in 2000. Meanwhile, he accumulated twenty-one England caps. Dennis left Chelsea for Leicester in 2001, and then led Millwall to an FA Cup final as player-manager, before moving to Southampton. Clearly he still has energy, experience and talent to unleash, and there is a strong feeling among the supporters that one day those virtues will again be channelled in the direction of SW6

Where did you grow up and what is your family background?
I grew up in Notting Hill and lived with my mum and dad in a pub that was run by my dad and I went to a local school called Christopher Wren.

What team did you support as a child and who were your heroes?
I supported Queens Park Rangers. My dad used to take me to Loftus Road when I was a young kid and I started following them after that. Stan Bowles was my idol. He was a cut above the rest and a class player.

What were your feelings about Chelsea at this time?
I didn't really have any. As I said, I was happy following QPR and I didn't really bother thinking about any other teams. I was just happy going out and kicking a ball about with my mates and playing football whenever I could.

How did you become a professional footballer?
I joined Southampton as a schoolboy, but didn't make it there. I signed for Wimbledon when I was eighteen years old and I went on from there.

What was it like going back to Southampton after all these years?
Strange. A lot has changed yet some of the faces that I remember from my first time there are still about. But now they've got a nice stadium, a good set of supporters and it's a great club.

Peter Crouch was better at Southampton than he is at Liverpool, wasn't he?
Give him time to settle in. He's a good young player and will do well. I've trained with him and I know what he can do. Liverpool have bought a good young player there. He's got a lot of skill and he's a determined man.

What was your first professional game and what are your memories of that game?
It was for Wimbledon against Cardiff City in 1985, the last game of the season. We won 2-1 and I set up the winner.

What were your first impressions of Chelsea when you came to the club?
It wasn't as good as it is now, but thanks to Ken Bates and all his work Chelsea became a big club, just like he said they would when I joined. If it hadn't been for Ken Bates the club probably wouldn't have survived. I have always admired him for what he did for Chelsea.

Who is the best manager you ever played under?
Luca, without a doubt. He was brilliant. He is the greatest manager Chelsea have ever had. He has got the love of the supporters, he's clever, knows his football, and he is the most successful ever Chelsea manager. He won five trophies while he was manager.

You like playing a round of golf together don't you?
(*Laughs*) We've played each other a few times.

But the truth is, that out of all of you, it's Franco Zola who's tops?
Yeah. I'm going to have to get some practice in.

What are your thoughts on the Dream Team and are there any other Chelsea players you would have included?
I'm glad that Luca is the manager, but to be honest I'm surprised that people like Gus Poyet and Robbie Di Matteo aren't in there. They were really great players who achieved a lot while they were at the club. I would definitely have them in my Dream Team, probably at the expense of Damien Duff. Ruud Gullit should be in there as well, and a few others that I played with here.

A lot of the votes came from younger supporters and to them Damien is a hero
I hadn't thought of it like that, but even so, I think that Gus and Robbie should have been in there somewhere.

Your votes for the Dream Team were split between midfield and the wing. Which position do you prefer?
Midfield, definitely. I feel I played my best football in midfield and developed as a player myself. I really enjoyed my football when I took on the role. It's a good position to play in when you're the captain of the team as you're in the centre of the action and can have a bigger influence on the game.

It has been said that playing with the likes of Zola and Vialli helped your game, and took you to another level. Would you agree, and can you tell us what it was like being in the same team as them, and also a player such as Ruud Gullit
When players like Luca Vialli and Franco Zola come to the club that you're playing for, everybody improves. My game, both skill-wise and tactically, went to another level when I started to train with them. When there are players like that around you, you can't help but improve. Ruud was a class act, and the same goes for Gus and Robbie and several others who came to Chelsea at that time.

What is your most memorable game as a Chelsea player?
The 2000 FA Cup final, the last one played at the old Wembley when we beat Aston Villa 1-0. Robbie scored the goal and we were all relieved that we'd won something after missing out on the league. I had the chance to take my son Henry onto the pitch and up the stairs to collect the FA Cup. I really enjoyed that day.

Your most memorable Chelsea goal is THAT goal then – in the San Siro?
Definitely. To score such a vital goal on a stage like that is something I will never forget. AC Milan in the San Siro. It was a great, great night and just to have played there was breathtaking. The atmosphere was incredible, and scoring in front of the Chelsea supporters was fantastic. It is one of the highlights of my football career.

And your favourite terrace song has got to be the San Siro song?
Yes, I love that.

A couple of times when you've come back to Chelsea and been introduced to the crowd and they've started to sing it to you, I've noticed that look on your face. You do love it, don't you?
Yeah, it's great.

We were singing it up at Bolton when we won the league
Were you? That's nice. I'm pleased to hear that.

Which team do you dislike the most, and why?

I don't really dislike any team. I just love playing football and being involved in the game. I don't hate anyone in football. We all have to just get on with it and there's no time for any of that. I know the supporters have teams they really dislike, hate even, but I don't think there should be any room for it there either.

What is your worst Chelsea memory?

The 1994 FA Cup final against Manchester United. It was a horrible day. The worst thing about it was that we could have scored three or four goals in the last twenty minutes but the chances just didn't go in. On the day, I suppose we didn't deserve to win, but we definitely didn't deserve to lose 4-0. That is definitely my worst Chelsea memory.

Who was your most difficult opponent?

Patrick Vieira. He is a brilliant player and was always very hard to play against. It's easy to see why Arsenal were successful when he was with them. He's an immense player and a really nice guy. We get on well together.

Which young player do you tip for future success?

That's a hard question for me to answer really, because I haven't been around Chelsea for a while but, looking back – and he's still young now – it would have to be John Terry. I knew him when he first started at Chelsea and I knew that he would go on to become a great professional. He's still young and he has a great future ahead of him, both at Chelsea and for England. He deserves everything he's got so far and there's plenty more to come. John wears his heart on his sleeve when he's playing and he will sweat blood for his team-mates. He is Chelsea through and through.

What do you dislike most about being a professional footballer?

Injuries. I've been lucky with them throughout my career and I haven't had any really bad ones, but when I haven't been playing because I've picked up a knock or a strain, it really annoys me. It is the worst thing that can happen to any professional footballer.

What is the biggest mistake you have made in your career?

Leaving Chelsea. It's the worst mistake I've ever made, not just in football but in my whole life. I wanted to stay, but Ranieri made it clear that there wasn't going to be any future for me at Chelsea. I was desperate not to leave, but I went before matters really came to a head. As soon as I made my mind up to leave I knew I would regret it, but it was something that I felt I had to do. The good thing, though, is that I've still got loads of good friends at the club, people like Thresa Conneely and Gary Staker, and others who have been at the club for years.

Do you wish you were playing for Chelsea now?
Definitely. I would love to be involved with what's going on now. I wish I could have stayed but, as I said, it didn't work out with Ranieri. I really regret leaving now, especially as I think that we could have done a lot more than what we did, especially under Luca. I felt that we could have gone further in the Champions League and we should have qualified for it a few more times if Luca had stayed. We would have definitely won a lot more than we did, but things didn't turn out that way

Steve Clarke's done well hasn't he?
Yes, he has, and I'm pleased for him. I used to room with Steve and we're still great pals. He loves the club and he's Chelsea through and through and deserves to be where he is at now.

What ambitions do you have for the future, and can you tell us what you have been doing since you left Chelsea?
At the moment, my ambition is to keep playing for as long as I can and to keep enjoying my football. Obviously, since I left, I've managed Millwall and now I'm back at Southampton.

You did well at Millwall didn't you? Are we right in saying that you got on well with Theo (Paphitis), but didn't really click with Jeff Burnage (his successor as Millwall chairman)?
That's about right. It's a good little club Millwall and when I was there we did well, but there's only so much you can do without any money. Theo was okay and we got on very well together. I'm glad I went there because I learned a lot from the experience, but football management is a tough business.

What is your big passion outside of football?
Obviously my wife Claire and my kids Henry and Amber. They're the biggest things in my life, even before football. Apart from them, together with a very good friend of mine I have been busy buying properties and renovating them. It's something that I've found that I really enjoy.

What is your favourite book, film, album?
My favourite film has got to be Once Upon A Time In America, and I have just finished reading a book about the Krays. Musically, I like soft soul – you know, the stuff from the Seventies, a bit of Motown and that kind of thing.

Do you have a favourite country or place you like to visit?
Dubai. I go there several times a year. I like it there a lot. I like the climate and the country. It is a great place to visit. I see Gus Poyet and Dan Petrescu when I'm out there sometimes. I wish we had that sunshine in England.

Duffer St Patrick – Chelsea and Ireland

Damien Duff

Damien Duff was born on March 2nd, 1979, in Ireland. Trevor Francis had just become Britain's first million-pound footballer. Elsewhere industrial disputes ravaged the country with rubbish piling up in the streets and even gravediggers refusing to bury bodies. Ominously, The Bee Gees were number one with Tragedy. Damien first came to prominence with Blackburn Rovers, making his debut for them in 1997. In 2002 he won the League Cup and also made a big impression for the Republic Of Ireland in the World Cup. Damien joined Chelsea from Blackburn Rovers in July 2003 for £17m and won the Premiership and League Cup in 2005

Where did you grow up and what is your family background?

I grew up in Dublin. Not in the city centre, but about twenty minutes outside in a place called Ballyboden. I come from a close family and have two brothers and two sisters. I'm the middle child.

What team did you support as a child and why?

Glasgow Celtic. With the Catholic connection, most people in Ireland support Celtic and obviously, being Irish, I support the Republic of Ireland.

Who was your favourite player as a youngster?

Ryan Giggs. He played on the left wing, which is my position, and I loved looking at him. I wasn't a Manchester United nut or anything like that, I just enjoyed watching Giggs, seeing the way he took people on, his dribbling skills and crossing ability. He scored goals as well, and he is still doing all those things today. Ryan Giggs is a great player.

What were your feelings about Chelsea in those days?

I didn't really take a lot of notice of them to be honest. As a professional, before I came to Stamford Bridge, all I had ever known was Blackburn after I signed for them. I loved it there and looked up to Tim Sherwood, who was the captain, and Alan Shearer, who was there at the same time. Players like that. But coming to Chelsea has been the greatest time of my life. Although I've only been here a while, I don't ever want to leave. I have fallen in love with the place.

How did you become a professional footballer?

Playing football is all I ever wanted to do. When it came to careers choice at school when I was about fourteen or fifteen, and you had to fill in the forms about what you wanted to be, I wrote down footballer. It got all the teachers laughing, but that didn't bother me. I knew what I wanted to do and I just went out and did it. I have always been strong-minded and if I make up my mind to do something I usually get it done. I was lucky because my whole family were behind me and at least *they* took me seriously. I am really grateful for the encouragement they gave me. My family, all of them, have been brilliant. They all come to watch me play and my dad is over for games all the time. He loves Chelsea and so does my ma.

What were your first impressions of Chelsea when you came to the club?

I was a bit nervous coming to such a great club as it was a totally different world from Blackburn. If you've been to that part of the world and been here in London, you will know what I mean. The north and south of England could be two different countries, with two different characters. I first met up with the rest of the Chelsea lads in Malaysia. They made me welcome from day one, although it took me about a year to feel that I'd really settled in. I feel right at home now.

What is the big difference between playing for a club such as Blackburn and Chelsea?

The facilities at Blackburn are top notch. After all, it is not that long ago they won the league. The people are nice up there and the fans are passionate. It's hard to put my finger on the difference, but there is something happening here at Chelsea. Something big, and we all know it. I'm a part of it and want to remain a part of it. That's the difference I suppose. History is being made.

What are your thoughts about the Dream Team, and are there other players you would have included?

It's a wonderful thing to get this honour after such a short time with the club. I would have been devastated if things had not gone well after I first moved here, as it was a big decision, especially as Chelsea are such a big club and they paid a lot of money for me. The transfer fee can weigh you down, but it has worked out well. I'm in love with the club, the rest of the players and the supporters. I couldn't have dreamed it would have turned out so well and they would nominate me for such an honour. I would like to thank everyone who voted for me. There are a lot of Irish people in London, and especially in West London, so maybe they all voted for me.

As far as the team goes, I wouldn't argue with the choice of the supporters. There are some massive legends in that side, Chelsea heroes such as Peter Osgood and Ron Harris, plus fantastic players such as Zola and my current team-mates John Terry and Frank Lampard. That is a side that could definitely beat anyone.

Who is the best manager you have ever played under?
Jose Mourinho without a doubt. There's only one man. I can honestly say he has been a massive influence on my career.

What is your most memorable game as a Chelsea player?
It's a whole new team now and what with Roman coming in, you could say it's like a new club in some ways. Winning the League Cup was the first trophy we'd won as a team and as a group, so if I have to choose a single game, it has to be that day in Cardiff when we beat Liverpool. That was a pretty good game, wasn't it? All the games in our Champions League runs were memorable, and winning the Premiership really was an incredible experience.

What is your most memorable goal?
I know it probably wasn't the prettiest, but the first one that got me off the mark for Chelsea against Wolves stands out. It is important to get off the mark and that one did the job. I enjoyed the fluke in the League Cup semi-final at Old Trafford against Man Utd. Seeing that go in the net was nice, in such an important match against our rivals. Obviously, that helped us reach the final where we beat Liverpool. Having said that I love every goal I score.

What is your favourite terrace song?
The Celery song is really funny.

Have you ever heard the other version, the one that goes 'if Damien Duff don't tickle her muff, then we'll send in Geremi'?
Well, yes, I have actually. I hope my mother doesn't hear it though. Thankfully, if she did I don't think she'd get the gist of it. I do like Ten Men Went To Mow as well. We were all singing that on the team coach on the way back from the League Cup final. I really like that one. It always gives us a buzz hearing that.

Which team do you hate the most, and why?
It has to be Glasgow Rangers. I'm afraid it's compulsory if you support Celtic. It is just something that you grow up with.

What is your worst Chelsea memory?
Without doubt it would be doing my shoulder twice. It's probably the lowest point of my career so far. I thought I was back, but then I went and hurt it again. I had a few injuries related to it as well. It ruined the season for me, especially after feeling that I was really settling in at the club. It was a tough time for me and I became quite down over it all. It was very frustrating. As

far as matches go it was a big disappointment losing to Liverpool at Anfield in the semi-final of the Champions League, and I was very disappointed not to be playing.

Who is your most difficult opponent?
Any full back in the Premiership is going to know his stuff. If I had to name some individuals I would say that Gary Neville and Danny Mills give me real problems, but once I'm out there, I just enjoy playing football.

Which young Chelsea player do you tip for future success?
Robert Huth. I know he hasn't played that many games, but it's only because he's at a club with three other world class central defenders. He's unbelievable and if he was at any other club in England, he would be in the first eleven every week. He's definitely one for the future.

What do you dislike most about being a professional footballer?
Losing I suppose. It's always been my dream to be a footballer and I'm doing it so I'm happy with that, but being injured or not being picked is pretty bad as well.

What do you regard as the biggest mistake you have made in your career?
I don't think I've made that many really, and I hope I don't in the future, but if I have then I believe they happened for a reason. I suppose the thing to do is to learn from your mistakes – that's what I will try to do anyway.

What ambitions do you have for the future?
To win a lot of trophies for Chelsea and to be here for many, many years to come. I am not thinking any further than playing for the club and doing well.

What is your big passion outside of football?
Family, friends and obviously my girlfriend, but I love football – it's up there with them. I have football on the television at home all the time and my girlfriend loves it as well, which is always a bonus. Football is my life really.

Tell us about your career to date with Ireland and how you see the Irish team developing.
My main aim is to get to another World Cup. I played in the 2002 World Cup and, as a young player who was still learning the game, the experience was great. I'm desperate to play in the competition again. Now, Robbie Keane and myself are probably regarded as two of the senior players. That puts a lot of responsibility on me, but it gives me something to think about and I love

it. I have known the Ireland manager Brian Kerr since I was a youngster and he gets the best out of me, so I'm totally comfortable within the set-up. We have some fine players and there is a lot of potential in the squad. I think we will do well.

How did the Roy Keane situation affect you?
It didn't really affect me at all. I can't say I was thinking about him too much. All I was worried about was myself and all I was concentrating on was trying to get into the side and playing well. Like I said, I was only a young player then and I just wanted to impress and try to establish myself.

Left-footed wingers seem to be in short supply in English football, but Chelsea have two. How did you feel when Arjen Robben came to Chelsea?
I wasn't worried when he joined the club. Competition is always good. That's what I think, anyway. It stops players becoming complacent and acts as motivation, makes you work harder on your game. When Arjen arrived, he got off to a great start and I was just trying to get into the team myself. At the time, I couldn't even get into the first twenty at Chelsea, and I was struggling with injury. It's great that Jose will play both of us in the same team. Arjen is a class player. He has great pace and skill and I am happy playing alongside him.

What is your favourite book, film and type of music?
The Da Vinci Code is a good book and because I have read it recently it sticks in my mind. Being a good Catholic boy some of the things in it seem controversial, but I am still one hundred percent Catholic. I suppose my favourite film is The Godfather Part 2, and I love all kinds of music, but the best band of all are U2. I'm not just saying that because they're Irish either. They really are a great band. I've met the drummer. They like their football as well, but I can't pretend they follow Chelsea.

Do you have a favourite place you like to visit outside of football?
I think Ireland is the centre of the universe. It's a beautiful country and full of great people, but I love it in and around Chelsea as well. I love the area, the buzz around the place on a match day, and I love the supporters. However when I'm not here, I like to be in Ireland, especially in Dublin. Those are the only two places for me.

If there was one thing about this country you could change, what would it be?
Some people say the weather, but the weather is as bad, if not worse, in Ireland, so it doesn't bother me. As for changing anything, I'm happy at Chelsea, so there's nothing I would change at all.

The King – pursued by George Graham and Tommy Baldwin

Peter Osgood

Peter Osgood was born on February 20th, 1947. Rationing from the war was still in force, England was in the midst of a fuel crisis and the freezing conditions almost brought the country to its knees. The cockney anthem Maybe It's Because I'm A Londoner was heard for the first time. Peter made his debut for Chelsea in 1964 having come up through the junior ranks. In all he scored 150 goals in 380 appearances for the club, featuring and scoring in both the 1970 FA Cup and 1971 European Cup Winners Cup victories. He later moved to Southampton where he won the FA Cup again. He was capped four times for England and played in the 1970 Mexico World Cup. He has frequently been voted Chelsea's Best Ever Player by the supporters

Where did you grow up and what is your family background?

Dad was a bricklayer and I followed him in the building trade for a while. Mum worked in a hotel, among other things. She's still with us, bless her. I was raised in a place called Dedworth, near Windsor, and went to the local schools. Martin Knight, who wrote my book, reckons that the Osgood name means Pagan God, but I don't know what sort of drugs he takes.

What team did you support as a child and who were your heroes?

My brother was an Arsenal fan and, dare I say it, I started to support Arsenal. My brother used to take me up there to see George Eastham, who they had signed from Newcastle. I thought he was a fantastic player, who played for England and ended up at Stoke. But then all of a sudden my Uncle Bob wrote to Chelsea for a trial and he started taking me to the Bridge and I became a Chelsea supporter. My idol was Jimmy Greaves. We even share the same birthday.

How did you become a professional footballer?

I was playing well at school and was captain of the school team. I got picked for the district side and then went to play for a great local side called Spital. I really motored once I was with them. I had a trial with Reading and then, as I said, my Uncle Bob wrote to Chelsea and I got a trial and they signed me up there and then as a junior.

What were your first impressions of Chelsea when you came to the club?

I used to play at Welsh Harp, the training ground, on Saturday mornings, and there was an old taxi driver called Wally who used to take me up to

Chelsea to see the first team play in the afternoon. He was a lovely man, and thought the world of us boys, and looked after us. He was a wheeler dealer and even though he was basically Chelsea, the club were dithering about whether I would be offered full terms and Tommy Doc was wavering about signing me, so he had a word with Bill Nicholson and said Bill was interested in signing me for Spurs. Luckily Tommy Doc did sign me and I went to Chelsea. It was brilliant going over to Stamford Bridge in Wally's taxi and watching the first-team.

Who is the best manager you have ever played under?
That's a very difficult one, but I would probably favour Tommy Docherty as he gave me my first chance as a raw seventeen year old. He dropped Barry Bridges and put me in the first team, which was a big thing at that stage in my career. I played under Lawrie McMenemy as well, when I moved to Southampton, and Dave Sexton. If you could have rolled the three of them together, the capabilities they had, that would have been very interesting. They would have made the perfect manager.

Tommy Doc was a great motivator, a terrific guy, and could handle players. Lawrie Mac was the same, could handle big-name players, while Dave Sexton was a brilliant coach. Dave was the best coach I ever worked under, an absolute genius as a coach. The only thing was he was a very average player himself and I don't think he could handle players like myself, Huddy and Charlie, who had lots of flair. He thought we abused our position, to be honest, because we had so much talent but didn't use it. That's the trouble when you're a flair player. You have to turn it on week in, week out, and sometimes you can't.

Guys like Johnny Hollins, Webby and John Dempsey would give a hundred percent every week and Dave liked that more than the flair players. It was a bit like Alf Ramsey to be honest. I played for England under Alf and he only had one flair player in his team, and that was Bobby Charlton. He even dropped Jimmy Greaves in the World Cup, just to play Roger Hunt, which was unbelievable. It is sad, but I think we (the English) have a problem with individuality in all walks of life.

What is your most memorable game as a Chelsea player?
I think you always remember your first game. I was seventeen years old and fresh off the building sites, and there I was playing at Stamford Bridge with a great Chelsea side, and it really was a fantastic Chelsea team, with people like Terry Venables, Peter Bonetti and George Graham. We won 2-0 against Workington at home, in a League Cup replay, and I scored both goals. That was special for me, but I was back in the reserves the following week.

The 1970 FA Cup Final Replay has to be the main one though. We went on to win it and beat a great Leeds side. They said they murdered us in the first game at Wembley, but we had two or three kicked off the line, on a muddy pitch. It was a great game and we conjured up four goals between us, and then we went to Old Trafford, where again it wasn't the best pitch, and we came through to win the Cup. We were behind three times in the two games and still came back to win. The fans were absolutely awesome that day. They kept believing in us and that's what pulled us through.

What is your most memorable goal?
It has to be the goal in that FA Cup final replay. It was a great ball from Charlie Cooke. I was sort of floating in mid-air, and thinking I'm going to score here, almost in slow motion. Charlie was unbelievable. He knocked it into that space and the defenders just couldn't do anything about it. David Harvey, the goalkeeper, went and checked and that gave me my chance to pick my spot. I think if Gary Sprake had been playing rather than Harvey he might have come out and clattered me. In the end all I had to do was glance it in. It really was a great ball from Charlie. Thank you, Chas.

What is your favourite terrace song?
It's got to be Osgood, Osgood, Born Is The King Of Stamford Bridge. That's such an accolade. When you think of all the great players who have appeared for the club over the last hundred years, and they call you the King, well, that's awesome. You can't beat that. And, even now, I hear it sometimes when I'm near the ground and people spot me. It makes me feel all warm inside.

When we were playing well we were concentrated on the game, but when we were down we used to hear the songs more, and those boys were there for us. Sometimes you needed a little pick me up and The Shed were great. The amazing thing was that when we were playing away and coming back on the train, we used to go down to the buffet bar and have a drink with them. That's different to how things are today. The lads were great with us, people like Geoff Paget and Mike Greenaway, the Zigger Zagger man. We became friends. They were lovely, lovely people and had an absolute unwavering passion for the club.

The great thing is that's what brought me into being with the boys. I've always been one of the lads, one of the fans. It's fantastic when you have that rapport. They appreciated me and I appreciated them. All the players were like that. We were very receptive to the Chelsea fans. They were great supporters and loved us to bits. [*Wags finger*] And I won't hear a word against them.

Which team do you dislike the most and why?
I don't really dislike teams, I'm not that sort of person. I could say Arsenal and Manchester United as they are our rivals today, and they dominate (or they did!), while in my day Liverpool were a fantastic side, but if there was one team I did dislike I would have to say Leeds. It was always a battle against

Leeds. They were animals, they really were, but we had some boys who could match them. They had a couple of little lads in there, who were great ball players, and unfortunately Billy Bremner's dead now, and he was a lovely little man off the pitch, and you shouldn't speak ill of the dead, but on the pitch he was a little shit. He really was. And Johnny Giles. He was another one. But he was a fantastic player, a great player.

What is your worst Chelsea memory?
Leaving the club. We lost to Stoke City at Wembley in the League Cup final, and 1972 wasn't a good year. I thought we were the better side, but we got beaten, and it all fell apart from then onwards. Leaving Chelsea was a big strain on me. I hated every minute of it. There was a period where there was a bit of a stand-off between a few of us and Dave over our differences and we thought, wrongly, that player power might win. We heard Dave Sexton had been given the sack and we got the champagne out on the Kings Road – me and Huddy and Hutch and all the boys – and then he was reinstated and I was gone. Leaving Chelsea Football Club in 1974 was devastating for me.

Who was your most difficult opponent?
I was very fortunate that I played a lot of European games and also played for England a few times. The Italians were hard to play against, but I would honestly say that the best footballer I ever played against was Bobby Moore. Roy McFarland wasn't far behind him. I thought Roy was a very good centre-half. He was very fair and hard and would give you a good game. But I would say Mike England was my most difficult opponent. I think I got the best of most centre-halves, but Big Mike was a handful. Frank McLintock was in the same mould, but I would say Mike England was the one. He was naughty, would elbow you and kick you off the ball, and we had some good battles. Full credit to him. Unlike the Leeds mob there was no malice.

Which young player do you tip for future success?
There's one lad there at Chelsea who's really come on, and that's Joe Cole. He has been fantastic and he's learnt his trade. Jose Mourinho has got hold of him and told him what he has to do to become a player and Joe's listened. He has become much more disciplined. Against Norwich he went in and won a tackle, and then knocked it in the top corner of the net.

He is a fantastic little player and a great lad. He has got a head on his shoulders and all of a sudden he has grown up, even though he is still young. He's a different breed to Charlie Cooke and Alan Hudson. This little fellow can go and score goals – Charlie and Alan couldn't. I'm not saying he's better, just different. He scored in both the games against Liverpool in the Premiership and changed them around. He still does his tricks, but now he does them in the right areas.

What did you dislike most about being a professional footballer?
Not having a drink on Friday night! No, I never disliked anything about being a professional footballer. I wasn't a lover of training to be honest, as I just liked to play football. They said we didn't train much, but we worked bloody hard under Dave Sexton. We did cross-country runs across Epsom Downs that were unbelievable and he was a hard task master. Dave wanted fit people, especially on the pitches we played on. Training was the bugbear for me. I didn't like it, just wanted to get the football out and play. If I had a football I would run all day. But it was fantastic to be a footballer and I've never regretted or moaned about it. How could I?

What do you regard as the biggest mistake you made in your career?
Probably falling out with Dave Sexton. That was the big one. I was an England player at that particular time and had just played against Italy. I was only twenty-seven years old and should have stayed, but unfortunately with Dave around one of us had to go, and at the end of the day it was me. Yes, that is my biggest regret, falling out with Dave.

Do you think the minimal-contact style of football today would have suited the way you played?
Yes, of course. In my day there were plenty of players who could kick you, and that's what they did. If you were a flair player, you were the first one they picked on. They knew you were a match-winner and they wanted to take the main man out. It's what Chopper used to do with Greavsie, when we played Spurs. He'd kick Jimmy in the first five minutes and you'd never see him after that. Lets be fair, at Old Trafford in the replay, after the first game at Wembley when David Webb got murdered by Eddie Gray, Chopper played at right back and kicked him early, really hurt him, and he never played. That doesn't happen now. I would have loved playing today.

What are the key differences between the modern game and when you were playing?
When you look at the pitches they play on now, the balls they use and the boots they wear, the improvement is incredible. During that FA Cup run we had in 1970, when we reached the final, we played at Loftus Road on an absolute mud heap and beat QPR 4-2, but the game would have been cancelled today. Then we played the semi final at White Hart Lane and won 5-1 against Watford, and again, the pitch wasn't very good at all, but we scored five goals. We went to Wembley and they'd had the horse show there two weeks before. The pitch was terrible, yet we scored two goals. We scored eleven goals in three games, playing on mud heaps.

We were a good footballing side, so imagine what we could have done on today's pitches. A few years ago, Zola of all people, moaned about the pitch and the club re-dug it and two weeks later they were playing on a new surface. If we'd said that in our day they would have laughed and told us to get on with it. The stadiums are another improvement and the facilities are just so much better.

People say football is quicker and faster now, and it is, because you're not allowed to bring players down and take them out. If you'd tugged Chopper's shirt, he wouldn't have fallen down. He would have told you to piss off. The cheating that's come into the modern game has spoilt it, and that's down to some of the foreign players who've come in. Our players have adapted to it, and that's a shame.

Who would you have most liked to have played with from the current Chelsea team?

I played with a great Chelsea side who weren't quite consistent enough to win the league, but on our day we could beat anyone. We proved that. I don't really like to go down that road, but there are certain people, like John Terry. He is in the same mould as John Dempsey and David Webb, but he's probably a better footballer. He has Chelsea at heart just like Chopper did, and he's a good leader. Maybe Chopper wasn't as strong a leader in the dressing room, but if he stood up and said something then we all listened.

Frank Lampard is another one who I would like to have played with, but the thought that really excites me would be lining up alongside Zola. I thought the little man was awesome. I have always been a fan of Jimmy Floyd Hasselbaink as well, and obviously Luca. I loved the runs Vialli made. He wasn't the quickest, but he made great runs for people to play and stick him in. Robben is coming on and he's another great player.

As The King Of Stamford Bridge, did you mourn the loss of The Shed?

Of course. You hate to see it go, but that's progress. It was a great thing to go down to The Shed, even though they were so far back from the pitch, and hear them shouting and singing. They were the best fans, the real Chelsea boys. We always appreciated them and went down and saw them first. That's what kicked off our game, hearing The Shed singing and cheering us.

Do you think you would have been England's centre-forward under Sven Goran Erikkson?

If Emile Heskey can be, then yes. I think I was very unfortunate in my career that I only had four caps. I played in Mexico twice, against Czechoslovakia and Romania, and I thought I would play against Brazil, but they chose Jeff Astle instead. That was the sort of fellow Alf Ramsey was. Again, he didn't want a flair player, he played a big man up front and thought the crosses were going to come in for Astle and Geoff Hurst, but it didn't work for him.

I was very disappointed. I'd played for the England Youth team and the England Under-23s and I think I was only ever in one losing team. I went into the full side in 1970 and we beat Belgium, then I played in the World Cup in the same year, and after that didn't play again until 1974.

I think Alf was too protective of his team. Some of the lads were too old and he didn't bring the youngsters in. The same happened with Manchester United and that's why they went into decline. Sometimes managers are too loyal to their players when they should be bringing some new blood in. Under Sven, I like to think I would have won more caps.

Which pubs did you use around Stamford Bridge?
The Black Bull and Rising Sun were right by the ground and we would pop in those sometimes, but we used to go down the Kings Road most of the time for our serious drinking. We used to use pubs like The Trafalgar, The Chelsea Drugstore and the Markham Arms. Alexander's was our main restaurant, and we used to go to the Pheasant Tree which was a great club restaurant. The Eight Bells was another pub we used, and that was a great place because we would sit at the table and there was a telephone there, so people used to phone us up and ask if they could come over for a drink, and we would say yes, or no. If they were pretty and female we tended to say yes. Those were our main hangouts really.

What are your thoughts about the Dream Team chosen by the supporters and are there any other players you would have included?
You could probably pick fifteen or twenty teams from all the great players who have appeared for Chelsea over the years, so it really is a privilege to be in the first eleven. That's fantastic to have been chosen by the fans. I'm very happy.

What ambitions do you have for the future?
To retire as quick as I can. No, I enjoy my after-dinner speaking, my hospitality work at Chelsea and Southampton, and I love meeting the fans. The travelling can be tough at times, staying in hotels and being away from home, and none of us are getting any younger, but I am very happy. I live in a great little village and love it down here in Hampshire; love popping in my local for an hour and seeing the lads. Hopefully I'll see my young son Darren do a little better at football. He's already doing really well and was Player Of The Year this season for his team. He's a good kid, a lovely kid. He takes after his mum.

What is your big passion outside of football?
Chardonnay! I love enjoying life, being with friends, watching my young son grow up, having a good time and meeting lovely people. Seeing Chelsea win

the Premiership was fantastic, it's just a shame the Saints went down. But there are highs and lows in football and we've had a few. It's been a great season for Chelsea and I'm sure there's more to come. We waited a long time to win the league.

Do you have a favourite book, film, album?
When it comes to music I prefer ballads, people such as Glen Campbell and Ronan Keating, and I liked Eddie Grant when we used to go to discos. I'm not a big reader, but I enjoyed Bestie's book, Blessed. That was very detailed and honest. I'm not a film-goer these days. I prefer watching TV, old movies and programmes like Morse and Frost. As you know, I appeared in a film not too long ago. I had a cameo in The Football Factory along with Huddy. That was fun and they got the champagne out for us as well.

Do you have a favourite place you like to visit?
I've been to Dubai a few times, and I like it there, and we got married in Antigua, and I loved it there, but I'm a Spain man basically, down around Marbella. I really enjoy it down there.

If there was one thing about this country you could change, what would it be?
Nothing. I love the place. I always remember coming back from the World Cup in Mexico, after we'd been knocked out by Germany, and we were all a bit dejected on that plane. Alan Ball stood up as we were landing and said: 'Chins up, you've just landed in the best country in the world.' And he was right. It was what we needed and he captured the moment perfectly. England is a great country and we should be proud and enjoy it.

Z-O-L-A – Zola. Sheer class

Gianfranco Zola

Gianfranco Zola was born on July 5th, 1966, in Sardinia. Race riots swept America and the Vietnam War raged on. In Britain, The Kinks were warbling about a Sunny Afternoon, the BBC had unleashed Alf Garnett on to the public and Barclays Bank quietly introduced something called a credit card. Having won the Serie A with Naples and the UEFA Cup with Parma, Franco joined Chelsea in 1996 for £4.5m. The following year he was part of the FA Cup winning side and won the Football Writers Player Of The Year award. In 1998 he helped Chelsea lift the League Cup and the European Cup Winners Cup, and in 2000 was in the team that won the FA Cup again. He played thirty-five games for Italy and scored eight goals. Zola left Chelsea in 2003 to join Cagliari and retired at the end of the 2004-05 season. He is the only other player besides Peter Osgood to have been voted Best Chelsea Player Of All Time by the fans

Where did you grow up and what is your family background?

I grew up in Oliena, a very small village in Sardinia. Like many others, my family lived a simple life. This was normal for the area from which I come. It was a nice place to grow up. My family were farming folk, as were most people on Sardinia. It is only in recent times that it has become a holiday destination. My father was a farmer and also drove a truck to make ends meet. My childhood was extremely happy and you could not have wished for a better place to have lived. That is why I am back here now among my family and childhood friends, and near the mountains where I can fish. Oliena is famous for its wine too.

My father was a great lover of football and he encouraged me to play. He supported Cagliari, our local team, and of course I supported them as well. They were my heroes. They are not the biggest club in the world, nor the biggest in Italy. The capacity of the ground is only 18,000, but the people are passionate and the football has always been good.

When was your professional debut?

It was in 1984 for a side called Nuorese and I was eighteen years old. It was a great feeling to play for the first time and a very special moment for me. They were a C2 side. There is C2, C1, Serie B and then the top division is Serie A. Nourese were in Nuoro, the third biggest city in Sardinia. I had always dreamed of becoming a footballer, but didn't plan anything. It all happened quite naturally. It was a very smooth path.

Did you know anything about Chelsea before you came to the club?

I knew a little bit about English football and I knew a little about Chelsea as well but, to be honest, not too much. They weren't such a big club at that time. Now Chelsea are having one of the best periods in their history. It is like the 1950s, when they won the First Division title. Today, Chelsea are known throughout the world. They are mentioned next to Real Madrid, Milan and Barcelona these days.

What were your first impressions when you came to Chelsea?

For me, it was perfect. It was a perfect start and a perfect ending. I made my debut away against Blackburn Rovers and it was a rough, tough game, but I really enjoyed it. Let me say, it was easy for me coming to Chelsea. The support I have had from the people here has been unbelievable, and playing for Chelsea has been the best experience of my career. I feel privileged to have been able to play for Chelsea Football Club. I can't imagine it would have been the same if I had played for another team in the Premiership. It felt like a marriage, and still does. Only today I have come here to attend the Chelsea Legends dinner and the fans, old colleagues, and the staff are all making a fuss. I no longer play at Stamford Bridge, but everybody makes me feel that I am part of Chelsea, and always will be. It is hard to describe how that feels, but it is nice to know you have two families.

How do you feel about being included in the Dream Team alongside Chelsea legends such as Peter Osgood and Ron Harris? Would you have liked the chance to have been in the same side with players such as these?

Yes, of course, but I would have played for Chelsea with anybody. Obviously, those players have been fantastic for Chelsea and for me to be listed among them is a great honour. To play alongside Peter Osgood would be interesting. I never saw him play personally, only in recordings, but he was a very special player and is a hero for the Chelsea fans. I think we would have done well together. He was a great player.

Of course, I know a bit more about the current players in the team. I know why the fans have voted for them. Frank Lampard is excellent. He makes everyone around him shine and he has the ability to change games. And John (Terry) is the best possible captain. You are happy he is behind you at the back. And they love Chelsea. They are desperate to succeed. They believe in the club and put the team before everything. This is the secret. Not every club has players like that. Chelsea are very lucky.

Who is the best manager you have played for?

I don't really want to say that one manager has been better than another, or that one was worse than someone else. It is not really the way I like to do things. I must say that I have learned something good from all of the managers I have played for and I would have a good word for all of them. I would like to mention one man, though. Giovanni Maria Mele was great for me when I was a teenager. At the time I was a Mr Nobody and he was the first one to spot that I had some talent. He believed that I could go on and become a professional footballer and was a big help to me. I am pleased that Ruud Gullit brought me to the club, and of course that Luca continued picking me when he became manager.

What is your most memorable game for Chelsea?
The Cup Winners Cup final against Stuttgart in 1998 was special, but for me the most memorable game was winning my first FA Cup in England in 1997. It is a day I still remember very clearly in my mind. We had a good team and tried to play entertaining football. Roberto Di Matteo scored early on and then Eddie Newton made sure with a second, and the Chelsea supporters were happy as they hadn't won it for so long, since 1970 against Leeds United. There is great passion for the FA Cup and I will never forget that match against Middlesbrough.

What is your most memorable goal?
The one against Norwich was good, because it was quite spectacular, but the one I scored against Stuttgart was, for me, my favourite. I wasn't even supposed to play in that game as I was injured. I had a torn muscle from the league match against Liverpool at Stamford Bridge and it was a bad injury. Normally, it takes four or five weeks to recover, but I was playing again after just twenty-two days. I was on the bench and came on when the score was 0-0. The Chelsea fans were chanting 'Hughesie, Hughesie', asking for Mark Hughes, who was also on the bench. They wanted him to get a game, but then I came on and scored very quickly, and it ended up as the winning goal. It was very special for me because, as I said, I was injured and wasn't really meant to be in the squad.

There were so many Chelsea fans there that night and the atmosphere was fantastic. They were everywhere and took over the stadium. The noise and support was incredible and the celebrations after showed how happy we were to win. I will always remember that goal. It was a great ball from Wisey and typical of him. He was very good at passing the ball, a great player for Chelsea. I just ran into the channel and I didn't think too much. The ball arrived and I managed to hit it perfectly. I really did not have time to think. Yes, I am very pleased with that goal.

How did you get yourself fit for the final?
I have strong muscles. Sardinian muscles are the best. Seriously, though, it was a mental thing. I had a strong enough will to recover. It was a difficult

game because Stuttgart weren't conceding anything. It was a strange game. I felt sure I was going to get on to the pitch, but I didn't know when.

What is your favourite terrace song?

'Gianfranco Zola, la la la la la la' was unbelievable, but the best one was written by a school. It was a version of The Kinks song Lola. When I heard that I was very impressed. The children sent it to me on a tape and then they came to a match at Stamford Bridge and sang it to me afterwards. That was very nice, very special. I have heard the original song many times now and I think the lyrics are about a man who thinks he is a woman. I am sure the Chelsea fans chose the song because Zola rhymes with Lola, not because I am a man who thinks he is a woman.

Can you remember the supporters singing 'thank you, Mrs Zola'?

Yes I can. That was very funny. My wife Franca was embarrassed. She prefers to keep things quiet, but she liked the song, and really enjoyed living in England. At first we were living in Central London, but then we decided to move out of the city and ended up in Oxshott, near Cobham. It is in a really lovely part of Surrey and close to the best golf courses. And I like playing golf.

Which team do you dislike the most?

I don't dislike them in a bad way, but Arsenal and Leeds were always very hard teams to play against. They were very tough, especially away from home. I dislike them in a professional way. Leeds was always a battle. The first time I played at Elland Road it was more like a hunt than a game of football.

It's a good job you didn't play in the 1970s then. Have you seen the video of the 1970 FA Cup final?

I have seen that match and it looked like a really tough game. It was very physical and must have been hard for the players at Chelsea.

What is your worst Chelsea memory?

Leaving Chelsea was very hard for me, but I knew it would happen one day. One tough moment was when we came third in the league under Gianluca Vialli. We were only four points behind the winners Manchester United. We were playing well in the league, but we lost at home to West Ham in a game we dominated to a very lucky goal, and could only draw with Leicester after leading 2-0. We had a very good team and some great players. We won trophies, but if those two games had gone differently then we could have been champions as well. That was very tough and disappointing. We really missed Pierluigi Casiraghi. What happened to him reminds us all how much luck decides our lives. He was a great player and a brilliant signing by Luca. But he was badly injured against West Ham and was never able to recover. It could have happened to anyone, but this time it was Pierluigi. It was very sad, because I think he would have become Chelsea's biggest star.

Who was your most difficult opponent?
Playing against Arsenal's Tony Adams and Martin Keown was always hard. You weren't just playing against those two either, but the whole of their back-four. They were very good together and when I played against them they used to give me a hard time, not letting me get into space, and their tackling was tough. Adams and Keown were very strong opponents. Rio Ferdinand was another defender it wasn't easy to play against. He is another tough player.

Which young player do you tip for future success?
Well, for the past couple of seasons I haven't been able to study the young players at Chelsea too closely, but Robert Huth has a great attitude and when you see that guy, you know he is going to get where he wants to go. Another good player is Joe Cole. He has some fantastic skills. As long as he can go on using those skills for the benefit of the team he is going to be an important player. He did very well last year, scored goals and is playing for England.

What did you dislike the most about being a footballer?
Sometimes, when it takes you away from your family or when it stops you enjoying yourself, it can be difficult. You can't always do what you want, when you want to. That, for me at least, is the bad side of football. I have just had my first proper holiday with my family for a long time and am beginning to discover what normal life is. I am really enjoying some of the simple things in life now.

When I was playing I couldn't do certain things because at the back of my mind I was worrying about my fitness. Now I can do them without worrying. But really, how can there be much to dislike about playing the game you love in front of the fans you love, and getting paid for it?

What is the biggest mistake you made in your career?
On the pitch I made many mistakes. Everyone does. I made some off the pitch as well. When I think how I could have played differently, I feel sure I wouldn't make them again, but I suppose it is easy to say that. Nobody is perfect, but I hope that the mistakes I did make helped me become a better player. The important thing is to learn from your mistakes. One thing I really regret happened during Euro 96 when I missed a penalty for Italy. I was nervous and didn't score, but I am sure that if I had the chance again, I wouldn't miss.

The Special Ones

When you scored for Italy against England, when Italy won 1-0, the following week the Chelsea supporters were singing 'Chelsea 1, England 0'. What did you think about that?
Yes, I remember. It was at Leicester and their supporters were giving me a very hard time. I got a lot of stick from them. It is a great memory for me, the way the Chelsea supporters treated me after I had scored against England.

What ambitions do you have for the future?
The rest of my life starts now. At the moment, I am just taking time to rest and think about the right thing to do. People have asked me if I might return to Chelsea in some role, but we will have to wait and see. It might be with Chelsea, or it might be doing something else. I don't know yet what opportunities will be there for me. I will have to let the book unfold.

What is your big passion outside of football?
Obviously, my family is important to me, and I can spend more time with them now. My son plays football and I try to help, but really it is down to him how far he goes. Nobody taught me how to play and it must come from within. If he learns to make the right sacrifices and improve his qualities, he may have a chance. My other big passion is golf, and I discovered this while I was in England. I am okay at golf, but not brilliant, though I am gradually getting better. I played a few times with Wisey, but my regular partner was Kevin Hitchcock. I got on with everyone at Chelsea, but especially with him. He was one of the best golfers at the club. Hitchy and myself have a special relationship.

Do you have a favourite book, film, album?
I am a big fan of Elton John. I have been to some of his concerts and love his music. I met him at a party, but we didn't really have much time to talk to each other, and no, he didn't ask me to join Watford. I will read almost anything and like to watch films with my children.

Do you have a favourite place you like to visit?
I went to the Maldives once, and it was very nice and relaxing, but most of the time I have my holidays in Sardinia. I know that some Chelsea supporters have come to Sardinia to see me play for Cagliari, and I have been told that when they mention my name the locals make them very welcome.

If there was one thing you could change about England, what would it be?
The weather. Without a doubt, it would be the weather. It's not always so great here, but I really like the people and the country. Mind you, English people tell me the weather is changing, becoming hotter, and it's funny,

144

because since I have been back in Sardinia it has rained a lot. Seriously, though, the way you view a country has a lot to do with the experiences you have had and what I can say about England is that, for me, my experiences have always been good. The weather may be cold, but the people are very warm. My first game at Blackburn was in November, and it was cold and the best place to start.

Were you surprised how the Chelsea supporters fell in love with you?
It was very unexpected. What really struck me was the patience that the supporters have here and had with me, especially when I was playing badly. One year, I think I scored only four goals and, to be honest, I didn't play well at all, but the supporters used to get behind me and there was no negativity from them. I don't think that would happen in some other places. There are clubs where the fans are very critical and negative, but the Chelsea supporters are very different. It was amazing for me.

When Ruud Gullit signed you, were you worried about coming here?
No, not at all. I was totally into my new experience. Obviously, when you change town, country, culture there will always be things which you are a little unsure of, but since the beginning of my time at Chelsea it has been great. Everybody at Chelsea helped me, especially Gary Staker, who Ken Bates asked to translate for me. My English is better than his Italian now. There is one word to describe Gary's Italian, but it is a bad word that Hitchy taught me. Kevin Hitchcock and Dennis Wise were very good at swearing. But everyone made me feel welcome and it was an exciting time. I am very glad I came to England, and experienced English football. I have always said that coming to Chelsea has been my greatest experience in football.

What were your feelings when Roman Abramovich bought Chelsea? You had signed for Cagliari the day before. Did you wish that you could have stayed?
No, I had made my decision. Cagliari needed me and so I had to go and help them. By the time Roman Abramovich came, I had already made my mind up to return to Sardinia and play for Cagliari. Things worked out well. I scored a few goals and helped them get promotion, and last year we avoided relegation and are safe for another season in Serie A. That, for me, is great. As I have said, Cagliari are my local side, the team I supported as a boy, my father's club, so it was a very nice way to end my career. It was the right thing to do.

Wee Pat – a classic talent in John Neal's classic team

Chelsea Legends

Gary Bacchus casts his blue-tinted gaze over the eleven players who finished runners-up in the Dream Team poll, the Chelsea favourites who are Carlo Cudicini, Dan Petrescu, Frank Leboeuf, Paul Elliott, Graeme Le Saux, Pat Nevin, Ray Wilkins, Ruud Gullit, Peter Houseman, Kerry Dixon and Jimmy Greaves, and the man chosen to manage them, Dave Sexton

Dave Sexton

Until recently, Dave Sexton was recognised as the most successful manager in the history of Chelsea Football Club. With an FA Cup and a European Cup Winners Cup safely on his curriculum vitae, alongside a League Cup runners-up place and some healthy First Division placings, it was to be near enough a quarter of a century before anybody challenged his position.

Sexton was originally employed as a coach at Stamford Bridge, but left in 1965 to try his hand at management. He had a spell in charge of Leyton Orient before once again reverting to a coaching role at Fulham and then Arsenal. Chelsea, after dispensing with the services of Tommy Docherty, were on the lookout for a new manager and when Sexton was appointed in October 1967 it was with the blessing of the first-team squad.

As a coach, Sexton was highly respected by all those he worked with. His technique and knowledge stood him in good stead and it was no surprise when he developed Chelsea into a side to be reckoned with. In his first season Chelsea climbed to a respectable sixth in the First Division. A couple of seasons later the trophy cabinet received the FA Cup, and a further twelve months on, the European Cup Winners Cup took pride of place at Stamford Bridge.

Prior to this, Chelsea had never won the FA Cup, while their success in Europe against the mighty Real Madrid was also a first. In the FA Cup final versus Leeds United in 1970, Eddie Gray had caused Chelsea endless problems in the first game at Wembley, ripping Dave Webb apart down the left flank. In the replay at Old Trafford, Ron Harris was put on Gray, while Webb switched over to central defence. Sexton's tactics worked. Harris shut down Gray, while Webb moved forward for Ian Hutchinson's extra-time long throw-in and nodded home the winner. This is just a blatant example of Sexton's tactical awareness.

Dave Sexton managed what for many supporters remains the all-time greatest ever Chelsea side, a mixture of flair performers such as Peter Osgood, Alan Hudson and Charlie Cooke, and solid, gifted professionals like Ron Harris, Peter Bonetti and Eddie McCreadie. It is a great testament to Sexton's abilities that those six players have been voted into the Dream Team, while Peter Houseman has been nominated in this Legends side. Dave Sexton's achievements have stood the test of time and he is still revered by the supporters. Sexton put Chelsea on the map. He made the club a serious proposition. Only Gianluca Vialli's classic Nineties outfit has compared, the cultured Italian's team going on to even greater success. But it was Sexton who set the standards.

The loss to Stoke City in the League Cup heralded something of a downward spiral in Chelsea's fortunes, and off the field problems eventually beset the manager. It has often been stated that Sexton had an uncomfortable relationship with some of his star players and matters came to a head in 1974 when Alan Hudson and Peter Osgood were dropped. Sexton watched on as the popular Alan Hudson was sold to Stoke City, and when the board wouldn't sanction the transfer of Peter Osgood, Sexton offered his resignation. Dramatically, his offer was refused and Osgood was sold to Southampton, much to the despair of the Chelsea faithful.

The 1974-75 season saw Chelsea start poorly. The club were suffering under the financial burden imposed by the building of the new East Stand and when the team slipped to 17th position in October of 1974, Sexton was unceremoniously sacked. His reign had lasted from October 1967 to October 1974. It is tempting to wonder if he would have fared even better in today's game than he did back in his heyday at Chelsea. He was an excellent coach, but in the end seemed dogged by more mundane things such as contracts and discipline.

After leaving Chelsea, Dave Sexton continued to have a successful career in football at both club and national level, and he remains one of the most respected figures within the game. When he attended the first of the Chelsea centenary events held at the Butcher's Hook public house he mixed eloquently with those he had coached to such marvellous success in the early Seventies. Little did we know that following his departure further success would be so long in coming. One of the greatest periods in Chelsea's history is owed to this man.

Carlo Cudicini

After arriving at Stamford Bridge from little known Italian side Castel Di Sangro, there were people who questioned the logic of signing Carlo Cudicini. Sure, Carlo's father had enjoyed a wonderful career with Milan, but in his youth he had been somewhat injury prone, and perhaps Carlo's Chelsea appearances would be limited. How wrong these people were. By the end of the 2004-05 season, Carlo had made 170 appearances and conceded a mere seventy-three goals – a superb games-to-goals ratio. After replacing the ageing Ed De Goey, Carlo also saw off the challenge of Mark Bosnich to make the Chelsea jersey his own. His displays were sensational and helped to inspire the defence ahead of him. In particular, his reading of situations and his ability to come off his line at pace ensured that one-on-ones rarely resulted in an opposition goal.

During one glittering part of his Chelsea career, it seemed he was almost unbeatable. An acrobatic save at White Hart Lane had Jamie Redknapp gasping in disbelief. Our Frank's cousin had delivered a stunning free kick but somehow Carlo arched his body and pushed the shot just over the bar. If you ever get the chance to see it again, focus on the Spurs supporters behind the goal, look at the anguish on their faces as they realise Carlo has saved it – pure theatre, pure class and an absolute magic moment. Another wonderful save drew gasps of admiration from those that regularly pack out the Theatre Of Dreams. Ruud van Nistelrooy thought he had beaten the agile keeper low down, but Carlo simply extended his arm and with the help of an incredibly strong wrist flicked it past the post. Ruud raised his hands towards his head, rendered speechless by a world-class save.

Carlo also developed a reputation for saving spot kicks. During one incredible run you just got this feeling that a giant leap and an outstretched hand would push the ball away. It became quite a spectacle waiting for the unbelieving penalty taker to turn around with the dreaded look of anguish cloaking his features. However, Carlo's Chelsea career has also suffered a couple of setbacks due to injury.

A hand injury deprived him of playing a part in the final stages of Chelsea's epic Champions League run during the season 2003-04. He missed the tie with Arsenal that culminated in a superb win at Highbury, and the first leg of the fateful semi-final against Monaco.

To this day, I still wonder if the outcome would have been different in the first leg, when Monaco opened up a 3-1 lead, if he had played. Would Carlo have guided us to a final with Porto? Could Chelsea have actually beaten a Porto team so expertly managed by Mourinho? If so, would 2004-05 have seen Ranieri still in charge and would we have been Premiership champions? Only the gods know.

Last season saw the arrival of Petr Cech and his subsequent rise to prominence. Despite proving himself to be the best keeper in the Premiership in the two previous seasons, Carlo found himself on the bench, hoping for a chance to impress, a chance to regain the jersey he had coveted for so long. Unfortunately, it never really happened. In a season when Chelsea set all sorts of records, the likeable Italian didn't even play enough games to earn a winner's medal.

Even Mourinho's plans to grant Carlo a Carling Cup final appearance against Liverpool went horribly wrong. Selected to play in the FA Cup tie at Newcastle the previous weekend, he suffered the indignity of receiving a straight red card late in the game, with an instant ban ruling out any chance of an appearance in Cardiff.

Having played so few games for Chelsea during the 2004-05 season, it was felt that Carlo Cudicini would move on, and perhaps return to Italy, but as the season started he was still with Chelsea and intent on regaining his place. This fine keeper typifies the spirit amongst the players at the club these days.

The top professional players enjoy a grandiose lifestyle these days, and this is clear to see in their choice of luxury cars. Hanging around the Stamford Bridge forecourt, it is not hard to spot those who play for Chelsea arriving. The list of cars – Bentleys, Ferraris, Porsches – reads like a motor-show brochure. Therefore, it may come as a surprise to learn that Carlo, for several seasons, opted to walk to work before a home game. With the flash cars descending into the underground car park, he simply strolled through the concourse, partially disguised in an overcoat and hat. Of course, it wasn't long before he was spotted, but he never shied away from signing autographs for the punters and, like his fellow countryman, Gianfranco Zola, is a model professional and massive favourite with the Chelsea supporters.

Dan Petrescu

Dan Petrescu was a player who somehow contrived to play for Sheffield Wednesday, of all clubs, before signing for Chelsea. If the strange folk of Yorkshire had been accustomed to the stylish Romanian, it was to be the fervent support of SW6 that would end up adoring a player who occupied the right flank with a presence not seen for many a year. Brought to Chelsea by Glenn Hoddle, for the princely sum of £2.3 million, Dan was to epitomise the style of football Hoddle wanted to bring to Chelsea.

His touch and vision were far superior to anything many of us had previously seen. More importantly, Dan was able to play as a wing-back, full-back or in a right-sided midfield role. In the latter role it is often suggested that he formed a quarter of Chelsea's best ever midfield along with Dennis Wise, Roberto Di Matteo and Gus Poyet. While his career flourished under the leadership of Hoddle, it encountered difficulties when first Gullit, and then Vialli, were in charge.

When things were not quite going well for the team it was Dan who was inevitably sacrificed. As time wore on he could have been forgiven for becoming disenchanted with life at Chelsea, and during the reign of Vialli it was often suggested that the club would listen to offers for the versatile right-sided player. Thankfully, he didn't want to leave, insisting that he loved life at the club and also in London.

In the summer of 2000, after being left out of the FA Cup final squad, Dan left and returned to Yorkshire to play for Bradford City. It is probably fair to say that he never prospered from the move and that perhaps the best times of his career were now behind him. He certainly left some wonderful memories behind. Who will ever forget the goal he scored against Arsenal in the

Coca Cola Cup semi-final? With Chelsea trailing from the first leg, and with Vialli in charge for the first time, Dan received the ball on the edge of the area and turned not one, not two, but three Arsenal defenders inside out before rifling home a superb goal.

On the international front, during his time at Chelsea he became the most capped international the club had seen. In one of those games he was to break English hearts by dancing past Graeme Le Saux to score a crucial goal for Romania. As some form of retribution I am quite positive that the gods convinced Dan to dye his hair yellow, along with the rest of the Romanian side – not the best thing he ever did.

Dan Petrescu left Chelsea after appearing 208 times and scoring twenty-three goals. He also left with FA Cup, League Cup and European Cup Winners Cup medals in his pocket and a healthy bond with the supporters. The song Dan, Dan, Super Dan was a favourite with the fans, and a fitting tribute to a classy footballer with a sharp eye for goal.

After leaving the Gianfranco Zola Tribute Dinner in August 2004, a quick saunter along the corridors in the West Stand saw two prominent writers associated with www.blueandwhitearmy.net and the popular fanzine, cfcuk, enter a lift. Glancing behind, we were aware we were being followed. Dan Petrescu joined us. Both parties smiled at each other before Dan was told, in no uncertain terms, that he was a Chelsea legend.

Before he had time to reply, the conversation had moved on and the words 'unlike Gus Poyet' had been boisterously added. Looking a little perplexed it was explained that Poyet had tainted his reputation by joining Spurs, whereas Super Dan had enhanced his by turning down a similar move, hence the legendary status. Dan's face lit up as he realised what had been said. Before any other pleasantries could be exchanged, the lift doors opened and the all too brief encounter was over.

Frank Leboeuf

When Frank Leboeuf arrived at Stamford Bridge, he was in all fairness the lesser known of the three signings made by Ruud Gullit. While Gianluca Vialli had become one of Europe's most familiar faces, and Roberto Di Matteo had carved out a successful career in Serie A, Frank had played his career out in the lesser known French leagues. In fact, when he was plucked from Strasbourg, many simply asked Frank who? It wasn't long before the elegant Frenchman had endeared himself to the Stamford Bridge faithful.

Leboeuf was able to deliver pin-point passes over distances ranging from ten yards to an impressive fifty yards. His elegant passing launched numerous counter attacks as Chelsea, under Gullit, added a new dimension to their game. Frank was also more than adequate defensively. What he may have lacked in brawn he made up for in skill and his unnerving natural ability to read the game. While some doubted his ability to absorb the punishment dished out in the Premiership, it should be remembered, that for all his moaning, Frank took his knocks like a thoroughbred. The egg-sized lump that appeared on his head after Wimbledon tried to rough him up being one such example.

The Frenchman also added another dimension to Chelsea's game with his ability to ghost into unlikely areas and notch vital goals, a typical example being in the early stages of his first season against Aston Villa. The visitors had taken a surprise lead before Leboeuf drifted in behind a static defence to side-foot home an equaliser. At the time it was almost lost on those watching the exquisite way Frank had simply tucked the ball away, wrong footing the keeper rather than going for sheer power. However, when the opportunity required it, Frank could unleash fearsome drives.

In a fixture against Leicester City, the game looked to be heading for a draw, when deep in injury time Frank received the ball, some thirty-five yards out, from a corner. With minimal back-lift the ball was struck with ferocious power and it sailed into the top corner of the goal. That strike signalled the start of a vociferous chant in Frank's honour. 'He's here, he's there, he's every fucking where, Frank Leboeuf, Frank Leboeuf' reverberated around Stamford Bridge.

Unfortunately, Frank wasn't too pleased with the chanting and objected to his name being associated with a song that included industrial language, his point being that his children were often in the ground and he didn't consider it apt for them to hear such words. Almost as if they had been scolded, future versions of the song were watered down by the Matthew Harding Lower with the offending word subsequently removed.

Frank's natural ability to deliver a precision ball also saw him granted penalty-taking responsibilities. Once again it was something he managed with unnerving ease, despatching penalty after penalty past bewildered keeper after bewildered keeper. He simply strolled up and tucked them away, neatly and precisely. The epic FA Cup tie with Leicester City in 1996-97 sticks in the memory. The tie had finished level after a replay and deep into injury time Erland Johnsen won a debatable spot kick. With furious Leicester players confronting the referee, Leboeuf remained ice-cool to steer the ball past the dive of Kasey Keller.

There were times when the coolness did evaporate and on one occasion Frank lost it big time, blatantly lashing out at a prostrate Harry Kewell and then seemingly refusing to take the long walk. But such antics shouldn't be allowed to gloss over the attractive side of Frank's game. Those who were there at the 6-1 demolition of Spurs at White Hart Lane will always remember his sublime long ball that saw Dan Petrescu score a fine goal. It was the perfect epitome of what he could offer Chelsea.

After establishing himself in the Chelsea side, Frank became a prominent member of the French national squad, culminating in a historic World Cup final appearance against Brazil. Some may say he was fortunate to play, after Laurent Blanc was harshly sent off in a previous round and missed the final through suspension, but you make your own luck in this world. After celebrating with a winner's medal, he was often chided for constantly telling the nation, on television, that he was a World Cup winner. Personally, I can't see the problem. After all, haven't the West Ham lot been telling us for nigh on forty years that they won the 1966 World Cup?

Frank Leboeuf made 204 appearances for Chelsea and scored twenty-four goals, and is fondly remembered by those who witnessed his time at Stamford Bridge.

Paul Elliott

Football, despite giving so many people such immense pleasure, can also be a harsh game. When Paul Elliott signed for Chelsea in July 1991, for the sum of £1.4 million, it is doubtful whether anybody could foresee the impact he would have on the club, or the personal horror that lay ahead.

Before signing, Paul had previously played for Charlton, Luton, Aston Villa, Pisa and Celtic. Despite having such an impressive curriculum vitae, he was still a relatively young twenty-seven-year-old when he arrived at Stamford Bridge. He seemed to almost galvanise team spirit overnight. Bought to shore up the middle of an inconsistent defence, Paul brought that something extra the team needed. The fist shaking antics immediately helped him gel with the supporters, and his defensive play was verging on the sublime.

Paul had an impressive physique, possessed superb athleticism and dominated the penalty area. He arrived at Chelsea as Scottish Player Of The Year and had reportedly come south in order to claim a place at the heart of the England defence. The experience he had gained playing for Pisa stood him in good stead for the ferocity of top flight football. It also enabled him to show his skill in bringing the ball out of defence. He further endeared himself to the faithful by scoring on his debut against Wimbledon, climbing high to head home a Dennis Wise corner, and he was to maintain the same standard throughout that season.

An indication of the heights he could rise to was evident in the FA Cup clash with Sheffield United. This was the game in which Vinnie Jones picked up a ludicrously early booking, and as United pressed for an equaliser Paul dealt superbly with the aerial threat of Brian Deane as Chelsea sought to continue an adventure towards Cup glory. However, fate has no feelings for performance and lady luck was to deal him an incredibly bad hand.

Playing away at Liverpool on September 5th, 1992, he went for a fifty-fifty challenge with Dean Saunders, and in the resulting collision suffered an injury that was to curtail his career. Immediately after the match, Paul had an emergency operation on the lateral complex to give a degree of stability to the leg. Later, he was to have surgery to the right anterior cruciate ligament. Unfortunately, despite showing incredible courage, he was never able to come back from such serious injuries and his career was over.

Before Paul retired, I was fortunate to bump into him in the early hours of a Sunday morning. Having played for Luton early in his career, he often returned to the town for social gatherings. This particular occasion I spotted him as he was about to enter a Chinese restaurant in Bute Street. When asked about his injury, he refused to give up hope and we had an amiable chat about his aims and ambitions. Despite having played only fifty-four games, scoring three times, Paul viewed Chelsea as his club. We supporters used to give him a fantastic reception when he was introduced to us from the Stamford Bridge pitch and he acknowledged this fact.

His retirement was officially announced before the FA Cup final against Manchester United and Paul, at the time Chelsea's second most expensive signing, was forced to concentrate on media work. I still wonder to this day whether we would have fared better against Manchester United in that match, if Paul had been facing Mark Hughes. Could history have maybe turned out different?

Graeme Le Saux

When Graeme Le Saux joined Chelsea in December 1987, very few people could have imagined just what lay ahead for the youngster from Jersey. Signed from St Pauls on a free transfer, the Chelsea career of Graeme Le Saux was to span two unique periods. The first of these lasted until 1993 when he was sold to Blackburn for a paltry £625,000, with Chelsea also receiving Steve Livingstone in part exchange.

During this first period, the young Le Saux impressed everyone with his attacking play down the left flank. Soxy, as he became known, was able to play in either a left-back role or as a left-sided midfield player. Although his skills were widely appreciated by the Stamford Bridge faithful, he also had a few tempestuous moments. In one game, a somewhat disenchanted Le Saux threw his shirt in the general direction of the Chelsea bench. Several hacks thought he may have played his last match for Chelsea after such an action, but others saw it as a display of passion, a trait that had been sadly lacking in several Chelsea teams over the previous few seasons.

If I were to pick one game from Soxy's first spell at Chelsea that lingers long in the memory it would have to be the League Cup fixture against Spurs at Stamford Bridge. Graeme was in superb form that night, tormenting the Spurs defence with some surging runs down the left flank. To this day I still can't believe that at least one of them didn't result in a goal in what was to become one of the most one-sided 0-0 draws ever. So good was his performance that night that I rushed back to leafy Bedfordshire intent on watching it on television. Sadly, I was denied by the little matter of the first Gulf War breaking out.

Soxy's sale to Blackburn wasn't popular with the faithful; once again it appeared that we had sold our youthful soul cheaply. Steve Livingstone being included as part of the deal did not improve matters, as Steve was a journeyman striker who was never going to placate the fans.

While at Blackburn, Graeme's game improved and he was part of the Premiership winning team that Kenny Dalglish assembled. He had also become England's best left back, a feat recognised by Ruud Gullit who was now pulling the managerial strings at Chelsea. In August 1997, Chelsea paid out £5 million to lure Graeme back to Chelsea. It is often suggested that it's not wise to return to a club you have previously left. Glorious memories can become tainted if things don't quite work out.

Thankfully, for Soxy it was to be different. Chelsea were emerging as a new force in English football and he reaped the rewards. During his second spell, Graeme picked up Coca Cola Cup and European Super Cup winners medals, as well a medal for being part of the European Cup Winners Cup squad. Unfortunately, injury prevented him from making an appearance in the final against Stuttgart, with a young Danny Granville taking his place.

During his second spell, Soxy created a wonderful left flank partnership with Celestine Babayaro. The pairing gelled naturally and it remains a mystery to this day why, in the twilight of his Chelsea career, Soxy was never given further opportunities to enhance his international career, when England were crying out for a naturally left-footed player.

Even though he was older and supposedly wiser, the famous temper, albeit disguised as passion, surfaced once or twice in his second spell at Chelsea. Two occasions that spring to mind are his return to Blackburn, where a touch-line tussle saw Soxy dismissed by the referee, while the second involved a spat with Robbie Fowler.

During his career, much was made of the fact that Graeme was different to your conventional footballer. Instead of studying the tabloids, he could often be found with his head buried deep in The Guardian. Rumours, which were untrue, circulated regarding his sexuality which culminated in Robbie Fowler making obscene gestures in his general direction while Graeme prepared to take a free kick against Liverpool. As the action progressed, Fowler was seen to crash to the ground, the victim of an alleged assault. The officials saw nothing and Soxy got away with something many of us would like to repeat on the Toxteth waif.

Sadly, injuries started to limit Graeme's appearances in the Chelsea side, and when Roman Abramovich invested his millions in the club, Soxy had already agreed to join Southampton, where he subsequently played out the remainder of his career. In his two spells at Chelsea the fresh-faced youngster from the Channel Islands made 312 appearances and scored sixteen goals, in a Chelsea career that endeared him to those who have Chelsea indelibly stamped through their bodies.

Pat Nevin

When John Neal signed a player from the Scottish club Clyde in 1983, for a mere £95,000, his slight build betrayed the stereotypical Glasgow image held by many. Stood before the assembled press that day was a young man who through pure football skill was to become a firm favourite of the Stamford Bridge supporters during the five seasons he played for the club. His name was Pat Nevin, and the mere mention of him is still enough to conjure up wonderful memories for those who were lucky enough to see him in action for Chelsea.

Pat wasn't your typical footballer. After being chased by Chelsea for a year or so, he only relented and signed on the understanding that it would perhaps be a two-year sabbatical from college. Upon first seeing him, Ken Bates sought reassurance from Neal that the slightly-built right winger in front of him would actually make the grade. Ken needn't have worried. Pat was to go on and play 242 games for Chelsea and score forty-five goals.

During his first season it soon became apparent that Wee Pat had something special. His balance and technique, allied with hours of practice on the training ground, ensured that he soon became popular with the fans. After forcing his way into the team for the Milk Cup fixture against Gillingham, he didn't miss another game all season, and it soon became commonplace for John Neal to simply suggest that his team give Pat the ball in order for Chelsea to win.

One example of how Pat Nevin could hold a packed Stamford Bridge in the palm of his hand came against Newcastle. Chelsea were leading comfortably when he decided to have a bit of fun. The wee man went on a mesmerising run, leaving player after player in his wake. Kevin Keegan, playing for Newcastle that day, was, like the rest of us, suitably impressed. That first season also saw him contribute fourteen goals as Chelsea roared to promotion.

If Second Division defences had struggled to control him, First Division defences fared no better. His intricate, exciting wing play provided the perfect ammunition for the strike partnership of Kerry Dixon and David Speedie to flourish. Unfortunately, his style of play also meant that he often suffered from some wild challenges, but he remained unflustered, simply dusted himself down and got on with things.

When John Neal was sidelined by ill-health, Wee Pat became somewhat frustrated playing for those that followed. John Hollins and then Bobby Campbell both failed to get the best out of him and, with Chelsea's fortunes waning and ending in relegation, he left for a fresh challenge at Everton.

During his time at Chelsea, though, Pat had this ability to do no wrong. In a fixture against Manchester City, Chelsea were once again winning easily when he decided to take a penalty. In all honesty, it was the worst penalty you are ever likely to see. He hit the ball so tamely the keeper could have dived, stood up and still had time to pick the ball up before it reached him. Normally such a kick would have resulted in a barrage of barracking from the terraces, but like Pat the crowd saw the funny side. As laughter rolled on to the pitch Pat tried, unsuccessfully, to remain composed.

Playing for Everton, he returned to Stamford Bridge and ended up scoring for his new team. Normally such an event would be celebrated in manic fashion by the former player, while the crowd watches in hushed silence, but not on this occasion. Pat acknowledged he had scored with the minimum of fuss, while the home crowd rose, as one, to applaud him.

On another occasion, Chelsea were playing at Goodison Park. Several of us made the long midweek journey to cheer on our team. Pat, meanwhile, had moved on to Tranmere Rovers after his Everton career had come to an end. Sitting high up in the away stand, I was aware of a slight figure heading in my general direction. With his head bowed he shuffled along the row of seats and sat immediately next to me. The instant he raised his head, thousands of Chelsea supporters spontaneously burst into a chorus of 'one Pat Nevin, there's only one Pat Nevin, one Pat Nevin'. The wee man had been rumbled, but he had shown two of his former paymasters exactly where his loyalties lay.

Ray Wilkins

To say that Ray 'Butch' Wilkins was a massive talent is stating the blatantly obvious. The fact that such a wonderful talent only played 198 games, scoring thirty-four goals, for Chelsea, is bordering on the criminal. Wilkins was signed by Chelsea as an apprentice professional, at the age of fifteen. He joined a youth system that was bursting with talent and arguably went on to become the pick of that particular bunch.

Wilkins was a born leader, a player who wasn't afraid to point the finger and prompt the others in his team in a way that belied his youthful years. A simple nod or a gesture of the hand in a certain direction was inevitably followed by a precision, often defence splitting, pass. Whether the distance was ten or thirty yards, it rarely missed its target as Chelsea's young midfield general pulled the strings at the heart of the side. Indeed, Wilkins was to become the fulcrum of Eddie McCreadie's much heralded Chelsea team.

Such was his ability and his enthusiasm, Ray found himself appointed captain at the tender age of eighteen, having made his senior debut in the 3-0 victory against Norwich in October 1973. His prominence in the Chelsea midfield meant that Ray made his England debut in 1976 against Italy, and was a regular by the age of twenty. This feat is even more remarkable when you consider that Chelsea were languishing in the Second Division at this period in time.

With Chelsea going through a transitional period both on and off the pitch, it didn't really come as a surprise that other teams were watching Ray. His departure to Manchester United after Chelsea were relegated during the

1978-79 season, for a fee of £825,000, meant that yet another great talent had been sacrificed.

Although Ray enjoyed a successful career at Manchester United, it is heart-warming to hear him still talk about his time at Chelsea with fondness. Indeed, during our Premiership-winning campaign you could see the pride he took from seeing his Chelsea win the title. I guess that being made captain of the club at eighteen left an indelible mark on one of the gentlemen of the modern game.

My most memorable recollection of Ray Wilkins doesn't come from his playing days, but after he had left Chelsea and was working in tandem with Vialli at Watford. Chelsea supporters had never had a chance to say goodbye to Vialli and so some of us decided to arrange a sort of pilgrimage to Vicarage Road. Obviously this beano didn't coincide with a Chelsea fixture.

Having been assured that Watford FC had no objections to a bunch of Chelsea supporters attending their fixture against Bradford City, we agreed to meet opposite the Red Lion public house. With a couple of hours to kick-off we were far from inconspicuous, but nevertheless made to feel very welcome. As we awaited the arrival of another of our group, a coach started to slowly meander through the traffic. On closer inspection, it was deter-mined that it contained the Watford team, who had obviously been to a local hotel in preparation for the encounter with Bradford.

As the coach neared our party we could make out the distinct features of Ray Wilkins sat nonchalantly on the front seat. With the Watford supporters making something of a commotion, Ray looked to his left and his eyes, betraying his normally calm exterior, nearly popped out of their sockets. Expecting to see a collection of Hornets supporters bedecked in yellow and red, he instead was confronted with a motley collection of Chelsea shirts. To say time appeared to stand still for Ray is something of an understatement. After what seemed like an eternity, he raised an arm and acknowledged us before turning to others on the coach to enquire why we were stood on a street corner in the middle of Hertfordshire. It was a really priceless moment and would have made excellent television.

Ruud Gullit

It is an indication of just how far Chelsea have progressed over recent years, and a startling realisation of just how strong the Dream Team is, that Ruud Gullit can only make our second eleven. However, his signing from Sampdoria, in the summer of 1995, heralded a new era in Chelsea's history. Prompted by Glenn Hoddle, Chelsea decided to try and make that quantum leap that would take them to another level – a level where we wouldn't always be viewed as a team that were content to be remembered for having one glamorous era in the 1970s. Ruud was to be the catalyst for that awesome bound.

Legend has it that Ruud only contemplated joining the club due to the fact that Chelsea wore white socks. The dreadlocked Dutchman supposedly believed that those who wore white socks had a penchant for winning trophies. At the time of his arrival, Stamford Bridge wasn't the stadium it is now. The site was littered with construction vehicles as Ken Bates, backed by his Eurobond, tried to fulfil his dream of creating his own little village. It was hard to see how two such strong characters could survive side by side without each one trying to steal the limelight – without each individual jockeying for attention.

Ruud started his Chelsea career marshalling a defence that had always looked shaky under pressure. His role as the sweeper saw the elegant Dutchman spray an array of passes around the pitch. Unfortunately, those somewhat ageing legs were not too keen on sprinting back when possession was inevitably lost. After suffering an injury, Ruud took up a more forward position in midfield. It suited his game and his natural silky skills enabled the man with an incredible aura about him to become the heart of the team. At thirty-three years of age many pundits had suggested that Ruud's career was all but over, that his knees, blighted by several operations, would not hold out, yet to us Chelsea supporters he was like a footballing vision, holding us spellbound with his sublime play.

Unfortunately, despite Chelsea only finishing eleventh that season, the club were unable to hold on to Glenn Hoddle, as the call came from the FA and Hoddle was off to manage the national side. Rumours suggested that George Graham was set to replace him, but supporter power was to prove otherwise. Hoddle's farewell match saw vociferous cries for Ruud to be given the management reins and Ken Bates, rather surprisingly, gave in to fan power. Almost immediately the dynamic Dutchman set about creating his own unique Chelsea side, and it was a side that was to finally prove that the quantum leap to another level had been achieved.

Using his football prowess Ruud recruited Leboeuf, Di Matteo and Vialli, and Chelsea were making headline news. The influx of world class talent meant that Ruud's appearances in the first team were now somewhat restricted. However, when he filled in at centre-back after Leboeuf was injured over the Christmas period he still looked the part. Chelsea were improving in the Premiership, but it was in the FA Cup that glory, under Gullit, was to be achieved. With Wembley beckoning, many Chelsea supporters hoped that Ruud would play an influential part in guiding us towards the twin towers from on the pitch, as well as off it. Sadly, a broken ankle sustained at Derby ruled him out for the season.

Nevertheless, it was a very proud, suited Dutchman who led Chelsea out on that sunny day on May 17th, 1997, as Middlesbrough were beaten 2-0. Ruud had elevated Chelsea back into the limelight and a defunct trophy cabinet was now being prepared for, hopefully, a glut of silverware. But things were to take a sudden and very dramatic turn the following season. With the squad bolstered by several more signings, Chelsea were going well on three fronts. In the Premiership we were lying second, in the European Cup Winners Cup we were handily placed, and in the Coca Cola Cup we had reached the semi-finals, when Chelsea made back-page news with a story that seemed to reveal the club hitting the self-destruct button. Ruud had been sacked.

To this day the reasons why remain murky, clouded by angst, rumour and pure speculation. Many suggested that Ruud had simply asked for wages to which the club were unable to commit, implying there had been a falling out over net or gross in the monetary stakes. Had the ego clash mentioned earlier finally come home to roost? Who knows? However, the relatively short time that he spent at Stamford Bridge is indelibly stamped on our memories. Ruud's Chelsea career may only have spanned fifty games, with seven goals scored, but his influence is partly responsible for the club having the world-class-thinking ethic it displays today.

Ruud Gullit left Chelsea in acrimonious circumstances, but since the new regime has taken over the wounds seem to have healed. The enigmatic Dutchman is often a guest on Chelsea TV and attended the first of the club's centenary celebrations at the Butcher's Hook, where he chatted very amiably with those now pulling the strings at Stamford Bridge. More importantly he still had that aura of class about him, and the ability to make a dramatic entrance while holding his audience captivated, just as you would expect from a man who is a former World Player Of The Year, but who has also sampled the magic of pulling on our beloved blue shirt.

Peter Houseman

Often it takes time for a player to be accepted by the supporters. Sometimes it can be an almost titanic struggle to win over those who berate a footballer without realising what they bring to the side. Peter Houseman was one such player. For one reason or another, he fell foul of The Shed support, often being made a scapegoat when things were not going well – until one monumental night during a famous season.

Peter made his Chelsea debut before his eighteenth birthday, against Sheffield United in December 1963. He was a local lad from Battersea, who had the persona of being gentle and slightly laid back. Despite making his debut at such a tender age, Peter wasn't to become a regular in the side for another five years, with Tommy Docherty regularly ignoring his considerable talents.

He possessed an exquisite left foot and during the 1969-70 season he forced his way into the team in a midfield role. However, the introduction of a young Alan Hudson saw Peter being moved to the left wing, and this change was to rejuvenate his Chelsea career. He became an ever present that season and was instrumental in making it one of the most vividly remembered in Chelsea's history.

Hugging the touchline, Peter displayed incredible crossing ability and work rate, and began to wow those who had previously berated him from the terraces with some excellent displays. A turning point in his relationship with the supporters came during the epic FA Cup run when he scored a wonderful goal against Burnley. Chelsea had drawn the original tie 2-2 at Stamford Bridge, but won the replay 3-1 up at Turf Moor with Houseman netting a brace.

Perhaps buoyed by the change in response to his play, Peter went from strength to strength, and when Wembley beckoned he put in the performances to match the occasion. At White Hart Lane he was instrumental in the 5-1 thrashing of Watford and also went on to play major parts in both the final at Wembley and the incredibly emotional night at Old Trafford when the FA Cup was won and Leeds United were finally defeated.

Despite being seen as laid back, Peter lived and breathed football, and while it was a club rule that suits were to be worn on away trips, he took great pride in wearing his for home matches as well. Also, while most players had hobbies away from football, Peter was often reported as implying that as well as his profession, football was also his hobby. Chelsea were renowned for being a swinging club in the Sixties and early Seventies, but Peter shunned that lifestyle, and despite his on-off relationship with the supporters often chose to take the tube to and from home matches.

The following two seasons saw Peter enhance his medal collection with a European Cup Winners Cup winners medal as Chelsea defeated Real Madrid, once again in a replay, as well as a League Cup runners-up medal in the defeat to Stoke City. In the 1974-75 season Dave Sexton chose to play him as a full back, though it wasn't a major success. He probably lacked the physical aggression needed for that role and in the summer he was transferred to Oxford United.

In 342 appearances for Chelsea, Peter Houseman scored thirty-nine times, and today he remains a firm favourite with many of the fans fortunate enough to see him play. Tragically, two years after joining Oxford, Peter and his wife were killed in a road crash on the A40 as they were coming home from a dinner dance. Those who knew Peter and admired his play were left to mourn the passing of a Chelsea legend.

Kerry Dixon

Kerry Dixon first made his mark in non-league football with Dunstable Town, his prolific goal scoring attracting several league clubs, Reading eventually taking the gamble on the blond striker from Luton. The Berkshire side were not to be disappointed. Kerry made the step up into the professional ranks with consummate ease, his prolific scoring record was maintained and he was soon attracting the attention of the talent scouts from the higher divisions. Thankfully, it was to be Chelsea that were to offer a fee substantial enough, £175,000, to tempt Reading into letting their prize asset leave in August 1983. John Neal was constructing a new Chelsea side and he saw the prolific striker as somebody who could lead the line and get the goals necessary to launch Chelsea on a promotion drive.

During that first season with Chelsea, Dixon formed a formidable partnership with David Speedie. The ex-Darlington striker was the perfect foil for the rampaging Dixon and although, off the pitch, he originally had a tempestuous relationship with the fiery Speedie, on the pitch it was a different story. The partnership yielded goals galore. Dixon netted twice on his debut and in a memorable fixture at Grimsby netted the goal that won Chelsea the Second Division championship.

After scoring with impressive ease in Chelsea's 1983-84 promotion season, the critics were split with regard to Kerry continuing in such a rich vein of form in the First Division. It didn't take long for the number nine to make his mark though. In front of a Clock End packed with Chelsea supporters, Dixon rifled home an equaliser to give Chelsea a well-deserved point in their first game back in the top flight. Indeed, his scoring record was maintained and Kerry forced his way into the England squad for the USA tour the following summer. On that tour he netted a brace against West Germany and the future looked very bright.

After again scoring with some regularity the following season, Kerry suffered a stomach injury playing against Liverpool at Stamford Bridge in a fourth round FA Cup tie. It was an injury that many felt took an edge off his game, almost as if it deprived him of that yard of extra pace that separated him from the other strikers around at the time. Even so, he was not to be denied a place in the Mexico World Cup squad that summer and he sealed his place in the final twenty-two with a brace of goals at Old Trafford. Both were scored in the second half as Dixon showed his natural prowess to despatch two exquisite efforts into the Old Trafford net. One came when David Speedie picked him out with a precision pass, and the other after Kerry raced on to a long through ball.

Unfortunately, Kerry wasn't quite able to dislodge Bobby Robson's preferred partnership of Gary Lineker and Peter Beardsley, and didn't feature in the World Cup itself. More worryingly, when Chelsea once again fell into the Second Division some people thought Dixon would be sold on as Chelsea sought to rebuild. This didn't happen, and twenty-five goals in the 1988-89 season ensured we romped away with the Second Division title for the second time in Kerry's Chelsea career.

With Bobby Tambling's all-time Chelsea scoring record in sight, there were many who felt sure Kerry would overtake it, but as the magical figure of 202 loomed on the horizon, the goals began to dry up. As a team Chelsea were struggling and new options player-wise were being implemented. However, it still came as a major shock when Dixon was transferred to Southampton in July 1992 for £575,000. Although he was not scoring as regularly as he had done in the past he had, under the leadership of Bobby Campbell, developed his game in other areas. Whereas Kerry had once been the recipient of some wonderful crosses from Pat Nevin, he had now become probably the best deliverer of a cross at Stamford Bridge, a classic case of poacher turned gamekeeper.

He wasn't the greatest of penalty takers, and a spot kick at Loftus Road will go down as one of the worst in Chelsea's history. To say it cleared the crossbar with ease is an understatement. Chelsea's leading fanzine at the time, The Chelsea Independent, printed a map of Shepherds Bush in its next issue, asking its readers to pinpoint exactly where the ball had landed. Even the most gifted have off days.

Upon his departure Dixon had made over 400 appearances for the club and netted 193 goals. It was definitely a case of so-near-but-so-far with regards that magical goal-scoring record set by Bobby Tambling, but Kerry is guaranteed a place in the affections of all those Chelsea supporters who saw him shine.

Jimmy Greaves

A strike rate of a goal every two games is usually considered exceptional, but Jimmy Greaves managed 132 goals in just 169 appearances. More amazingly, he seemed able to score at will. Jimmy wasn't a striker who notched the odd goal every other game, he regularly took teams apart.

Who else scored five times in a match, on three separate occasions? Who else could visit Deepdale, when Preston were top of the pile, score three to put Chelsea 3-0 up, watch on as Preston pulled it back to 3-3, before scoring a fourth. When Preston had the impudence to make it 4-4, Jimmy simply stepped up to score a fifth and win the game 5-4.

The writing was on the wall when Jimmy Greaves first arrived at Chelsea. In the season before he made his first-team debut he notched up an amazing 114 goals in junior football. It was therefore little surprise when he scored on his debut away to Spurs at the start of the 1957-58 season. Chelsea were trailing with only five minutes to go when a young Greaves notched up his first goal. He wasn't about to lose his place and stamped his mark on the game by scoring an incredible four times against Portsmouth on Christmas Day.

When, in November 1960, Greaves notched a hat-trick against Manchester City, he became the first player to score a hundred league goals before his twenty-first birthday. According to the statistics, it didn't seem to matter how many the opposition scored, as Greaves would ensure Chelsea could still win. Indeed, his club record of forty-one goals in the 1960-61 season is a record that is unlikely to be beaten.

Unfortunately, his prowess was attracting attention from other clubs. At the time English football was operating under the maximum-wage restraint, whereas Europe wasn't. Therefore, a young Greaves jumped at the opportunity to bolster his wages by joining AC Milan. Thankfully, for Chelsea supporters, he still had one magical display up his sleeve. His last game for Chelsea, against Nottingham Forest, saw Greaves turn in a masterful performance, scoring all four goals in a 4-3 win. He was carried off the pitch by jubilant Chelsea supporters. His spell in Italy wasn't a happy one and to this day Jimmy feels aggrieved that nobody from Chelsea made serious attempts to re-sign him. Instead, he drifted off to Spurs.

Of all these eleven players, Jimmy Greaves is the only one I never saw play. I had heard about the great man, and seen him on video clips, witnessed the electric pace and deadly finishing secondhand, but I had never sat down and thought about it, never really accepted just how great this man was. Sure he had his quirks and his excesses, but his scoring record really is second to none and I wish I had seen him. As a renowned bad trainer, with a tendency to enjoy life off the pitch, I wonder how he would have done in the modern game, and how the current Chelsea manager would have coped with this irrepressible talent?

The Chelsea fans enjoyed this trip to Millwall so much they wrote a song about it

Blue Is The Colour

Chelsea used to boast some of the most consistently noisy supporters in England and had more than their fair share of terrace composers. The Shed was famous across the country and remains legendary today, widely respected for the loyalty and fanaticism of those who gathered in the home end. During the darkest days of goal famines and empty East Stand seats, The Shed kept the club alive, attending home games in large numbers and taking thousands away. These Chelsea fans never wavered in their vocal support. The arrival of all-seater grounds and the high price of attending a match has driven many such supporters away from Stamford Bridge, and the atmosphere has suffered as a result. Nick Brown presents a brief history of Chelsea songs

It is unlikely that the Chelsea support started chanting 'you're gonna get your fucking heads kicked in' as Stockport County scored the winning goal in our opening fixture of the 1905-06 season. The Football League had been running for nearly twenty years when Chelsea were formed, as an after-thought once Fulham had refused founding chairman Gus Mears' invitation to play at his newly-built stadium at Stamford Bridge. Though the club did attract good attendances in its early years, and for some time after, early Chelsea crowds tended to be spectators rather than supporters. While other clubs did have supporters who backed their team vocally during this period, crowds at Chelsea tended to watch the spectacle of football and often applauded the opposition for good play.

The immediate inhabitants of Chelsea, which even then was a well-to-do area, were more likely to attend West End theatres than football matches. The working class support in the area already had Fulham, who were a Southern League club at the time, established down the road. Chelsea were refused permission to join the Southern League, so opted to join the thirty-six club Football League, which wanted to expand to two twenty-club divisions. The Football League was dominated by Northern and Midland clubs, the only team south of Birmingham in the league being Woolwich Arsenal. Chelsea thus got elected straight into the league.

With Chelsea being the closest club to the centre of London, it attracted much floating support from visitors to the capital and early migrants from other parts of the country and overseas. The fact that there was no local opposition in the League also saw supporters tending to go to Chelsea to watch players from Northern clubs, who would not be seen at Fulham, rather than support the team.

By the time Chelsea reached the Cup final in 1915, known as the Khaki Cup final as the crowd was in army uniform, ready to go to war in France, it is likely that early terrace songs were heard, though these were probably patriotic ones about fighting for England rather than Chelsea.

During the inter-war years, there are no records of vocal support at Chelsea. The crowd still applauded both their own and opposition players, waved a rattle, and heckled the ref for bad decisions, or the players for rough play. In fact, Chelsea and their 'supporters' were the butt of music hall jokes, due to their Pensioner club badge and image, and lack of vocal support. Though widespread chanting at other clubs still wasn't the norm, many did vocally support their clubs.

By the mid-Thirties, Chelsea had become the local club for the people of Battersea and Wandsworth, and were pulling in support from large swathes of South and West London. However, the song Come On You Pensioners was not forthcoming. Other clubs had formal identities and were now over fifty years old. They had been set up by factory workers and the like, had built up their support and rivalries, and sang songs based on work and local identity.

After the Second World War support at Chelsea changed. In 1948 a group of Chelsea fans set up the Chelsea (Away) Supporters Club, enabling fans to club together and support the team at away matches. Supporters started giving vocal backing, though it was limited to a hardcore few and widespread chanting had not yet begun. When Ted Drake became manager in 1952, he was concerned with Chelsea's image and support. He made a number of changes, which the directors took on board. This helped set up a new identity which Chelsea fans wanted to belong to and encouraged vociferous fanatical support, though it did not happen overnight.

Chelsea took the bold step of ridding itself of the Pensioner image and replaced the badge with a Standing Lion Rampant, while the club's nickname changed to The Blues, something which supporters identified with, as could be seen with the early Battersea Blues and Stockwell Blues. The club also totally redeveloped its youth side. For nearly fifty years before, Chelsea had tended to be a buying club, bringing in players to entertain the fans. With the new youth set-up home-grown players were developed, who supporters could relate to, and this also ensured Chelsea became part of the local community, as youngsters could play for the various Chelsea youth sides and dream of making it to the first team.

One of the major changes at the supporters' level was Ted Drake's impassioned plea. He basically asked them to stop welcoming and applauding opposition teams. He asked them to stop being spectators and become supporters. By the time Chelsea won the league in 1955, chants of CHELSEA could be heard on the terraces. The early chanting supporters tended to watch the game on the halfway line on the large West Terrace, known then as the Popular Terrace. The Shed, or Fulham Road End, as it was called then, was yet to become vocal. The roof at The Shed end was already there, and had been built for the bookmakers who attended the dog racing held at the ground since 1933.

The 1950s also saw great changes in society, after the end of rationing in 1952, as the country enjoyed an economic boom. Fashions and trends changed dramatically, and youth culture began with the rise of teddy boys, mods, rockers and skinheads who ran riot on the streets of England, and also attended football, and the music and songs from the day were adopted into chants on the Chelsea terraces. Exactly when it all began is questionable, but certainly by 1960 the Chelsea fans were singing, though it would be the mid-Sixties when it took off big time. As away support grew, so did the selection of songs, while the televised broadcasting of football matches encouraged supporters to sing and invent new songs, as these rituals could be seen throughout the country.

The Fulham Road End became vocal in the 1960s and adopted their own anthem from a Bud Flanagan song called Strolling.

> Strolling, just strolling,
> In the cool of the evening air,
> I don't envy the rich in their automobiles,
> For a motor-car is phoney, I'd rather have Shank's pony,
> When I'm strolling, just strolling,
> By the light of the moon above,
> Every night I go strolling,
> I know my luck is rolling,
> When I'm strolling with the one I love,
> CHELSEA.

In 1965, the Popular Terrace was closed down to make way for the new West Stand, built amazingly over one summer. With the Popular Terrace gone, the Fulham Road End became the home for Chelsea's more vociferous supporters. Mr C Webb of Ockendon, wrote a letter to the club, which was published in the match-day programme on September 7th, 1966.

He said: 'From now on we wish for the Fulham Road End to be called The Shed. That is the section where the fanatics stand – and, while we are on the fanatics, why don't more people come in The Shed and join in the singing and chanting, instead of just at big matches like last season's Fairs Cup. If we could have had that support all through the League and Cup, we would have won them both. This year we must have this attitude at every game, so please help us make The Shed as fanatical as The Kop.

The reference to The Kop in Cliffy Webb's letter was because many supporters admired the noise it made. Liverpool fans had adopted the music of

The Beatles and other Mersey bands as their own when they came up to the First Division in 1962, and they had the largest and most fanatical support. By the mid-Sixties other supporters wanted to emulate this, including those at Chelsea.

By 1967 a new sport had begun on the terraces – the taking of the opposition's home end. Visiting supporters would arrive in numbers and try to take over the terrace where the home fans gathered. The songs took on a new menacing edge.

> *To the tune of: My Old Man Said Follow The Band*
> My old man said be a Chelsea fan,
> And don't dilly-dally on the way,
> We'll take the Tottenham in half a minute,
> We'll take the Arsenal and all that's in it,
> With hatchets and hammers,
> Carving knives and spanners,
> We'll show those Tottenham bastards how to fight!
> Cos you won't take the Shed with the North Stand in it,
> Cos Chelsea rule the South.

> *To: Messing About On The River*
> We went up to Wolves,
> We took their North Bank,
> We came down to Arsenal,
> They're not worth a wank,
> So take my advice,
> There's nothing so nice,
> As kicking the fuck out of Tottenham.

> *To: I Get Around, by the Beach Boys*
> Round, round, get around, we get around (repeat),
> My buddies and me are getting real well known,
> The North Banks know us and they leave us alone,
> We've taken Molineux, The Kippax and Filbert Street,
> We take the ends of every mob we meet,
> We get around.

There was also the mournful...

> On a Wolverhampton Terrace,
> In the pouring rain,
> A young Chelsea supporter,
> Got a bullet in his brain,

As he lay there dying, blood pouring from his head,
He looked up to the clear Blue sky,
This is what he said,
You're gonna get your fucking heads kicked in!

Rivalry with Tottenham seems to go back to the 1960s and is reflected in many songs. In January 1964 over 70,000 were at Stamford Bridge for an evening Cup-tie, which saw one-time Chelsea hero Jimmy Greaves return to the club in the colours of Tottenham. By 1967, when the two clubs met in the FA Cup final, the rivalry was truly born. In the intermediate years, a number of Chelsea players had moved on to Tottenham. Tottenham's location in North London, in a predominantly Jewish area, was also highlighted in many songs of the day. Some songs were just a basic offer to the Tottenham fans, while others took on the Jewish bigotry.

To: Let's Dance, by Chris Montez
Hey Tottenham, do you wanna fight?
Fight the lads in blue and white,
Oh let's fight...
(Clap, clap, clap, clap, clap),
Oh let's fight.

To: Run Rabbit Run
Run Tottenham, run Tottenham, run, run, run (repeat),
We are the Shed Boys,
And we've all got a gun,
So run Tottenham, run Tottenham, run, run, run.

To: Let Him Go, Let Him Yarry
If you are feeling tired and weary,
And you've got a Jew boy's nose,
You'll get your fucking head kicked in,
If you walk down the Fulham Road,
You walk into the Rising Sun,
You'll hear a mighty noise,
Fuck off you Tottenham bastards,
We are the Chelsea boys.
Now Big Jim is a fairy,
But he's got a heart of gold,
He hasn't had a foreskin,
Since he was one-day old,
He walks into the Park Lane End,
And all the Jew Boys wail,

171

Big Jim is our leader,
The King of Israel.

To: My Bonny Lies Over The Ocean
If I had the wings of a sparrow,
If I had the arse of a crow,
I'd fly over Tottenham tomorrow,
And shit on the bastards below.

To: Marching Through Georgia
Hello, hello, we are the Chelsea boys,
Hello, hello, we are the Chelsea boys,
And if you are a Tottenham fan, surrender or you'll die,
Cos we all follow the Chelsea.

Not all songs around this time were devoted to violence and the taking of ends. The Chelsea fanatics also sang songs on the virtues and love of supporting Chelsea, and the following were heard on the terraces in the late Sixties.

To: Blaydon Races
Whooo, me lads,
And all you lovely ladies,
Walking down the Fulham Road,
To see the Chelsea aces,
Hooray for Doc and all the Chelsea team,
Best team the Fulham Road has ev-ev-ever seen.

To: Peek A Boo
I would grow much weaker,
Weather would be bleaker,
If I spent a week away from Chel-el-sea,
Stamford Bridge, you're the only ground for me,
That's where I go, it's my home, to see Chelsea.

To: Milord
Come on and cheer again,
Cos Chelsea's here again,
We are the finest football team,
You've ever seen,
We are the best in town,
We are the best around,
We are the greatest football team you've ever seen.

To: Oh Come All Ye Faithful
Oh come all ye faithful,
Joyful and triumphant,
Oh come ye, oh come ye,
To Stamford Bridge,
Come and behold them,
Born the kings of football,
Oh come let us adore them (repeat three times)
Chel-el-sea!

To: Grocer Jack
Dave Sexton, Dave Sexton,
Is it true what people say,
We're gonna win the Football League.
(Sometimes sung as FA Cup)

To: Lambeth Walk
Any evening, any day,
Any time you're Chelsea way,
You'll see them all,
Playing the best football – oi,
Chelsea are the boys in blue,
Chelsea are the best, it's true,
You'll see them all,
Playing the best football – oi.

To: When Johnny Comes Marching Home
Chelsea's gonna win the league this year,
Cos there's not a single team in the land that we fear,
Everton or Liverpool,
Tottenham, Leeds or Arsenal,
Cos Chelsea are by far the best team in the land,
La-la-la-la-la-la.
(Repeat last two lines)

Chant... Chelsea rule, Chelsea rule,
We sing louder than the Kop at Liverpool.

To: Bless 'Em All
So come on you Chelsea and score,
When you get one you'll get more,
We'll sing you (in) assembly,
When we get to Wembley,
So come on you Chelsea and score, score, score.

173

Another favourite was...

> You can talk about the Arsenal or the Tottenham Hotspur too,
> Or even Man United,
> Or the Wolves from Molineux,
> Or any Continental team you care to name for sure,
> But give to me the Chelsea, the team we all adore.

With The Shed formally named in 1966, the supporters in this area also began singing songs about this area of the ground, highlighting their support and love for the club and also their new found notoriety. These songs included the following.

> *To: I Was Born Under A Wandrin' Star*
> I was born under the Chelsea Shed,
> Boots are made for kicking,
> Guns are made to shoot,
> Come up in the Chelsea Shed and we'll all stick in the boot.

> *To: Teddy Bear's Picnic*
> If you go down to The Shed today,
> You're sure of a big surprise,
> If you go down The Shed today,
> You'll never believe your eyes,
> For Jeremy, the Sugar Puff bear,
> Has bought some boots and cropped his hair,
> And is going to fight for Chelsea.

> *To: Bless 'Em All*
> Fuck 'em all, fuck 'em all,
> United, West Ham, Liverpool,
> We are the Chelsea,
> And we are the best,
> We are The Shed boys,
> So fuck all the rest.

> *To: All You Need Is Love*
> SHED, SHED, SHED,
> Clap-clap, clap-clap.

> *To: Those Were The Days*
> We are The Shed my friend,
> We took the Stretford End,

We'll sing and dance and do it all again,
We live the life we choose,
We fight and never lose,
For we are The Shed, oh yes we are The Shed.

Two more Shed specials went...

Chelsea are the team that play at the Bridge,
The Shed is a part of the ground,
When The Shed sings it is so loud,
It can be heard for miles and miles around,
Oh Chelsea, oh Chelsea, oh Chelsea,
The greatest team in history.
(Repeat last two lines)

As I was walking down the Fulham Road,
I met some brand new faces,
And they said to me,
Are you going to see those famous Chelsea aces,
So I took them up to the mighty Shed,
To see the Great Eleven,
And they said to me, 'oh this must be that place they call Blue
    Heaven'.

As well as celebrating their home end, the Chelsea support of the late
Sixties began saluting the Chelsea players of the day with their own songs.
The first two songs, sung about Tommy Baldwin (1966-74) and Peter Osgood
(1964-74 and 1978-79), are still sung in the stands today, long after these two
left the club. The Osgood song was applied to Ray Wilkins between 1976-78,
but after Wilkins left the club and joined Manchester United, the song
returned to Osgood and has never been awarded to another player since.

To: MacNamara's Band
His name is Tommy Baldwin,
He's the leader of the team,
What team?
The finest football team that the world has ever seen,
Weeeeeeeeeee're...
The Fulham Road supporters,
And we're louder than The Kop,
If anyone wants to argue,
We'll kill the fucking lot.

To: Noel, Noel
The Shed looked up and saw a great star,
Scoring goals past Pat Jennings from near and afar,
And Chelsea won, as we all knew they would,
And the star of that great team was Peter Osgood,
Osgood, Osgood, Osgood, Osgood,
Born is the King of Stamford Bridge.

To: Lily The Pink
Peter Houseman, played terrible football,
And The Shed all called him names,
So Chopper Harris, gave him a kick in the bollocks,
And now he plays in all the games.

In general, individual songs for players or the simple chanting of the player's name did not really start until the Seventies. However, by then the Chelsea faithful would often sing everyone's name. Some Chelsea players had songs dedicated to them, bestowing the fact that they were better than their opponents, while other songs were just blatant abuse of opposing players and managers and highlighted Chelsea's more notorious support.

To: Knick, Knack Paddywack
Lee bums Bell,
Bell bums Lee,
Lee and Bell bum Summerbee,
With a knick knack paddywack give the dog a bone,
Why don't City fuck off home.

To: Smoke Gets In My Eyes
They asked me how I knew,
Chivers was a Jew,
I of course replied,
The thing between his eyes,
Is twice the normal size.
(The last two lines of this was later changed to 'because he's
    circumcised')

To: Noel, Noel
Gilzean, Gilzean,
Gilzean, Gilzean,
Born is the king (queen) of Golders Green.
(Later applied to Glenn Hoddle)

To: Standing On the Corner
Standing on the Stretford End,
Throwing bricks at Denis Law,
Manchester is one big brothel,
Denis Law is the biggest whore.

Or... Standing on the Spion Kop End,
Throwing bricks at Roger Hunt,
Liverpool is one big brothel,
Roger Hunt's the biggest cunt.

Player comparisons were made in the following two songs...

The Arsenal have Radford,
The Palace have Queen,
West Ham have Geoff Hurst,
And Tottenham Gilzean,
But Chelsea have Osgood and he is the King,
And also Keith Weller,
Who plays on the wing.
Keithy, Keithy Weller, Keithy Weller on the wing (repeat)

Ei-ei-ei Bonetti is better than Yashin,
Osgood is better than Eusebio,
Man United are in for a thrashing.

The Shed also adopted some well-known classics. Many of these, which first appeared in the late Sixties and early Seventies, have stood the test of time and are still delightfully sung in the stands today.

To: The Dambusters March
We all hate Leeds and Leeds and Leeds,
Leeds and Leeds and Leeds and Leeds,
Leeds and Leeds and Leeds,
We all fucking hate Leeds.

To: I'm Forever Blowing Bubbles
I'm forever blowing bubbles,
Pretty bubbles in the air,
They fly so high,
They reach the sky,
And like West Ham they fade and die,
Tottenham always running,

Arsenal running too,
We're the Chelsea boot boys,
And we're running after you.

To: Land Of Hope And Glory
We hate Nottingham Forest,
We hate Arsenal too,
We hate West Ham United,
But Chelsea we love you.

To: Tramp, Tramp, Tramp, The Boys Are Marching
The famous Tottenham Hotspur went to Rome to see the Pope,
The famous Tottenham Hotspur went to Rome to see the Pope,
The famous Tottenham Hotspur went to Rome to see the Pope,
And this is what he said... FUCK OFF!

Who's that team they call the Chelsea?
Who's that team we all adore?
We're the boys in blue and white,
And we'll fight with all our might,
And we're out to show the world the way to score.

Bring on Tottenham or the Arsenal,
Bring on spastics (later Scousers) by the score,
Barcelona, Real Madrid,
Tottenham are a load of yids,
And we're out to show the world the way to score.

To: Oh When The Saints Go Marching In
Oh when the Blues, oh when the Blues,
Go marching in, go marching in,
Oh when the Blues go marching in,
I want to be in that number, oh when the Blues go marching in.
(Later the choruses were sung at a much higher tempo, with
    'marching' replaced by 'steaming')

A firm belief that success was only just round the corner was expressed
with...

We shall not, we shall not be moved,
We shall not, we shall not be moved,
Just like the team who's gonna win the Football League,
(or FA Cup),
We shall not be moved.

Celebratory songs like Knees Up Mother Brown were normally sung straight after Chelsea scored, along with much jumping up and down and pushing. This continued near enough until the end of terraces and was an amazing sight.

There were an infinite variety of chants based on the team name, ranging from CHELSEA, followed by hand clapping, to the continuous rendition of CHELSEA, CHELSEA, CHELSEA. The latter really took off in the Eighties. Liverpool's own anthem of You'll Never Walk Alone was also adopted with fans holding their early knitted Chelsea scarves in the air. In later years, the song was banished and a new derisory version adopted.

In 1970 the Chelsea Shed was skinhead land. Ska and reggae was the music and the team came out to Liquidator by Harry J & The All Stars, a song which remains a big favourite to this day. The Shed would clap along and add CHELSEA to the song, and would also perform the skinhead moonstomp. A new section of the ground, the North Stand, was also coming to the fore in the Seventies, and this was recalled in a number of songs.

To: From The Halls Of Montezuma
In the dark back streets of Liverpool,
Where the Mile End's never been,
Lies a mutilated body of a Scouse git,
Where the North Stand kicked him in,
To hell with Liverpool, to hell with Man City,
We will fight, fight, fight for Chelsea,
Till we win the Football League.

To: Snoopy And The Red Baron
Ten, twenty, thirty, forty, fifty or more,
The Chelsea North Stand were running up the score,
Eighty Arsenal died in that spree,
When Chelsea ran riot at Highbury,
And out from the corner a hero arose,
A funny looking geezer with a big red nose,
His name is Harkins,
They say he's insane,
And the North Bank Highbury was taken again.

While The Shed end used to chant 'come and have a go if you think you're hard enough', it was the older boys in the North Stand who they encouraged to fight opposition supporters, with chants like 'North Stand, North Stand do your job'. The North Stand Chelsea also had their own song, which exemplified their higher ranking in the hooligan stakes among Chelsea supporters at the time.

North Stand here, North Stand there,
North Stand every fucking where,
We're all mad, in the head,
We're the North Stand, not The Shed.

The Seventies saw no let-up on the more aggressive Chelsea songs. If anything, the crowd became more menacing. While the Sixties had seen Chelsea
rise to the top and enjoy their most successful period so far, the Seventies saw
the demise of the club's fortunes after the successful FA Cup and European
Cup Winners Cup wins of 1970 and 1971. The Shed still had a repertoire of
new songs, some of which were useful for the purpose of abusing the referee
or opposition players, as the club slid down the table.

To: Clementine
Where's your lipstick, where's your lipstick,
Where's your lipstick, Charlie George,
In your handbag, in your handbag,
In your handbag, Charlie George.

Chant... Stanley, Stanley, Stanley Bowles,
Stanley Bowles, Stanley Bowles,
Stanley, Stanley, Stanley Bowles,
Stanley Bowles, Stanley Bowles,
Oh, wank, wank, wank, wank, wank, wank, wank,
Wank, wank, wank... wank, wank, wank.

To: God In Heaven
Referee, referee,
Your old lady is a whore,
Your old lady is a whore.

Or... Referee, referee,
You're not fit to wipe my arse,
You're not fit to wipe my arse.

To: Clementine
Where's your glasses, where's your glasses,
Where's your glasses referee?
You ain't got none, cos you're a blind cunt,
You're a blind cunt referee.

Or... Where's your father, where's your father,
Where's your father referee?

You ain't got one, cos you're a bastard,
You're a bastard referee.

By the late Seventies, with the club now firmly in the Second Division, the song of abuse for the referee was a straightforward chant of 'who's the wanker in the black?' Opposition supporters at the Bridge were taunted with the following throughout the Seventies, with some lasting longer.

To: In Our Liverpool Slums
In your Liverpool slums,
In your Liverpool slums,
You look in the dustbin for something to eat,
You find a dead cat and you think it's a treat,
In your Liverpool slums.

To: The Red, Red Robin
When the red red robin,
Comes bob-bob-bobbing along,
Shoot the bastard,
Shoot the bastard,
Shoot-shoot-shoot the bastard.

To: Distant Drums
They're over there,
They're over there,
And do they smell,
Like fucking hell.

To: She'll Be Coming Round The Mountain
There won't be many going home,
Oh there won't be many going home,
There won't be many, won't be many,
Won't be many on the train.

To: It's A Long Way To Tipperary
It's a long way to Fulham Broadway,
It's a long way to go,
It's a long way to Fulham Broadway,
It's a long way to go.

More threatening chants were You're Going Home In A London Ambulance and You'll Never Make The Station. During the game itself, if trouble did occur the Shed End might respond with rhythmic, militaristic hand clapping and...

> A-G
> A-G-R
> A-G-R-O
> AGRO!
> Come and have a go,
> At the Chelsea aggro!

One of the most menacing chants, usually sung after the opposition scored and with much finger pointing and out-stretched arms, was the delightful You're Gonna Get Your Fucking Heads Kicked In, urgent clapping filling in the gap between each repetition. Another friendly chant was We Are E-vil, with the emphasis on the E in evil. When Gary Glitter released Hello, Hello, I'm Back Again in 1974, within weeks it was being used as a battle cry.

> Hello, hello,
> Chelsea aggro,
> Chelsea aggro,
> Hello...

The police were also targets of abuse, with some of the following directed their way. Harry Roberts murdered three policemen in Shepherds Bush in the Sixties, and was convicted and locked away, but his name was heard for many years after in The Shed.

> *To: London Bridge Is Falling Down*
> Harry Roberts is our friend, is our friend, is our friend,
> Harry Roberts is our friend, he kills coppers,
> Let him out to kill some more,
> Harry Roberts.

> *To: Campdown Races*
> Who's that twat in the big blue hat,
> Doo-dah, doo-dah,
> Who's that twat in the big blue hat,
> Doo-dah doo-dah day.

The Shed also used to sing or whistle the Laurel And Hardy theme tune when any police walked in front of the end, and in 1975 when Chelsea were relegated, they still managed a dig at Tottenham.

> *To: Blaydon Races*
> All the yids, you should have seen them running,
> Running out the Park Lane End,

Because The Shed were coming,
Big Jim and Sammy Skys,
You should have seen their faces,
Running from the mighty Shed,
All dressed in boots and braces.

Another two went as follows...

We walk with a wiggle and we smile with a grin,
Whenever there's a bundle we all join in,
We are the boys who make the most noise,
We are the Chelsea, boot boys.

Bertie Mee said to Bill Shankly,
Have you heard about the North Bank Highbury?
Shanks said no, I don't think so,
But I've heard about the Chelsea, aggro.

By the late Seventies the Chelsea faithful had humour in their plight, as they regularly sang We're Gonna Win The League, or Champions, despite the club languishing in the middle of the old Second Division. Other ditties included We All Agree, Super Chelsea Are Magic. With The Shed now fully established, it began segregating itself into different areas – The White Wall, Middle, West Side and Tea Bar. Each had its own song, such as We're The Middle, We're The Middle, We're The Middle Of The Shed. At big games they would group up to sing...

We're The Shed End, we're The Shed End,
We're The Shed End, Stamford Bridge.

During the 1976-77 season, Muhammad Ali fought George Foreman, and Johnny Wakelin wrote a song about it called In Zaire. Within weeks the Chelsea North Stand had put the tune to good use.

Once there was a battle there,
In Mill, in Millwall,
Hundred thousand North Stand there,
(Later changed to 10,000 Chelsea there),
In Mill, in Millwall,
All the Millwall gathered round,
In Mill, in Millwall,
Chelsea battered them down into the grou-ound,
In Millwall, in Millwall.

Chelsea fans also vented their anger at Sports Minister Dennis Howell, who banned them from travelling to away matches after various outbreaks of trouble. The ban proved unworkable. ·

> Chelsea boys are back again,
> If we meet Dennis Howell,
> We'll slash his veins,
> We'll kick him in the balls,
> We'll kick him in the head,
> We'll kick the fucking bastard till he's dead.

There are other songs that came out in the late Seventies and which are still sung cheerfully today.

> *To: Lord Of The Dance*
> Carefree, wherever you maybe,
> We are the famous CFC,
> And we don't give a fuck,
> Whoever you may be,
> Because we are the famous CFC.

The We Hate Nottingham Forest song, meanwhile, mutated into We Will Follow The Chelsea.

> *To: Land Of Hope And Glory*
> We will (all) follow the Chelsea,
> Over land and sea – and Leicester,
> We will (all) follow the Chelsea,
> On to victory,
> Altogether now (repeat song).

The 'and Leicester' was originally added to the We Hate Nottingham Forest version, but was the only line which stayed in the new adaptation. As times were bad, eternal love for Chelsea was also announced.

> *To: You Are My Sunshine*
> You are my Chelsea, my only Chelsea,
> You make me happy, when skies are grey,
> You never noticed,
> How much I love you,
> Until you've taken, my Chelsea away,
> La-la-la-la-la.

The 1976-77 season was a bright time in that Chelsea got promotion back to the First Division and The Shed was back singing as vocally as ever, after a dismal year before. Chants such as Eddie McCreadie's Blue And White Army (repeated over and over again) began, and this was also adopted for Johnny Neal and, to a lesser extent, Johnny Hollins in the Eighties, and would reach a deafening crescendo as the speed increased. Years later, the same song would be dedicated to Matthew Harding.

Chelsea had a brief spell in the First Division at the end of the Seventies, and it was during this period that On A Wolverhampton Terrace was heard, as well as the enjoyably long Great Man United song, which is still remembered by many pub dwellers today.

> I went down to Wembley one fine day in May,
> Full of supporters so happy and gay,
> And when it was over and when it was done,
> Benfica were beaten by four goals to one.
>
> The first was scored by wee Georgie Best,
> The second was scored when Bobby out jumped the rest,
> The Stretford End chanted but I never did,
> And the third was scored by young Brian Kidd.
>
> The Stretford End cried out, they cried out for more,
> And Bobby obliged by making it four,
> A team to remember, a team to recall,
> Was the great Man United, the best of them all.
>
> They came down to Chelsea in '75,
> They took up the North Stand, The Shed and the side,
> But Chelsea were many, too many to ruck,
> And the great Man United got battered to fuck.
>
> We went to Old Trafford in '78,
> The whole of Manchester was lying in wait,
> But Chelsea went mental because we had our pride,
> And the whole of Manchester Uniiiited died,
> Tood-a-loo, tood-a-loo,
> And the whole of Manchester Uniiiited died.

The end of the Seventies still saw Chelsea fans believing in themselves and the team, with chants like We're So Great It's Unbelievable and We Are The Famous, The Famous Chelsea arising. The theme song for the television comedy classic The Liver Birds, set in Liverpool, had its words rewritten by The Shed.

If you're standing, on the corner,
With a red scarf round your neck,
Chelsea boys, will come and get you,
And we'll break your fucking neck.

While the Chelsea support had been riding the crest of a ska and reggae music wave in the late Sixties and early Seventies, racism and the rise of the National Front in the mid-Seventies meant songs about 'Paki-bashing', 'knifing niggers' and 'gassing Jews' were not uncommon during the late Seventies and early Eighties. The National Front used Chelsea as a recruitment ground and many young white males were all too happy to join in, the Front, like football, offering a good excuse for a punch-up.

West Ham, whose first black player was Clyde Best in the late Sixties, received racist chants based on the Banana Splits children's TV series, while into the Eighties they were treated to You're The Pride Of Bangladesh. The age-old abuse of Tottenham continued into the Eighties with Does Your Rabbi Know You're Here, racist and anti-Semitic versions of Spurs Are On Their Way To Wembley, and a chant about Garth Crooks and a tree.

When Chelsea's first black player, Paul Canoville, made his debut in 1982, he was given horrendous abuse by sections of the Chelsea support, with 'Chelsea are white' songs being sung. Canoville made the grade and, like many black and Asian supporters who followed the team at the time, he became an 'honorary white' to some. Other black players received abuse after Canoville, with the likes of Keith Dublin and Keith Jones suffering as they were subjected to monkey noises. 'You black bastard' was also chanted at opposing black players during this time.

The Munich songs directed at Manchester United also hit the scene in the late Seventies and early Eighties and were sung against them up until 1989, after then being restricted to pubs.

Many of the old favourites were still being sung in the Eighties, but as the crowds and visiting support dried up The Shed often had to sing among itself. Banter between the Middle and White Wall of the Shed grew as there were little or no away fans to abuse. Abuse of other areas of the ground grew at this time, with the cardboard cut-outs in the Benches receiving stick.

The 1981-82 season saw a good Cup run, which allowed the Chelsea fans the treat of abusing the visitors from both Tottenham and Liverpool, with the Scousers subjected to Does The Social Know You're Here? During the Falklands War, The Shed sang songs about bombing Argentineans, to the Captain Pugwash tune, and Tottenham's midfield player Osvaldo Ardiles was treated to...

Ossie's cousin,
He is dead,

British helicopter on his head,
Ooh-ooh-ooh...

A similarly-tuned song about a Tottenham fan dying on the escalators at a tube station was also aired at this time. During the Miners' Strike, Forest fans were subjected to Scab chants as they broke the strike, and when we went up the road to Sheffield Wednesday, Chelsea sang Get Back To Work You Lazy Bastards or Arthur Scargill Is A Wanker. While down in the Second Division, Chelsea still had the enjoyment of playing Leeds and West Ham, and a new-found rivalry with QPR.

Leeds matches were built up over the season, with The Shed counting the number of weeks to the match. An incident at Piccadilly Circus tube station between Chelsea and Leeds supporters was revered in The Shed, the single word Piccadilly sung at subsequent matches between the clubs as Chelsea reminded Leeds of the ambush. In these desolate days, loyalty was important and The Shed would sing at every home match If You're All Going To Barnsley Clap Your Hands, or whatever the next away fixture was, and the whole end would respond. West Ham's Chim-Chiminey song was adapted and a new ending added – 'we hate those bastards in claret and blue'. QPR, the joke team from up the road who were getting mouthy, had two chants dedicated to them.

Go by train,
Go by car,
Go and laugh at QPR.

QP-R, QP-R,
QP-Ha, ha, ha...

A song that more likely came from the late Seventies, but was sung occasionally in the early Eighties, derided both Tottenham and QPR.

To: Sham 69's Hersham Boys
Tottenham boys, Tottenham boys,
No pork pies (chops) or saveloys.

Or... Rangers boys, Rangers boys,
Make more noise with Tonka Toys.

Or... Chelsea boys, Chelsea boys,
Laced-up boots and corduroys.

An early Eighties song by the Gap Band, Oops-Up-Side Your Head, was adapted within weeks.

187

> You'll get a boot, wrapped, round your head,
> A boot wrapped round your head.

The all-time low in Chelsea crowds, but not necessarily in terms of singing, came in 1983 as Chelsea slid towards Third Division football. Though attendance figures were down, a hardcore of 5,000 Sheddites would still sing for ninety minutes in a 6,000 crowd. Away from home, Chelsea fans were as vocal as ever, with a never say die attitude. The continuous chant of CHELSEA, CHELSEA, CHELSEA began at away games, and sometimes lasted the whole of the second half without a break. The arrival of Gate 13 in the East Stand as the new home of a young and lively support livened up the Benches and the West Stand during 1982-83, and for several years after, meaning there was now vocal support all around the ground.

New 'unique' Chelsea songs such as One Man Went To Mow began, while away from home the Chelsea fans taunted the Old Bill with chants like Bring Out Your Riot Gear, Chelsea's Here, Chelsea's Here. The early Eighties saw various bans on Chelsea fans travelling to away games, and chants ranged from the blatant You'll Never Ban The Chelsea, to the humorous We're Not Here.

Chelsea's large away following in the Second Division days gave rise to questions directed at home fans such as What's It Like To See A Crowd? and Is That All You Get At Home? When less than 1,000 visitors turned up at the Bridge they were treated to Is That All You Take Away? In fact, at this time some teams only bought ten or twenty fans and were derided with Did You Come In A Taxi? and Is Your Tandem Parked Outside?

After five years in the Second Division, Chelsea were on their way back to the First Division and a new array of songs were being sung.

> Come along, come along,
> Come along and sing this song,
> We're the boys in blue,
> Division Two,
> We won't be here for long.

Shortened versions of old classics were also heard.

> And it's super Chelsea, super Chelsea FC,
> We're by far the greatest team,
> The world has ever seen.

An age-old favourite which was usually sung at home, You've Come All This Way, And You've Lost, was changed on a memorable Friday night in Manchester when Chelsea took 7,000 up to Maine Road.

We've come all this way,
And we've won, and we've won.
(Repeat)

Players' names were sung wholeheartedly, and the introduction of There's Only One... began. Nippy Scottish winger Pat Nevin got his own crescendo of Wee Pat Nevin, La, La, La, which just became faster and faster. When Chelsea were back in the First Division in 1984, Chelsea Are Back and Tottenham, Tottenham Here We Come chants became all the rage, and instead of Chopper's Gonna Get You the chant Rougvie's Gonna Get You arrived. But it was a bad night for Doug in the Cup at Sheffield Wednesday, though a good result in the end for Chelsea, that really immortalised him in song.

3-0 down,
4-3 up,
Dougie Rougvie fucked it up,
La-la-la-la-la.

As in the Sixties and Seventies, the Chelsea fans took up songs of the day. Thankfully, though funny at the time, many were short-lived, as was the case with Christmas tunes like Nellie The Elephant and the Frog Song. On the subject of totally non-football-related songs, whether concerned with violence or supporting the team, Celery hit the Chelsea terraces around 1986-87.

Celery had three very good years before the police clamped down on the throwing of celery at matches. The song died down, but still gets an airing now and again, and occasionally a few bits of celery are tossed, but nothing like its heyday when 5,000 Chelsea fans were throwing it around. Just for the record, the words are...

Celery, celery,
If she don't come,
I'll tickle her bum,
With a lump of celery,
Celery, celery.

The Celery song arrived when hooligan firms were busy giving themselves names. Where's Your Famous Service Crew? was directed at Leeds, while ICF Stands For I Can't Fight, or Ice Cream Firm, was directed at West Ham. Some Fulham Road stalls also sold Inter Celery Firm t-shirts to take the mickey out of West Ham.

The late Eighties also saw the brief (thankfully) E-I-O chant, an attempt to replace the more traditional Knees Up Mother Brown, which involved jumping up and down and singing E-I-O. An early Nineties version was Here We Go, and was another one which didn't make the grade. Along similar lines, Let's All Have A Disco and Let's Go Fucking Mental were Nineties-style, jumping-up-and-down songs, which I quite enjoyed.

The Eighties chant of You're Shit, And You Know You Are changed into the more polite, but still very funny You're Not Very Good in the Nineties. I remember this one first being sung at Everton away. As we got stuffed 7-0 at Nottingham Forest in April 1991 the Monty Python classic Always Look On The Bright Side Of Life emerged, and in the following weeks other clubs adopted the same song. But it was first heard on the Chelsea terraces. The Nineties saw a few new songs, and many adaptations of tried and tested material.

> I'm Chelsea till I die,
> I know I am,
> I'm sure I am,
> I'm Chelsea till I die.

Others, like Blue Flag, were a revival of old songs but with new words.

> From Stamford Bridge to Wembley,
> We'll keep the blue flag flying high,
> Flying high, up in the sky,
> We'll keep the blue flag flying high.

Perhaps the most enduring and pleasantly surprising was the Sixties Shed boot-boy classic song Fuck 'Em All, the only revision in the words the replacing of 'we are the Shed End' with 'we are the Chelsea', which to me was an improvement.

Certain matches earned their own songs during the Nineties, like our great win over Liverpool in the FA Cup.

> 2-0 down,
> 4-2 up,
> We knocked Scousers out the Cup.

> *And...* Da-oh, da-oh,
> Vialli scores and the Scousers go home,
> Not one, not two, not three, but four,
> Vialli scores and the Scousers go home.

Vialli received folk status at Chelsea, along with a select few other players, and he has his own song, just for scoring at Old Trafford.

When the ball hits the back of the Old Trafford net,
It's Vialli,
When the boys in the blue make it two fucking nil,
It's Vialli.

While Bob Geldof sang about feeding the world, the Chelsea faithful changed it to Feed The Scousers, while the abuse of opposition players has continued, though probably more politely. Ian Wright received Stanley Bowles type treatment with Ian Wank, Wank, Wank; Nottingham Forest's Jason Lee's hairstyle earned several renditions of He's Got A Pineapple On His Head; Arsenal's Martin Keown was awarded He's Got A Monkey's Head; and Newcastle's Peter Beardsley received Esmerelda, The Bells chants, or just a basic You're So Ugly It's Unbelievable.

Many opponents' songs have been turned against them in recent years, and the one that follows has been adapted for a number of managers and teams in the last ten years.

To: Daydream Believer
Cheer up Bobby Robson,
Oh what can it mean,
To a sad Geordie bastard,
And a shit football team.

Indeed, player abuse has become increasingly popular, especially when it comes to the more high-profile names, and the first years of the the 21st Century have seen David Beckham tormented with references to his wife, while Wayne Rooney will have to suffer a few years of granny-shagging abuse.

While opposition players have borne the brunt of many new songs in recent years, the Chelsea choir has also seen fit to make tribute to its own players. Dennis Wise and Gianfranco Zola, for example, have had superb songs dedicated to them.

Oh, Dennis Wise,
Scored a fucking great goal,
In the San Siro,
With ten minutes to go.

A 5-0 League Cup victory at Highbury saw the brilliant...

Who put the ball in the Highbury net?
Arthur,
Arthur fucking Chelsea.

And... One, two,
One, two, three,
One, two, three, four,
Five-nil.

With The Shed closed down and the ground all-seater, the Matthew Harding Stand has become the vocal area of Chelsea's support. The rest of the crowd do join in, although the East Stand still needs a kick up the arse sometimes. Did singing at football stop when the terraces were closed? No, of course not. Chelsea have seen vociferous seasons since the demise of The Shed, and to a certain extent the loss of the old West Stand and Benches. Chelsea fans still sing, and new songs are still invented, though whether we sing as much, or as loud, is obviously debatable. In the old days you had singing an hour and a half before kick-off, and throughout the game, but was it every game? Was it fuck. It is certainly a lot quieter today, but then I have rose-tinted memories of the days when I used to start songs off in The Shed, with everyone joining in – and if they didn't, you were given a derisory chant of Solo! Nowadays, though, we only seem to sing when we're winning or scoring.

As we celebrated one hundred years of Chelsea Football Club in style, there was one new I chant was more than happy to join in.

Have you ever seen Chelsea win the league?
Have you ever seen Chelsea win the league?
Have you ever seen Chelsea, ever seen Chelsea, ever seen Chelsea
    win the league?
YES WE HAVE.

I have every faith that the next generation of Chelsea fans will create fresh songs. While the old Rising Sun, Wheatsheaf, Ifield and so on have gone by the wayside, there are the likes of The White Hart where the next wave of football songs will be produced or, maybe, there will be a spontaneous new one, created inside Stamford Bridge. But the old ones won't be forgotten, because they are the true classics.

There are many chants and songs I have missed out in this brief look at the history of Chelsea songs, and no doubt memory loss or other errors have changed the words of some of the older ones. There are many songs and chants which lasted, say, a pre-season tournament, European trip, or just one or two games, which are not included.

When it came to singing, there was one supporter who was Mr Chelsea, though maybe that wasn't the exact term used. To me, Mick Greenaway emphasised what supporting Chelsea was all about. He became famous for his Zigger Zagger chant, which in later years was exclusively his. All Mick was interested in was Chelsea fans singing their hearts out for the team and if his Zigger Zagger chant got them going, then so be it. Mick would supply the Zigger Zagger, Zigger Zagger, and the hundreds of Chelsea boys around him would supply the Oi Oi Oi. Mick would keep this call and response going for ages, before slowing down and seeing the chant drift into When The Blues Go Steaming In.

My knowledge of many of the songs in this chapter are through Mick and his friends, who I first met in the Second Division days. Mick is sadly no longer with us, but I can imagine him up in heaven now, singing Chelsea, Chelsea, Chelsea Are The Champions, and stretching God's tolerance to its very limits.

The Shed develop their writing skills as they tell the players what is required

Having A Say,
Having A Laugh

With their roots in the punk fanzines of the late Seventies, when home-produced publications touted the likes of The Sex Pistols and The Clash, football equivalents were perhaps inevitable given the number of fans who bought them in pubs and around music venues. Marrying the same DIY ethic with terrace concerns, the explosion of football fanzines saw ordinary supporters dodging official censorship and getting their views into print. Chelsea were no exception and there was plenty that needed saying. Mark Meehan looks at an area of football culture that has developed over the years and is still going strong today

There were a number of unpleasant sidelines to watching Chelsea play at home in the 1980s, and the concept of Category A matches blending nicely with a visit to the Gents toilet at the back of the old West Stand was certainly one of them. Another was the high charge being levied for a souvenir programme.

This was at the fag end of John Hollins' managerial tenure at Stamford Bridge and when the short lived reign of Booby (sorry Bobby) Campbell was about to begin. Chelsea and souvenir programmes were always good bedfellows, with the club being the first in the country to launch their own magazine-style format in 1948, something that everyone else followed. Then there was the small pocket-sized programmes that ran from 1961 to 1974 with so much information and detail in them that they would keep your average logarithms fanatic happy.

If people can take exams in studying soap operas, then the Chelsea programme era of the 1960s and 1970s is a subject worthy of its place on the national curriculum. In 1974-75 the club moved to an A4 format which played havoc with us saddos who had all those programmes neatly packed and labelled in the same size shoe boxes, or in the binders the club used to provide. I know of at least one Chelsea fan who thought our relegation that year was down to our new-style programme format. He said it was some kind of curse, and this was a couple of years before the magician Romark tried to do the same thing to Eddie McCreadie's Blue And White Army. (I spoke to his nurse last week and he is still taking the medication as he enthrals her with tales of what Mrs Hudson used to cook for husband Alan, the poetry of Eddie McCreadie, and which luvvy would be sitting with Lance Percival and Rodney Bewes in the old East Stand this week.)

Our programme slightly shrunk in size over the next decade or so, but shrunk even more in terms of decent content. We did have one or two good programmes. The 1983-84 season brings back many happy memories on the pitch, while off it there used to be one page in the programme that was written by supporters and was worth reading. But other than that, reading what Gordon Dimbleby (who he?) had to say, or whether or not the former bingo ticket seller from Wimbledon FC was going to help us with Save The Bridge, did not make the Official Matchday magazine worth shelling out for. Better to buy another pre-match pint in the pub instead.

Ken Bates' column was always worth a look to see which poor hack was getting the raw end of his wrath this week. I remember Harry Harris receiving more stick than most and yet he ended up being one of Ken's regular lunch companions. Somehow I cannot see the mid-Eighties editor of The Daily Mirror believing Harry when another law suit from Peter Carter Ruck arrived on his desk and he said 'don't worry boss, in a few years we will look back on this and laugh as we share a bottle of champagne in Ken's penthouse in Chelsea Village.'

The blandness and bullshit contained within the forty or so pages beggared belief at times. Even when the team was struggling on the pitch, throwing away three-goal leads at Oxford and drawing 4-4, everything was presented as being upbeat when the supporters knew different. Also not helping the situation were the digs at the fans, either by the manager or the chairman in his programme notes. An early letter writer to the Chelsea Independent pointed out that despite having purchased every Chelsea home programme and read every copy of Bridge News he had never seen a letter printed about the club's trains to away games. Although the club did at least in the Eighties regularly print the names of the supporters who went on the official train and thank them for their support, you never read a complaint about the service.

How often did the train break down on the way to an away game? How many times did the six hundred supporters that travelled miss the kick-off? How often were there only peanuts or Wagon Wheels left for the long journey home? Did these things never happen? They did, but you never read about them until the arrival of fanzines. The quality of the Chelsea programmes rose with the dawn of fanzines at Stamford Bridge, the club even nicking ideas and writers for the official publication.

At other clubs around the country the situation was not dissimilar and, coupled with crucial events such as Heysel and Bradford, supporters and supporters' groups started getting active and soon began to produce their own alternative publications to rival the official mouthpieces. There was also the first alternative football magazine since FOUL folded in the 1970s, one which soon achieved national distribution and is still doing well today – When Saturday Comes.

So was this how and why fanzines arrived at Chelsea? Yes and no. Clearly, once the first fanzines were up and running, supporters started getting involved and sending in their contributions for inclusion, and soon there was also an expanding audience of supporters wanting to read something different, a publication that would actually say that Kerry Dixon might just need a kick up the arse and that John Hollins should go, or give them the chance to read about great away games of the past such as the trip to Bolton in 1977.

However, at Chelsea the starting point was shaped by another issue. The first fanzine at Chelsea was the Chelsea Independent. The Indie was started in April 1987 by a small group of Chelsea supporters deeply concerned about the goings on with our future neighbours Fulham Park Rangers, and with a certain David Bulstrode talking about the possibility of ground sharing with QPR. These supporters thought it was time to act.

Having attended a demonstration at Hammersmith Town Hall against the proposed merger with QPR and Fulham, a number of Chelsea fans decided to form their own supporters' group and an inaugural meeting of the Chelsea Independent was set up in the Kings Head pub, now the Slug And Lettuce. Nearly a hundred Chelsea supporters turned up, and from those who attended that first meeting twelve people paid £12 each to produce the first ever issue of the Chelsea Independent. It was a twelve-page magazine and 500 copies were printed, all of which were sold without ever going on sale outside Stamford Bridge. They were sold in pubs and clubs and certain outlets in London such as Sportspages in Charing Cross Road, or by word of mouth as news quickly spread about this magazine produced by the supporters themselves.

The second issue went on sale at the start of the 1987-88 season with a print run of 2,000 and sold fast. Early issues of the Indie allowed supporters to air their views, which were currently being ignored at club level, or they could raise such issues as racism, policing, the lack of atmosphere, pricing policies and ticketing arrangements.

An early letter that was sent to Ken Bates highlighted eight areas where the fanzine thought the club might want to hear some positive suggestions.

These were – (1) Ticket sales: Better ticketing arrangements for away games and flexible box-office opening hours. (2) Attracting new Chelsea supporters: Attract young supporters with free tickets to local schools. (3) Marketing team shirts: Sell versions of the late Sixties and early Seventies team shirts. (4) Saving the Bridge: Shares in the club. (5) Facilities for supporters: A supporters' social bar in the new stadium that would be open on match days and during the week. (6) Match programme: Reintroduce a column along the lines of Terrace Talk. (7) Membership: Each member should be able to bring a guest at an identical cost. (8) The team: Simple. Buy back Pat Nevin.

Soon after the Independent hit the streets the second Chelsea fanzine arrived in the shape of Red Card. In the same-sized A5 format, the Red Card was, as one Chelsea fan said to me at the time, for Sun readers, while the Independent appealed to those who preferred The Guardian. Complete tosh I know, but it might have been interesting if early on Alan had made Big Al from Portsmouth go topless.

There was a period when readers of both fanzines seemed to think the Red Card and Independent were involved in a war of words, in the same way The Sun and The Mirror have competed against each other over the years. It even saw letters appearing from supporters asking for both sides to call a halt to slagging off their rivals. I am not sure where this phoney war came from as all the fanzines at Chelsea made efforts to get along with each other, and sometimes editors would swap articles which were more suited to another publication. This also applied to those fanzines that have long since bitten the dust, or which only appeared for a couple of issues.

Credit has to go to Alan Collis and Red Card, which is still going strong today and, as the front cover occasionally reminds us, is the longest running fanzine at Chelsea. Although Big Al and Pugs' pages have gone West some time back, the Red Card is still worth a read. It also now has its own developed youth policy as Alan's son Oliver has been known to edit the odd issue. This fanzine has clearly got its long-term future secured and will soon celebrate its 20th anniversary

Going back in time, an early campaigning issue in the Chelsea Independent was for the return of the old badge. The club had produced a new Millwall-style lion badge in 1986, despite the club registering the old badge as a trademark in 1970 and achieving the registration on June 13th, 1972. In no time at all a petition of 2,000 signatures was delivered to the club, and the theme of the old badge cropped up regularly in more than one fanzine for the next seventeen years. This was to no avail during the Bates era, despite being raised at frequent intervals by the Red Card and later by Matthew Harding's Blue And White Army.

The badge remained the registered trademark of Chelsea until 1991 and the club could have at any time in those three years from the petition restored the badge. It was not until the new management of Kenyon and Buck arrived that Chelsea did the decent thing and brought the badge back (at least partially), to coincide with the club's centenary season.

Matthew Harding's Blue And White Army changed its name to cfcuk and launched a campaign to reinstate the old lion badge. The founder/editor of the fanzine, David Johnstone, was told by current Chelsea chairman Bruce Buck that the club was inundated with completed petition forms that first appeared with the arrival of the new regime under Roman Abramovich. At least 20,000 signatures were collected (11,000 by the editor himself). Who said fanzines did not change anything, even if it was better late than never.

Earlier on the Independent also highlighted the issue of ground safety following the horrifying incidents of overcrowding at White Hart Lane and Old

Trafford early on in the 1987-88 season. Remember, this was before Hillsborough, and having been at the Tottenham game I can remember the crush inside the ground as the Tottenham stewards only opened one section at a time, until they thought the relevant part was full and they moved on to opening a new section. From memory, as a result a crash barrier collapsed due to the crushes and this was never reported despite a number of Chelsea supporters being injured that day. It took till half-time for the final section of terracing to be opened to give the Chelsea supporters some breathing space and air. The justification for not opening the section was that it was being kept as a no-man's land of segregation between the two sets of fans. For the historians among you, it was also the last time Chelsea lost in the league at Three Point Lane.

That 1-0 defeat by Tottenham in August was a disaster in that we lost a game that really should have been there for the taking. But it was nearly a disaster in terms of supporters being seriously hurt or even killed. In the section behind the goal which was so overcrowded, people were so crushed that many lost their shoes, one barrier towards the back of the section collapsed, while those attempting to get out of the crush by climbing over the fence to the adjacent section were beaten on the hands by police.

There was no enquiry. Two years later Hillsborough happened.

Another area where the pages of the fanzines were inundated with the written word concerned the current playing staff – who should join Chelsea, who should leave Chelsea, and how So & So was a complete and utter tosser and what possessed Hollins/Campbell/Webb/Porterfield/Hoddle to buy him in the first place. There has always been a school of thought that the supporters should get behind whatever eleven players wear the blue shirt, never mind who they are and what their ability, but that did not stop people putting their five-pence worth in. The Rougvies, McNaughts, Murphys and Darren Wood's stranded starfish impersonation all got a mention, but in the early days of his Chelsea career one player more than any other came in for a fair amount of stick – and that was Dennis Wise.

Having been scapegoated by being dropped early on by Bobby Campbell, and then to have supporters getting on his back, it was a surprise that Wise did not up sticks and leave. But following an article in the Independent which urged people to give him a chance, get behind him and remember, you are a Chelsea supporter, Wise went on to become one of the most popular Chelsea players of all time.

There were other sides to the Independent, one of which was humour. One of my own particular favourites was the regular updating of the East Stand Top Tier Club, also known as the Mickey Droy Memorial. This was a spoof award dedicated to those supreme athletes who, in their services to the art of football, went beyond the call of duty – and reached the third tier of the East Stand. Early award recipients included Mickey Droy (naturally), Keith Dublin, Gordon Durie, Ken Monkou and Eddie Niedzwiecki.

Personally, I would not mind a small plaque on a wall somewhere inside the new Stamford Bridge corridors dedicated to the Mickey Droy Memorial. Every time someone achieves the feat of clearing the ball to the top tier we could invite Mickey back to Stamford Bridge to award a certificate to said player. It would be fun and a lot more interesting for Mickey than being walked round the pitch with Neil Barnett for the first game of the 2005-06 season, with Barnett saying 'East Stand – Mickey Droy... Shed End – Mickey Droy... West Stand – Mickey Droy' and cringing as some of the Johnny Come Latelys ask 'Mickey Droy? Who's he?' Having said that, though, how many of the current Chelsea squad would be likely to join the Top Tier Club? Maybe a stray goal kick from Petr Cech will hit some of the old moaners sitting in the front row of the top tier, but somehow I cannot see Arjen Robben or Damien Duff ever becoming members.

There are people who believe fanzines became too serious. As most of the stuff that goes into fanzines comes from the Chelsea supporters themselves, was there a period in the 1990s when Chelsea supporters lost their sense of humour? I don't think so. Douglas Coombs did not, and when Ian Porterfield finally got the sack, Douglas gave the following possible reasons for his dismissal – (1) Before home games he had attempted to replace Blue Is The Colour with Marvin Gaye's What's Going On. (2) He said 'whatever happened to that nice Robert Bates?' once too often. (3) He objected to the chairman's plan to name the new North Stand the Grange Farm Dairy Cattle Artificial Insemination Stand. (4) In the executive lounge he observed to club sponsors Commodore that their new computer-enhanced graphics weren't exactly Sonic The Fucking Hedgehog!

Among the Indie pages there was also the odd Monty Python sketch, plus Fawlty Towers, Fast Show and Only Fools And Horses spoofs, but one of the funniest things to appear in the Independent was in Issue 65, when 'Gulliver's Travels' put together his own musical extravaganza called Oliver Fleck The Musical, with a supreme casting list of Dennis Wise playing the Artful Dodger, Robert Fleck as Oliver Twit, Matthew Harding as Bill Sykes, Glenn Hoddle as Nancy and, naturally, Ken Bates playing Fagin. The grand finale was a jolly old smelly pong around the old Joanna Lumley in homage to the newly arrived Dutch master. Shame The Shed never picked up on Ruud Glorious Ruud.

Probably one of the biggest compliments one can give to the writing in the fanzines at Chelsea is what happened to some of the regular contributors. At least four by my calculations ended up working on the club programme or Onside. A number have since gone on to write for FourFourTwo, Shoot or some publications now out of print such as Goal, Football Monthly, Total Football, Action Replay and the Chelsea Magazine, or have gone on to publish books of their own.

Another use for the fanzines was as a place to highlight examples of poor policing, or instances where a Chelsea fan might have been arrested or convicted unfairly. When both the Red Card and the Chelsea Independent reported the problems of policing at Stamford Bridge and the fact we had the highest arrest rate in the league, it saw an opening of a dialogue between all the fanzines at Chelsea.

For a while in the early Nineties there were regular letters sent in about the police on Merseyside or Sheffield or some other wasteland UP NORF, where the Old Bill looked for an early collar to feel and eject from the ground so their day's work was done. Sometimes, though, the letters got it wrong. One suggested that during half-time of a home game with Everton the legendary Paperman had to be carried rather than escorted from the ground due to over-zealous policing, but it later transpired he had had a heart attack and they were trying get him medical assistance as quickly as possible. Despite his heart attack, the Paperman was apparently none too pleased to have been taken out of the ground as he missed the end of the game.

The Independent also organised a number of meetings where officers from Fulham Police Station came along and spoke to Chelsea supporters. Those who were regulars during the relegation year of 1987-88 may recall heavy-handed policing and at the first meeting the police admitted they had an arrest policy. The meetings were an opportunity for both sides to meet and for supporters to air their grievances and vice versa. The ban on the carrying of celery into the ground was also sensibly lifted as a result. These meetings continued for several years and I would like to think brought about a change of police policy at Chelsea. I should particularly mention Inspector Brookes from Fulham Police Station, who not only came along to the meetings but now, having retired, gets to come to Chelsea every week as a fan rather than a policeman. He did more than most to build a dialogue between the police and, through the fanzines, the Chelsea fans, and should take credit for that achievement.

I am not sure though what the Fulham Old Bill made of the regular You're Nicked article, which gave Chelsea supporters the opportunity to complain about unfair arrest or ejection. From being chucked out at Oldham and then released from jail five minutes after the last train back to London, to the tale of the Chelsea fan arrested at Sunderland in 1985 for complaining to a police officer that he had been hit in the face by a greasy hamburger, this regular feature redressed some balance for Chelsea supporters.

The best You're Nicked came from someone who should be known as Jon from Walsall, arrested at Upton Park, but not for what you might think. At half-time some of our East London neighbours paid a visit to the away end to exchange scarves, pennants and some chit chat as they used to do in the old days at West Ham. On this occasion no-one had any scarves to exchange so it all kicked off. Jon, sitting on a crash barrier, had a good view of the lack of scarf exchanging and the odd punch being exchanged, so he decided to provide a commentary of events in his best David Coleman accent. Unfortunately, one of the local constabulary was a member of the David Coleman Fan Club so took him out and down to the police room. He then gave Jon a choice – a police van full of our nicked East London friends, or the street outside where by now the memorabilia-exchange activity had kicked off big time and all hell had broken loose. Jon chose the street and lived to tell the tale, but never did a David Coleman impersonation ever again.

With the advent of new IT hardware and improved software, all the Chelsea fanzines moved away from the cut-and-paste, back-of-a-fag-packet look to more professional publications with colour covers and designed layouts. I for one was pleased, as some of those early Chelsea Independents were not stapled in the right place, or even properly, and you could easily stab yourself with an exposed piece of metal. It is not uncommon for memorabilia collectors of all things Chelsea to remark that some of those early issues, on closer examination, have the odd bloodstain not obtained scrapping at Villa Park or Goodison Park.

Despite the advance of technology and the godsend that was Spell Check, the fanzines were still littered with spelling mistakes, reinforcing the 'enthusiastic amateurs' jibe Ken Bates once made. And you cannot talk about fanzines at Chelsea without mentioning their love/hate relationship with Bates. There were many supporters who did not bother reading fanzines, or stopped buying them, as they were perceived – and this particularly applied to the Independent – to be Bates knockers. Some fans also believed that by criticising Ken Bates the fanzines were therefore anti-Chelsea.

Interestingly, it only took until the third issue before the two parties crossed paths. The Independent had written to Bates after appealing for supporters to tell them which issues they wanted to raise with the club. Coincidentally, in the following month's issue of Onside, Bates answered a number of questions which, surprise, surprise, were the same questions the Independent had sent into Chelsea on the supporters' behalf.

At the same time the Independent was saying: 'None of us want to see the demise of Bates as that could ultimately mean the end of Chelsea. After all, it is his money and reorganisation that has kept the club going. Nobody will ever forget that he rescued the club in April 1982.'

The fanzines versus Bates debate was there from the start, with one side arguing that Bates saved Chelsea from the Mears regime and certain extinction, the other that since he had saved the club it had stood still and the supporters were paying the highest prices in the country for very poor facilities – poor toilets, poor catering, a rundown stadium and a team that had not won anything significant under his reign other than the Full Members Cup/ Zenith Data Systems Cup. Personally, I never had much of a problem with the old goat. My kids met him once and thought he was Father Christmas. In Issue 23 of the Independent Alex Baldock from Oxford declared Bates 'our saviour', while in Issue 38 the editorial was praising Bates for his tenacity, commitment and sheer bloody determination in securing the ground at Stamford Bridge.

Over the years the Red Card and the Independent had a few cross words with Grey Beard, but there were also times when Ken was quite genial and he invited all the fanzines to look around the Matthew Harding Stand before it opened in 1994, laying on mulled wine and mince pies. There was also the Portergate saga when Bates sued both the Red Card and Independent for believing The Sunday Mirror and repeating allegations made by Ian Porterfield about the sale of Gordon Durie and the purchase of Robert Fleck, and repeating said libel. It cost both fanzines ten Chelsea Pitch Owners at £1,000 to keep the wolf that was Peter Carter Ruck from the door.

Strangely, this incident showed a different side to Bates when, as part of the bollocking he gave the Independent, he recognised that fanzines had their place and were fully entitled to criticise, especially those first-team players who were not earning the wages the supporters were paying. He also agreed to be interviewed for the fanzine, provided the offending issue was shredded – Chelsea memorabilia collectors should hang on to Issue 43, as very few ever got into circulation.

Where the parties truly fell out was over Matthew Harding. To put it another way, the fanzines backed the wrong horse in a two-horse race. Ken Bates was always from the Keep Your Friends Close But Keep Your Enemies Closer school of thinking, so despite the occasional slagging both ways, the fanzines did still enjoy a dialogue with Captain Birdseye. That primarily changed for the Independent when they sided with and supported Matthew Harding, and started to ask questions about Chelsea Village, the albatross around the club's neck. For some reason that seemed to nark old Birdseye.

Ken Bates once said that ultimately the club belonged to the supporters. This wasn't quite true, the Independent pointing out that ultimately it belonged to the likes of RHK Nominees, Rysaffe Ltd and Hei See Ltd, who at the time owned over fifty percent of Chelsea Village. While Chelsea supporters were getting excited about names such as Vialli, Gullit and Di Matteo, they had never heard of Dr Fritz Schumaker, Han Rudolf Gyr, Konrad Annashon and Mrs Evelyn Reinhardt. Who were they? Well, they owned the club. Let's not forget Ashraf Marwan, either, who is well worth a search on the internet.

When Roman arrived as our saviour Tony Banks started asking lots of questions about who Abramovich was, and if this man was going to own our club then we as supporters needed to know where his money came from. I wish he had been as bothered about the previous owners.

It would be interesting to know what and where Chelsea would be today if Matthew Harding had not been killed in that fatal helicopter crash, and whether or not Roman Abramovich would have taken over the club. I suspect that if Harding had lived Ken Bates would still be Chelsea chairman and that

Harding would be out of the picture. It might be tempting to think that the supporters could have forced Bates out, like his old buddy Peter Swales at Manchester City, but that was not going to happen. His owning almost all of the club left Harding in a no-win situation, and Bates was in no mood to leave. He was too stubborn to let objections from the supporters bother him.

What clearly happened after the Harding versus Bates saga was that what little time Bates had for the fanzines went West, with the Independent bearing the brunt of much of his fire and angst. Although the fanzine continued for a few more years, it folded in 2001, after more than a hundred issues.

Red Card and Matthew Harding's Blue And White Army continued to have the odd cross word with Ken Bates, but two years after Roman took over how many would prefer to have Ken at the helm? If he was still here would we have won the league? Would we have Jose Mourinho as manager? Since leaving Chelsea, Bates tried to take Chelsea to court and then took over Leeds United of all teams. Most would have understood if he took over QPR, as that was the team he supported as a boy, but Dirty Leeds? Surely he must know how much the Chelsea supporters hate them. Drawing Leeds in the FA Cup would be interesting.

Ken Bates was genuinely and rightly held in high esteem for all his efforts in saving the club, but Chelsea had to move on to another level to compete regularly for the Premiership and the Champions League.

There were times when some of those writing into the Independent must have thought that Christmas and their birthday had come together, when something they had written about became reality. Back in 1991, Terence Lang wanted Glenn Hoddle as manager, while in the same year Paul Knight from Crawley said the club should introduce an away-match season ticket. An Independent reader was the first to suggest having a benefit game for retired goalkeeper Eddie Niedzwiecki, and as early as Issue 4 Sean McGovern from Kingston Upon Thames wanted a campaign to restore the old white socks, blue socks having replaced them at the start of the notorious, and briefly-lived, Chelsea Collection kit era. Long before Bates thought of it, Robert Rea was saying that the club needed its own Megastore and should do tours of the stadium, and he was also suggesting that members could have a pass-word (introduced in 2005) to buy tickets. Ironically, in the same article Robert joked about the Independent being Hardingite conspirators backed with Kremlin gold. Well, we have our Russian gold now.

Just before the demise of the Independent, another new fanzine arrived. Matthew Harding's Blue And White Army, which is now called cfcuk, is currently the third longest-running fanzine at Chelsea, and in 2005 passed the fifty-issue mark. Named in memory of Matthew, it also carried the title as most of the people who submitted articles sat in the lower tier of the Matthew Harding Stand.

From the first issue, the fanzine tried to establish a pool of regular writers, a practice still employed today, with each giving their own particular slant on one topic or another. All who contributed to Issue 1 had previously written for the Chelsea Independent, but by Issue 3 they were joined by others, including those involved in the Carefree 1992-93 fanzine. The Blue And White Army has always encouraged new writers and some who joined the fanzine in the early days are still writing for it today.

The lack of atmosphere at Stamford Bridge was first debated back in the early 1990s, with supporters writing in and complaining that The Shed was in danger of becoming like the North Bank. One suggested reason for the lack of atmosphere was that the fans in there were either too pissed or too stoned, and could only just about muster enough energy to stand for ninety minutes. These days it is due to the fact that we have lost a lot of our traditional support.

Today, in the pages of cfcuk, Red Card and the new kid on the block, Carefree, long-standing supporters are again highlighting their concerns about our support and the lack of atmosphere at Stamford Bridge. Gone are the days of unique terrace songs made up on the spur of the moment, and gone are the days of rivalry with the opposition as, unless it is a London derby, or Man United Red Sox visiting, most away supporters number no more than 1,500. Gone too are the days of everyone going mental and surging down the terraces when we score. While the Chelsea supporters love being champions, they also want the great atmosphere of days gone by. If this happened, Stamford Bridge would truly be a terrifying place to visit.

Back in Issue 25 of the Independent, Nick Brown wrote about seeing Ken Bates speak at a Football Supporters Association meeting, where Ken set out his vision for a future Chelsea. Nick talked about what would happen if the yuppies priced out those loyal supporters who had been around during the 1970s and the Gloomy Years of the 1980s. As Nick wrote at the time: 'We do not see fights among rich and poor Chelsea supporters along the Kings Road, but if the yuppies take over there will be a few pissed off Chelsea supporters with a certain amount of resentment.'

Times have changed at Chelsea since the early days of fanzines in the late Eighties. Chelsea have a 42,000 all-seater stadium, play to full houses nearly every week, and we are champions for the first time in fifty years and regularly playing in the Champions League. But the Chelsea fanzines are still appearing, and reading through their pages many of the same issues still arise – the club's pricing policy, ticket arrangements, the atmosphere at Stamford Bridge, and the thorny subject of new supporters versus old supporters. The more things change, the more they stay the same. There are plenty of pieces from Chelsea supporters unhappy about the arrival of new fans post-Gullit, post-Vialli, and now post-Mourinho. These glory hunters and Johnny Come Latelys have changed the face of Stamford Bridge.

Looking back at the fanzines over the years you could say that they have not changed the world. Chelsea supporters are still paying high prices for their football, no matter how successful the side. Nevertheless, the Chelsea fanzines have provided an alternative view and a voice for the supporters for the last eighteen years, and long may they thrive. The problems for fanzines now are the same as before. They are all going concerns due to the hard work and effort of a handful of people who put the things together and then, through wind and rain, have to sell them to prevent their lofts filling up with boxes of unsold copies.

So is there still a place for fanzines in a world where Chelsea are one of the biggest clubs in Europe and regularly win trophies, the days of hopeless underachievement in the dim and distant past? Yes, there is, and some of the issues from 1987 are even more relevant today. The lowest price ticket at Stamford Bridge is £35, and that is if you are a club member sitting in the Family Section. There is the long-running tandem issue of atmosphere at Chelsea and the differences between old and new Chelsea... or CHELSEA, as CFC Cathy highlighted scarily in an issue of cfcuk.

Don't get me wrong. I want to see Stamford Bridge full every week, but at what cost? We don't want the Highbury Library or the 60,000 Muppets of Old Trafford, but that is the way things are heading. I want to sit in a full Stamford Bridge each week, not amongst a coach load of Dutch tourists who only know who Arjen Robben is. Or the person who sits behind me and sings about Jose Mourinho pronounced with a H, when any decent Chelsea fan should know it is Jose with a J. Yes, you might call me picky, but daft though it may seem the measure of being a Chelsea fan is not how much they spend in the Megastore or who dines in the Sherpa Tensing suite, or whatever name it is. We keep getting told by Arsenal, Liverpool and Man United Red Sox supporters that we have no history. We may not have as much history as those clubs in terms of winning trophies, but this club has plenty of history in its supporters and what they invested in this club over the last thirty years. That is a part of our history and heritage we cannot afford to lose. If the fanzines continue to exist, and succeed in retaining or improving the atmosphere at Chelsea, then their place will be preserved as a voice for Chelsea supporters for many years to come. Also there needs to be a place where supporters can write and read about drinking bucket loads of beer at away games, and how we found that pub that stayed open all night in Barcelona, and was Doug Rougvie sinner or saint?

One important area where the Chelsea fanzines can take some credit, as they banged on about it for some time, was the issue of the supporters being able to buy tickets for European away games without being forced, almost Ronnie and Reggie style, to buy the official travel package. First there was Elizabeth Duff Travel and then there was Chelsea Village Travel. A key issue when Chelsea started playing regularly in Europe was supporters being able to choose whether to travel to matches independently or with the club. The propaganda coming out of the club from when we first played Viktoria Zizkov (remember her, nice girl), to later in the Champions League, was that if you did not travel with the club, you did not get in.

However, reading through all the Chelsea fanzines each time we played in Europe, the pages were filled with tales of supporters who had travelled to Europe under their own steam and got into the ground no bother. In Prague, Vienna, Bruges, Zaragoza, Bratislava, Tromso, Seville, Vicenza and so on, time and time again Chelsea fans booked flights themselves and either bought tickets locally or paid on the door at supposedly all-ticket games.

The European Parliament has probably not done much for Chelsea supporters down the years, but one thing that did happen was that the issue of ticket and travel sales was debated and the EU ruled it a restraint of trade, that any club selling tickets only as part of an inclusive travel package was breaking European law.

When fronted with the evidence from the fanzines, Bates tried to front it out, saying EU directives were contradictory. But with all the interested fanzines and fan groups, including Ron Hockings from the original Chelsea Supporters Club (whose Chelsea Blue publication could be argued to be the forerunner of the Chelsea fanzines), having got together on this subject, and Ron himself lobbying Tony Banks, soon the club had to back down. So today, as you log on to easyjet or Ryanair every time Chelsea play in the Champions League, and then you click on-line with Chelsea to buy the European away tickets, remember it was not that long ago that the club expected you to travel with them or else you did not get a ticket.

Finally, having gone through my loft and garage I have done a quick head-count of all the different Chelsea fanzines, with my apologies to anyone I have missed out. By my calculations the following titles have either been around for many years, or have appeared for a couple of issues and then faded into obscurity, while leaving their mark on the Chelsea fanzine movement. In no order of appearance, they are: Red Card, the Chelsea Independent, cfcuk (aka Matthew Harding's Blue And White Army), Cockney Rebel, Weststanders, Chelsea Till I Die, SW6, Blues Brothers, Carefree (1992 version), Carefree (2005 version), Balti Blue, The Chelsea Historian, Chelsea Fanatical, Curious Blue, One Nil Up Two One Down.

Special Ones 2005 – the drog's ollocks of a season

Champions

It had to be. The omens were just too powerful. One hundred years on from the inception of Chelsea Football Club. Fifty years since the club's only ever league title. The arrival of a manager who declared he was The Special One. A vintage season was on the cards and not only Chelsea die-hards could feel a championship in their bones. The 2004-05 season delivered everything it promised – and more. The Premiership was secured with aplomb. The League Cup was popped into the trophy cabinet almost casually. The European Champions League was nicked from us in the semi-final. But most satisfyingly was the flowering of a marvellous team. They were a revelation and some players in particular achieved greatness. John Terry displayed a masterful solidity and leadership. And Super Frank Lampard – what can be said? When was the last time our game boasted a midfielder who can open up defences so sleekly and find the net with such regularity? Damien Duff terrorised defences with his pace and dribbling ability. Others shone and the likes of Petr Cech and Joe Cole have the potential to become Chelsea legends. The famous cfcuk was at every game during this historic campaign and this is their account of how Chelsea won the Premiership in the club's centenary season

Manchester United. Home.Win.1-0. Gudjohnsen
Attendance: 41,813
Referee: G Poll. Date: 15.08.04
Chelsea: Cech, Ferreira, Gallas, Terry, Bridge, Geremi (Carvalho), Makelele, Lampard, Smertin, Drogba (Kezman), Gudjohnsen (Parker). Non-playing subs: Cudicini, Mutu
Report: A scrappy 1-0 victory in the opening fixture will always do, the bonus was of course that this one was against Man Utd. A solitary goal from Eidur was enough to earn the three points, after he picked up a headed pass from debutant Didier Drogba and bundled the ball over the line. Other Chelsea new faces were Petr Cech, Paulo Ferreira, Mateja Kezman, Ricardo Carvalho and Alexey Smertin who, after a season's loan at Portsmouth, finally put on the Royal Blue and was, despite the fact that John Terry got the official award, the 'people's' Man Of The Match. Good to see that Eidur is off the mark early.

Birmingham City. A.W.1-0. Cole
Att: 28,559
Ref: B Knight. Date: 21.08.04
Chelsea: Cech, Ferreira, Terry, Carvalho, Bridge, Geremi (Cole), Makelele, Lampard, Smertin (Tiago), Drogba, Gudjohnsen (Kezman). Non-playing subs: Cudicini, Gallas
Report: Another 1-0 victory, this time against Steve Bruce's Birmingham City. Bad boy Robbie Savage welcomed Mateja Kezman to the Second City with an elbow in the

face. Joe Cole came on as a substitute and won Chelsea the game after running into the box from the left and shooting a deflected ball past Taylor in the Birmingham goal. Didier Drogba had a couple of chances but failed to convert. Although Gray hit the inside of the post for the home side, Chelsea deserved the victory in what was always going to be a hard game against a resolute Birmingham side. Even John Terry, when asked if Chelsea deserved the win, smiled and said 'just about!'

Crystal Palace. A.W.2-0. Drogba, Mendes
Att: 24,953
Ref: C Foy. Date: 24.08.04
Chelsea: Cech, Ferreira, Terry, Gallas, Babayaro, Cole (Geremi), Makelele, Lampard, Tiago, Drogba (Gudjohnsen), Kezman (Mutu) . Non-playing subs: Cudicini, Carvalho
Report: Chelsea broke the hearts of every Chelsea supporter who was, after the opening two games, hoping that their side might win 38 consecutive league games 1-0. However, after a powerful first half header from Didier Drogba, there was only ever one team in it. After mixing with several of the Chelsea squad at the Zola dinner, former ECWC winner with Chelsea Danny Granville must have decided that he couldn't score against his old mates and headed his Palace side's only clear cut chance over the bar. Tiago Mendes became an instant hit with his first Chelsea goal and Jose Mourinho had his praises sung by the Chelsea faithful. At the end of the game, John Terry led the Chelsea players in mimicking Palace's pre-match huddle.

Southampton. H.W.2-1. Beattie (og), Lampard (pen)
Att: 40,864
Ref: S. Bennett. Date: 28.08.04
Chelsea: Cech, Ferreira, Terry, Carvalho, Bridge, Cole (Duff), Makelele (Geremi), Lampard, Tiago, Drogba, Gudjohnsen (Kezman). Non-playing subs: Pidgeley, Gallas
Report: There were thousands still trying to fight their way into the Matthew Harding end when Southampton's James Beattie scored after just 12 seconds. The away support couldn't have been that loud because no-one outside heard them cheer for the goal. Anyway, Beattie redeemed himself by slotting the ball past his own keeper to level the score. Super Frank Lampard stepped up to convert a penalty that gave Chelsea a 2-1 half-time lead. Although Saints gave Chelsea the odd scare in the second period, Chelsea always looked comfortable and, after four league games unbeaten, are starting to play like a team.

Aston Villa. A.D.0-0.
Att: 36,691
Ref: R. Styles. Date: 11.09.04
Chelsea: Cech, Ferreira, Terry, Carvalho, Babayaro, Makelele, Tiago (Smertin), Lampard, Cole (Mutu) Kezman (Gudjohnsen), Drogba. Non-playing subs: Pidgeley, Gallas
Report: Once again, Chelsea didn't manage to overcome what seems to be a psychological fear of home side Aston Villa. The Blues battled out a 0-0 draw against

an Aston Villa side that always looked dangerous on the break, although there were periods of the game in which Chelsea were in total control. However, after Didier Drogba had hit the woodwork in the latter stages of the first half, he was then booked (later rescinded) for diving in the second period after going down in the Villa box after a challenge that the majority (including both managers) inside the ground thought was a clear-cut penalty. Joe Cole, Chelsea's star performer on the day, was only given an hour before being replaced. However, the biggest bugbear was the dreadful support that came from the Chelsea end. While the majority were probably waiting for a goal to get them going, it's a sure thing that the players could have done with a song or two – something that might have helped them get going themselves!

Sp*rs. H.D.0-0.
Att: 42,246
Ref: M Riley. Date: 19.09.04
Chelsea: Cech, Ferreira, Terry, Carvalho, Bridge (Smertin), Cole (Duff), Makelele, Lampard, Tiago (Kezman), Gudjohnsen, Drogba. Non-playing subs: Pidgeley, Gallas
Report: A game in which Chelsea totally dominated but through a combination of wasted chances, bad luck and an upright, failed to score. The opposition took the plaudits for escaping with a point and the Blues might well reflect on the missed chance to make up ground on leaders Arsenal. Apart from not getting the run of the ball in front of goal, Chelsea were awesome but, when Eidur Gudjohnsen's effort came back after hitting the post, most Chelsea supporters realised that it wasn't going to be their day and that they would have to settle for a draw. Petr Cech made a stunning save in the second half, palming away the ball when many thought that it was a goal. Apart from that, he had nothing to do. Chelsea maintain their now world beating record of consecutive league games against a single club without defeat. One downside to the game however, was the woeful support from the home crowd. If Chelsea are to be the best in the country, they'll need the supporters to match – wake up Chelsea supporters.

Middlesbrough. A.W.1-0. Drogba
Att: 32.341
Ref: M Halsey. Date: 25.09.04
Chelsea: Cech, Ferreira, Terry, Carvalho, Gallas, Smertin (Tiago), Makelele, Lampard, Duff (Huth), Drogba, Gudjohnsen (Kezman). Non-playing subs: Pidgeley, Cole
Report: Yet again, Chelsea's defence and midfield remained solid and gave the opposition one clear chance at Petr Cech's goal. Former Chelsea striker Jimmy Floyd Hasselbaink came off second best when his head connected with John Terry's boot and needed stitches. The Dutchman even brushed John away when he went over to apologise. Up front, Didi smashed the ball against the woodwork and Billy Gallas hit a clear chance skyward. In the second half, again with the final ball just seeming to be a foot too high or behind the forwards, Didi powered a great chance over the bar and the game looked set for 0-0. However, he popped up in the right place with only minutes remaining to hit a low shot into the Boro goal to earn Chelsea all three points. Again, and at the risk of sounding very boring indeed, Chelsea's away support did

themselves no favours with their, at times, half-hearted support. A big pat on the shoulder must go to Drogba who, in the second half, motioned for the Chelsea supporters to raise their voices.

Liverpool. H.W.1-0. Cole

Att: 42,028

Ref: P Dowd. Date: 03.10.04

Chelsea: Cech, Ferreira, Terry, Carvalho, Gallas, Smertin (Tiago), Makelele, Lampard, Duff (Geremi), Drogba (Cole), Gudjohnsen. Non-playing subs: Cudicini, Huth

Report: Chelsea came out of the starting blocks on double time and were on top within minutes. Damien Duff, Super Frank Lampard, Didi 'The Drog's Ollocks' Drogba all came close before Drogba was taken off after just 37 minutes, suffering with a groin strain that served to put him on the injured list for several weeks. Joe Cole came on in his place but it was not until the 63rd minute that he made his mark. He had already had an effort cleared off the line before he flicked Frank Lampard's ball home in a well worked free-kick routine. However, the player was subject to some 'harsh' words from Jose Mourinho who commented that the youngster should have worked harder after scoring the goal. The second half followed the pattern of the first, with Chelsea creating chances but not putting them away. Late on, Smertin was replaced by Tiago, and Duff by Geremi. Cole and Eidur Gudjohnsen wasted further chances, and it wasn't until injury time approached that the visitors had their first real attempt on goal with Cech producing a fine save. Before the game, the first sitting of the Supporters Forum came to the conclusion that the DJ should change the timing of the 'Chelsea records'. It seemed to work with the home support more than fired up for this one. A radical improvement in atmosphere but there's still a lot to do...

Manchester City. A.L.0-1.

Att: 45,047

Ref: H Webb. Date: 16.10.04

Chelsea: Cech, Ferreira, Terry, Carvalho (Geremi), Gallas (Bridge), Tiago (Cole), Lampard, Makelele, Duff, Kezman, Gudjohnsen. Non-playing subs: Cudicini, Parker

Report: So Chelsea lose their unbeaten record. In the 11th minute the Sky Blues scored the only goal of the game. After Billy Gallas slipped on the sodden pitch, Man City stole possession. As Paulo Ferreira chased the long ball over the top, he challenged Anelka and the Frenchman went flying, while the Blue received a yellow card. Although the initial challenge was outside the area, the ref pointed to the spot. Anelka himself took the penalty and sent Petr Cech the wrong way. While Chelsea dominated the game, the luck still wasn't running for them in front of goal. Eidur Gudjohnsen was the most serious offender when it came to missing chances, the Iceman blasting the wrong side of the upright late on in the game. Mateja Kezman still looks a little short of pace and it looks like we're seriously missing Didi 'The Drog's Ollocks' Drogba up front. Super Frank Lampard was shown a yellow card. The good thing is that we are still in second place, albeit with a five-point gap between ourselves and the Gooners. The raucous home support outshone the visiting Blues although, when they did get going, those in Royal Blue were giving as good as they got. It won't be the first time that it's been said but, once again, remember you're a Chelsea supporter and it's 'win or lose, Up The Blues!'

Blackburn Rovers. H.W.4-0. Gudjohnsen 3, Duff
Att: 41,546
Ref: G Poll. Date: 23.10.04
Chelsea: Cech, Johnson, Carvalho, Terry, Bridge, Smertin (Tiago), Parker, Lampard, Cole (Robben), Duff, Gudjohnsen (Kezman): Non-playing subs: Cudicini, Gallas
Report: Chelsea legend and still favourite Mark Hughes again returned to Stamford Bridge, this time as recently installed Blackburn manager. However, the club that Sparky supported as a boy and for whom he gave sterling service were not about to give his side any favours. Chelsea started at a pace and could have taken an early seventh minute lead when a 20-yard thunderbolt from Super Frank Lampard was deflected over the bar by a Rovers defender, their keeper well beaten. Glen Johnson and Joe Cole then linked to create a superb opening but no-one was able to get a foot on the ball when the cross was delivered. Ricardo Carvalho, Damien Duff and Scott Parker then came close and, while some might have thought it was going to be 'one of those days', the majority of the faithful knew it would just be a matter of time. Then, in the 35th minute, after Wayne Bridge had linked with Joe Cole, Eidur Gudjohnsen pushed Cole's pass past Friedel in the Blackburn goal to score his and Chelsea's first. Two minutes later, he was on the score sheet again after he picked up a superb pass from Super Frank Lampard and pushed the ball into the far side of the goal. The second half ended on a somewhat sour note with Parker picking up a yellow card after getting involved with Rovers' Dickov. Four minutes into the second period, Eidur completed his first ever professional hat-trick after being brought down in the box while moving in on goal and persuading Super Frank to let him take the resulting spot kick. The Iceman coolly sent the keeper the wrong way to score. On the hour, he might have had a fourth but narrowly failed to get on the end of a cross from Glen Johnson. Arjen Robben made his debut, replacing Cole while minutes later, Alexey Smertin was replaced by Tiago. In the 74th minute, Duff made it four after cutting inside the box and hitting the ball into the corner of the goal. Almost straight from the restart Robben picked up the ball and waltzed through the Blackburn defence but was cynically cut down just outside the box. Kezman's luck was still against him as he smashed a shot against the bar and, moments later, pushed an effort just past the post. As well as a great performance from the team, Chelsea's support was probably the best it has been so far at Stamford Bridge this season. Well done all round.

West Bromwich Albion. A.W.4-1. Gallas, Gudjohnsen, Duff, Lampard
Att: 27,399
Ref: B Knight. Date: 30.10.04
Chelsea: Cech, Ferreira, Gallas, Terry, Bridge (Carvalho), Smertin, Makelele, Lampard (Tiago), Duff, Cole (Robben), Gudjohnsen. Non-playing subs: Cudicini, Kezman
Report: West Brom, like many other teams Chelsea have faced this season, came out of the starting blocks at an electric pace and, within two minutes, forced Petr Cech into a vital save, the keeper palming a header clear, before William Gallas was forced to clear off the line from the resulting scramble. The home side were getting around

the Chelsea backs and it was a good job for The Blues that West Brom's target men were having a bad day. As the half went on, Eidur Gudjohnsen was denied several on-goal chances as he narrowly failed to beat the off-side trap. Joe Cole, receiving a ball from Gudjohnsen, fired towards goal, bringing a good save from the home keeper. Just as it looked as though the first half would end goal-less, John Terry headed a Super Frank Lampard corner towards goal with Gallas adding his head to the momentum of the ball just to make sure, to send Chelsea in for the break winning 1-0. The second half saw Chelsea start with two changes, Wayne Bridge and Joe Cole coming off in favour of Ricardo Carvalho and Arjen Robben respectively. The changes almost brought fruition straight away as a rampant Gallas had a shot pushed away by the keeper, with Robben coming close with the follow-up. With five minutes of the second half played, Gudjohnsen headed Duff's low cross into the goal to double Chelsea's lead. Albion came back strongly and reduced the deficit after Cech could only parry a fierce shot, but could not react quickly enough to stop the ball being fired home from 20 yards. The fact that Chelsea had conceded momentarily stunned the, up until then, excellent travelling Chelsea support. However, within moments of resuming their vocal domination of the game, they were rewarded with a third goal from Chelsea as Super Frank Lampard's run and pass was picked up by Duff who simply ran into range and easily beat the advancing keeper. Despite restoring the two-goal advantage, Chelsea were not having things all their own way as Cech was made to perform heroics as he twisted at close-range to deny a firm Kanu header. But with 10 minutes left, Super Frank latched onto a ball from Robben and smashed it home from at least 20 yards out. As the Chelsea supporters celebrated and Super Frank Lampard earned a well deserved early bath as he was replaced for the remaining few minutes by Tiago, news came through that the Gooners were losing against Southampton which, for the few moments that 'We Are Top Of The League!' resounded from the Chelsea end, they were. However, fate saw to it that Arsenal would steal an injury time equaliser that would relegate Chelsea back to second position. Still, a great day was had by all – 'Champions League, we're having a laugh.'

Everton. H.W.1-0. Robben
Att: 41,965
Ref: M Riley. Date: 06.11.04
Chelsea: Cech, Ferreira, Carvalho, Terry, Babayaro, Makelele, Lampard, Tiago (Kezman), Duff (Huth), Robben, Gudjohnsen (Geremi). Non-playing subs: Cudicini, Cole
Report: With David Moyes' Everton side riding high in the Premiership, chasing at Chelsea's heels, the home crowd was highly charged and expectant for a game that The Blues had to win in order to prove their title challenge was serious. Petr Cech had already been forced into two crucial saves before Arjen Robben, fast becoming a key man at Chelsea, lead the attack and midway through the first half took the ball on brilliantly and smashed it towards goal, causing the Everton keeper to tip the ball onto the bar before it bounced away. Damien Duff also saw an effort cleared off the line. Robben again came close before the half-time break, a 45-minute period that also saw Super Frank Lampard come close twice and inadvertently cause a handbags-at-ten-paces incident. Ten minutes into the second half, Paulo Ferreira was replaced by Mateja Kezman. Robben and Eidur Gudjohnsen missed further chances before the Dutchman scored a brilliant goal in an end-to-end move. Gudjohnsen was replaced

by Geremi while Robert Huth was sent on in place of Duff. It was a great performance in a totally enthralling end-to-end game of football. Chelsea's win enabled them to leapfrog over the Gooners who lost to Man Utd earlier that morning. However, Jose Mourinho's comments about the home support made the news, after he said that Chelsea supporters needed to do more in order to lift the team. As in everything else the manager has said since his arrival at Chelsea, he's right.

Fulham. A.W.4-1. Lampard, Robben, Gallas, Tiago
Att: 21,877
Ref: U Rennie. Date: 13.11.04
Chelsea: Cech, Ferreira, Carvalho, Terry, Gallas, Smertin, (Tiago), Makelele, Lampard, Duff (Kezman), Robben, Gudjohnsen (Huth). Non-playing subs: Cudicini, Bridge
Report: The morning's action had seen the Gooners return to the top of the table after beating Sp*rs 5-4 at Three Point L*ne and this left Chelsea with a point to prove. However, it was Fulham who had the first chance, forcing Petr Cech into an early save. Twenty minutes into the game, Super Frank Lampard had a header well saved before John Terry made a surging run through the Fulham defence but only managed to stab his final effort wide. Chelsea were by this time rampant, with Arjen Robben leading the line and coming close on several occasions. Alexey Smertin and then Eidur Gudjohnsen had chances but the game remained scoreless. Claude Makelele was booked after bringing down Boa Morte. The deadlock was finally broken in the 34th minute when Chelsea were awarded a free-kick, following a foul on William Gallas. A well worked routine featuring Robben and Damien Duff was finished off by Lampard, who hit a right-footed shot into the top corner of the goal – the lead was nothing less than Chelsea deserved. Gudjohnsen then came close, but the half ended with Lampard receiving an undeserved booking for alleged diving. Fulham started the second half by attacking, forcing John Terry to clear after Gallas had a pass intercepted in his own half. Gudjohnsen, latching onto Robben's pass, had a shot blocked but then the almost unthinkable happened when Fulham equalised. Chelsea were on the back-foot as Ricardo Carvalho headed the ball out but Diop shot from 25 yards out to leave Cech standing. However, the Blues replied almost straight away after Robben danced his way past three defenders to slot home from 10 yards out to notch his fourth in four games. Tiago replaced Alexey Smertin just after the hour mark. In the 71st minute, Gallas got down low to head in a ball from Lampard to put Chelsea 3-1 up and firmly in control although Cech was asked to save another on-target effort. Soon after Mateja Kezman came on for Duff, Tiago received a return ball from Robben to smash the ball home for his second of the season and Chelsea's fourth on the day. While Chelsea supporters taunted the home fans with 'Carling Cup, YOU'RE having a laugh!', Robert Huth was given a run out for the last eight or so minutes, Mourinho resting Gudjohnsen and tightening up at the back. With Chelsea at the top of the League and the prospect of The Selecter at Club Ska, a top weekend was assured.

Bolton. H.D.2-2. Duff, Tiago
Att: 42,203
Ref: D Gallagher. Date: 20.11.04
Chelsea: Cech, Ferreira, Carvalho, Terry, Gallas, Tiago, Makelele, Lampard, Duff (Kezman), Robben, Gudjohnsen (Johnson). Non-playing subs: Cudicini, Bridge, Parker
Report: For the first time in as long as many can remember, the ground was full in time for the kick-off. Even those arriving past the three o'clock deadline found themselves having to wait until 3.30pm for the kick-off – it was delayed due to a combination of a traffic accident at Hammersmith and the planned engineering works that ensured that a large part of the London Underground's District Line was not operating. Thankfully, when The Blues took to the pitch, they didn't hang about. Within the first minute Damien Duff had latched onto Super Frank Lampard's through ball and rounded the Bolton keeper to slide the ball home. A perfect start. Bolton however – as all Chelsea supporters know – are no mugs and set about getting themselves level straight away. Duff then forced a good save from Bolton keeper Jaaskelainen in the 19th minute, and in the 27th Super Frank Lampard saw a powerful header go over the bar. Up until half time, the visitors had only one serious chance on goal, but Chelsea had Ricardo Carvalho to thanks as his header cleared the danger. Three minutes after the break Tiago flicked the ball home after a well worked corner routine involving Robben and Duff. In the 52nd minute, Petr Cech made his first serious mistake in a Chelsea shirt and allowed Bolton to get back into the game. Attempting to reach a ball sent in from a free kick, he struggled to get through a crowded six-yard box and flapped vainly at the cross. Bolton's Davies got his head to it and sent it into the goal. Twenty minutes later, however, Cech redeemed himself with a good save from Bolton's Speed. As the scoreboard flashed up the rest of the results as they came in, the Chelsea players seemed to lose concentration as they realised that the Gooners had dropped two points at home to West Brom. With ten minutes left Duff came off for Mateja Kezman and, a minute later, Gudjohnsen gave way for Glen Johnson. With four minutes to go and as the Chelsea supporters chanted 'Top Of The League', the inevitable happened and Cech was beaten for a second time after a 20-yard blast from Jaidi. It was the first time during Jose Mourinho's time in charge that Chelsea had surrendered a lead and they had the chances to win it – Eidur Gudjohnsen missed an easy chance as well as smashing the ball against the bar. Mourinho was not very happy about the game, but hopefully he'll take solace in the fact that we, as supporters, have seen it all before, though the difference this time is we're still top of the league and there are many of us confident that we will still be there come the end of the season.

Charlton. A.W.4-0. Duff, Terry (2), Gudjohnsen
Att: 26,355
Ref: M Clattenburg. Date: 27.11.04
Chelsea: Cech, Ferreira, Carvalho, Terry, Gallas, Tiago, Makelele, Lampard, Duff (Geremi), Robben (Babayaro), Gudjohnsen (Drogba). Non-playing subs: Cudicini, Smertin
Report: Charlton came out of the starting blocks at pace, hoping for a repeat of the first-minute lead that they took in the corresponding fixture last season. Just as they had done the previous week, Chelsea took an early lead. The game was into the fourth

minute when Damien Duff ran onto a fine through ball from Eidur Gudjohnsen. As Duff cut in from the right, he made short work of putting the ball past the advancing Charlton keeper Kiely. The Addicks came back several times and were denied by Petr Cech and then Paulo Ferreira. Ricardo Carvalho headed just over from a corner sent in by Super Frank Lampard then, at the other end, dived to intercept a cross and the Portuguese defender was fortunate when he watched the ball bounce back off the post. John Terry then picked up a booking for an innocuous challenge before Arjen Robben forced Kiely into a good save from a well-struck volley. Two minutes into the second half, Terry rose high to head Chelsea's second and, seven minutes later, the Chelsea captain collected his second of the game. As the ball was sent back across the goal and was missed by everybody, Terry was on hand to side foot the ball into the net. Chelsea were playing some of the best football they have played and Robben and Gudjohnsen again combined before the Iceman just failed to make the most of the cross. On the hour mark however, Gudjohnsen finally got his just rewards after picking up Super Frank Lampard's ball at the edge of the box and getting in front his defender to put the ball home. Two minutes later he was rested as Didi The Drog's Ollocks Drogba came on in his place. In the 70th minute, Geremi made his 50th Chelsea appearance, coming on in place of Duff before Celestine Babayaro replaced Robben. Although Chelsea were in cruise control, they seemed to go down a gear and remain content with the four-goal advantage. This was the fourth game in six Premiership matches that Chelsea had scored four. 'Top of the league, we're having a laugh.'

Newcastle. H.W.4-0. Lampard, Drogba, Robben, Kezman

Att: 42,328

Ref: R Styles. Date: 04.12.04

Chelsea: Cech, Ferreira, Carvalho, Terry, Gallas (Bridge), Tiago (Kezman), Makelele, Lampard, Robben, Duff, Gudjohnsen (Drogba). Non-playing subs: Pidgeley, Parker

Report: Both sides started the game tentatively – it might have had something to do with the early kick-off – and it wasn't until the 13th minute that Chelsea had their first attempt on goal. Claude Makelele passed a short free-kick to Super Frank Lampard. His ball found Damien Duff who tried to square it to Eidur Gudjohnsen, but the ball was placed just behind the Iceman. A minute later, John Terry headed into the net following a cross from Super Frank, but the Chelsea captain was ruled offside. Three minutes later, a last ditch tackle by Ricardo Carvalho earned the defender a booking as he felled Jenas outside the area. Petr Cech pulled off a stunning save from the resulting free-kick from Robert. In the 23rd minute, Cech was called into action again, saving a goal with his legs by diving at the feet of the on-coming Bellamy after Dyer had put the Welshman through. On the half-hour mark, Tiago was unlucky with a speculative shot that the Newcastle keeper Given made hard work of saving, but The Blues were still unable to break the deadlock. Minutes later Gudjohnsen had the chance to score, but placed his chip-cum-shot just wide after stealing the ball from the Newcastle defence. As half-time approached, Arjen Robben tried his luck, having two bites at the same cherry, but on both occasions his shots failed to hit the target. The second half began with Didi The Drog's Ollocks Drogba coming on to replace Gudjohnsen, but the stalemate remained. Just on the hour mark, another last ditch tackle from Carvalho gave Newcastle another chance to take the lead and Cech was again called upon to save from Robert's free-kick. In the 61st minute, William Gallas was replaced by Wayne Bridge and Tiago gave way for Mateja Kezman and, within two minutes, Chelsea had taken the lead. Super Frank Lampard finally made the breakthrough when he collected Drogba's cleverly chested pass after he received the ball from Makelele. The England midfielder took one touch before burying the ball past Given. Five minutes later, Drogba doubled the lead as he picked up Super Frank Lampard's ball and curled it into the Geordie net. Chelsea were now rampaging forward as Newcastle's defence began to crumble and Super Frank Lampard came close again with a long range effort. With a minute left, Duff put Robben through and November's Player Of The Month made no mistake after dancing his way through the defence before placing the ball into the goal. With injury time fast running out, Mateja Kezman took the chance to open his league account from the spot after Duff was brought down in the box. As the referee blew the final whistle, for the fifth time in seven games the Chelsea faithful cheered their side's victory, having scored four goals.

Arsenal. A.D.2-2. Terry, Gudjohnsen
Att: 38,153
Ref: G Poll. Date: 12.12.04
Chelsea: Cech, Ferreira, Carvalho (Bridge), Terry, Gallas Duff, Tiago (Drogba), Makelele, Lampard, Robben, Gudjohnsen (Parker). Non-playing subs: Cudicini, Kezman
Report: In a game that really mattered, Jose Mourinho had already won the psychological battle with his opposite number by claiming that it wouldn't make any difference to Chelsea's position at the top of the Premiership if indeed his side went on to lose. After two minutes, the Gooners looked like they might well maintain their hoodoo over Chelsea as they took the lead through Henry. He was left unmarked and made no mistake as he hit the ball past Petr Cech from the edge of the box. Chelsea, despite being on the back foot, pushed forward bravely in search of the equaliser and Super Frank Lampard forced a save from Almunia in the Gooners' goal with a fierce long-range shot. From the resulting corner, in the 17th minute, Chelsea drew level. John Terry rose to Damien Duff's corner to out jump everybody and place the ball in the back of the net. As the Chelsea supporters celebrated, a full-blooded London derby was being played out on the pitch. Arsenal almost replied straight away when Cole's cross just failed to find the boot of Henry. Moments later, Eidur Gudjohnsen unleashed a shot from 25 yards that knocked the Gooner keeper over as he attempted to block. Arjen Robben then tormented the Arsenal defence before setting up Tiago, but the Portuguese saw his shot go over the bar. In the 29th minute, Pires picked up the ball and ran between two Chelsea defenders. Although there appeared to be no contact, the Frenchman tumbled forward, earning his side a dubious free-kick some 20 yards from the Chelsea goal. While the wall was being organised, Henry took a quick free-kick before Chelsea were ready and after fending off heated protests from the Chelsea players, Poll allowed the goal to stand. Robben was booked as tempers frayed as no quarter was given by either side. At half-time, Wayne Bridge replaced Carvalho and Didi The Drog's Ollocks Drogba came on for Tiago. Within a minute of the restart, Chelsea were level. Super Frank Lampard's free-kick was headed on by William Gallas. As the ball came to Gudjohnsen he headed a looping effort that crept in on the far side of Almunia. Five minutes later Super Frank Lampard missed a great chance with a free header, his effort going high over the bar. The 67th minute saw The

Drog's Ollocks booked for tripping Pires as Arsenal threatened. Moments later, Robben danced past half of the Arsenal defence but his shot went just wide. Super Frank Lampard was the next Chelsea player to enter Poll's book after he tangled with Lauren. Scotty Parker made an appearance in the 77th minute, replacing Gudjohnsen as Chelsea looked to shore up midfield. Chelsea nearly took the lead when Terry headed goalward following a corner from Duff but the ball was headed over by Gallas directly in front of the Arsenal goal. Henry had the chance to settle the game as well as notch his third but he managed to hit the ball over an open goal after Cech had missed a cross sent in by Pires. The game ended 2-2 with Chelsea the more satisfied of the two sides as the point they earned maintained their five point lead at the top of the table. 'Top of the league, we're having a laugh.'

Norwich City. H.W.4-0. Duff, Lampard, Robben, Drogba

Att: 42,071

Ref: M Dean. Date: 18.12.04

Chelsea: Cech, Ferreira, Terry, Gallas, Bridge, Tiago (Parker), Makelele, Lampard, Robben (Kezman), Duff, Gudjohnsen (Drogba). Non-playing subs: Cudicini, Johnson

Report: For the first few minutes of this contest it looked as though the visitors would make a brave fight of things, but they were unlucky when an injury forced a seventh-minute change as the injured Svensson was replaced by McKenzie. After just ten minutes, and with Norwich still trying to reorganise, Damien Duff continued his amazing habit of scoring Chelsea's opening goal after picking a gift pass from Norwich's Helveg and smashing a low drive in past Green in the Canaries' goal. Chelsea should have been awarded a penalty in the 19th minute when the ball was clearly handled inside the area, but both the referee and linesman contrived to miss the incident. Although City were winning a fair amount of possession, they never really came close to troubling Petr Cech and, in the 34th minute, Chelsea doubled their lead. Another dreadful pass from a Norwich defender, this time Doherty, was seized upon by Arjen Robben. He played the ball on to Super Frank Lampard, who, after seeing two earlier attempts come close, made no mistake this time and smashed the ball home from 25 yards. Ten minutes later, Chelsea scored a goal that will surely rank among the best they notch this season. Robben picked up the ball on the right and played it to Super Frank Lampard. He took it on to the edge of the area before cutting it back to Tiago who was just inside the box. He then cleverly back-heeled the ball out to Robben who made no mistake, crashing the ball home from 18 yards. As the teams came out for the second half, many Chelsea supporters were expecting the floodgates to open but although Tiago and Super Frank Lampard came close, stout defending from Norwich served to keep The Blues at bay. On the hour mark, Gudjohnsen came off for Didi The Drog's Ollocks Drogba who saw his first chance blocked by the Norwich keeper. Both Robben and Super Frank Lampard then went close, and Tiago made way for Scotty Parker in the 76th minute. With Chelsea now in complete control and with 12 minutes left, Robben was given the chance of a rest and was replaced by Mateja Kezman. Super Frank Lampard then had another effort well saved by Green but despite Chelsea creating chances, the fourth goal still would not come. However, Didi The Drog's Ollocks changed all that in the 82nd minute. Claude Makelele had won a corner and from Duff's dead-ball kick The Drog's Ollocks jumped high to emphatically power his header low past the keeper and into the goal. Even though it looked like Chelsea had taken their foot off the accelerator to a certain degree in the second half, it was a stroll for The Blues and the result confirmed, for the Christmas period at least, that we would still be top of the Premiership.

Aston Villa. H.W.1-0. Duff
Att: 41,950
Ref: P Walton. Date: 26.12.04
Chelsea: Cech, Ferreira, Terry, Gallas, Bridge, Tiago, Makelele, Lampard, Duff (Smertin), Gudjohnsen (Drogba), Robben (Johnson). Non-playing subs: Cudicini, Kezman
Report: On a bitterly cold morning, Chelsea started well, with Arjen Robben prising open the Villa defence but his ball back to Damien Duff was just behind him and he couldn't adjust his body to pick it up. In the fifth minute, John Terry came close with a header that was just over the bar after a good ball was sent in from a free-kick taken by Super Frank Lampard. Petr Cech was then forced to make a save after Angel and Hendrie combined to carve out an opportunity. At the midway point of the first period Chelsea's passing game began to make headway with Claude Makelele and Super Frank Lampard dictating things in midfield. Duff and Robben again linked up and it took some desperate defending from Villa's Delaney to halt the attack. On the half-hour mark and just after Chelsea had kept out another effort from Hendrie, Robben created the opening that the home supporters had been waiting for. The Dutchman cut inside from the left and evaded a couple of tackles before laying the ball off to Duff. He then took the ball on his left before hitting home a low drive with his right foot past the keeper's near post. Five minutes later, Delaney was in the right place to prevent Chelsea scoring a second, clearing off the line after Super Frank Lampard's quick thinking and back-heel gave Robben the chance. With two minutes to go to half-time, Terry saw his header from a Robben corner go just past the post. Just as the referee was about to blow for the break, Robben earned himself a needless booking after he had blatantly tripped Villa's Ridgewell. From the resulting free-kick Cech was called upon to save after Whittingham's ball had been missed by everyone else. Chelsea had a good chance as soon as the second period began when Duff skipped around the defence to put in a ball that William Gallas headed wide. Eidur Gudjohnsen then had an opportunity to score but he was unable to get the ball out from under his own feet before it was cleared to safety by a Villa defender. Two minutes later, the Iceman was replaced by Didi The Drog's Ollocks Drogba and, two minutes after that, Tiago became the second Chelsea player to have his name taken. With 15 minutes remaining, Robben charged down the left wing but his eventual pass was too far in front of the Drog's Ollocks. Alexey Smertin came on in place of Duff with ten minutes remaining. Terry picked up a yellow card in the 86th minute for a strong challenge on Mellberg, a tackle which another referee might well have shown a red. With less than a minute of time remaining, Glen Johnson entered the fray, replacing Robben, but by then Chelsea had just done enough to seal victory. Although Chelsea didn't look as though they had played that well, it was Villa who had made things difficult. After Chelsea's first Boxing Day win for years, it was a pity that the Chelsea support didn't match the efforts of the players. Still, at least they had seen their side continue their domination of the League. Here's to 2005.

Portsmouth. A.W.2-0. Robben, Cole
Att: 20,210
Ref: A Wiley. Date: 28.12.04
Chelsea: Cech, Ferreira, Terry, Gallas, Johnson, Makelele, Lampard, Smertin (Cole), Robben (Geremi), Duff, Drogba (Gudjohnsen). Non-playing subs: Cudicini, Bridge
Report: Chelsea started this game tentatively, although Didi The Drog's Ollocks Drogba had an early chance, but his shot was well saved by Hislop in the Portsmouth goal. The home side, playing free-flowing attacking football, began to push Chelsea back and it was only stout defending from John Terry and William Gallas that ensured that the score remained 0-0. In the 20th minute, Petr Cech made another brilliant save, stretching to push a thunderous 30-yard shot from Portsmouth's Quashie over the bar. In midfield, Alexey Smertin and Frank Lampard weren't having things all their own way and there were periods when it looked like the Chelsea players were struggling to string more than two or three passes together. Up front, things were not much better, with the Chelsea attack being thwarted by a resolute and very well organised defence. As half-time came, many Chelsea supporters were looking at a 0-0 result. The second half began much as the first half had ended with some scrappy play and the home side looking the better of the two. On the hour mark, Damien Duff picked up a loose pass and headed for goal. He passed to Didi The Drog's Ollocks Drogba but he could only hit his shot straight at the Portsmouth keeper. Moments later, Eidur Gudjohnsen was sent on in his place. The first corner following his introduction saw Gudjohnsen attempt an overhead kick after Glen Johnson had headed on Arjen Robben's corner. Chelsea began to take command of the game and started to press forward. Robben made another run forward to supply Gudjohnsen but the Iceman's effort was well saved by Hislop. In the 73rd minute Smertin was replaced by Joe Cole and, as the Russian left the pitch, he was sportingly given a standing ovation from the home support for whom he used to perform when he first came to England. Chelsea, not playing the best of football, continued to press and again came close when Johnson made a good run to the goal line before cutting the ball back to Robben who saw his shot blocked. Paulo Ferreira was booked as Pompey's Fuller threatened the goal, the Portuguese defender cautioned for holding the player back. With 11 minutes to go, Chelsea finally made the breakthrough after Super Frank Lampard picked up the ball from Gudjohnsen. The England midfielder passed it on to Robben who shot from the right-hand side of the goal, the ball deflecting off a defender before hitting the back of the net. The Dutchman celebrated by removing his shirt and running from one end of the pitch to the other but, despite receiving a yellow card for the 'offence', there was no hiding the smile on Robben's face as his team-mates mobbed him. Minutes later, having picked up the caution, Robben was replaced by Geremi. Moments after this, one stupid booking was followed by another as Super Frank Lampard was shown a yellow for kicking the ball away while play had been stopped. As injury time at the end of the game was running out, Gudjohnsen made a good run around the back before pulling the ball back to Cole whose shot found the bottom left-hand corner of the goal to give Chelsea a two-goal win and all three points.

The Special Ones

Liverpool. A.W.1-0. Cole
Att: 43,886
Ref: M Riley. Date: 01.01.05
Chelsea: Cech, Ferreira, Terry, Gallas, Johnson, Tiago, Lampard, Makelele, Duff (Cole), Robben (Kezman), Gudjohnsen (Drogba). Non-playing subs: Cudicini, Geremi

Report: Chelsea travelled to Anfield where, in the past, success had only ever come in extremely small doses. This time however, with Chelsea riding high at the top of the table, it was the home side that were the underdogs. Liverpool came out fighting and looked determined to get a result. Early pressure from Liverpool's Riise tested Glen Johnson but the Chelsea youngster recovered and cleared the ball away. Petr Cech proved himself more than ready when he spread himself in front of a fierce effort from Traore. A minute later, it was Chelsea's turn to attack with Arjen Robben running on to Tiago's ball. After turning inside the defender and with just Dudek to beat, Chelsea's Dutch sensation could only manage to shoot the ball directly at the grateful Liverpool keeper. Chelsea could not take advantage of the resulting corner and it was Liverpool who broke away with the ball to leave The Blues dangerously exposed with only two in defence. Thankfully for Chelsea, Claude Makelele, tracking back, was able to do enough to ensure that the resulting Liverpool cross was impotent. In the 21st minute, Super Frank Lampard was booked for a foul on Alonso, a tackle that looked a lot worse than it actually was, but it meant that the Englishman would now face a one-match ban, having picked up a season's total of five cautions. Both Tiago and then Robben had long range efforts at the Liverpool goal but Chelsea's attacking play was being stifled by resolute and well-organised defending on the part of the home side. With the half-time break approaching, Liverpool stepped up a gear and began to put real pressure on the Chelsea goal. When Gerrard sent his free kick into the area, the ball bounced off Tiago's arm but the referee decided against pointing to the spot. Moments later, Paulo Ferreira cleared the ball away from Liverpool's Nunez before Cech acrobatically seemed to change direction in mid-air to keep the ball out. With only seconds of the half remaining, Carragher had a chance but hit his volley over the top of Cech's goal. Following the interval, Chelsea came out looking a little more determined than they had in the first half and began to string passes together and take the game to Liverpool. Robben took the ball forward and it took three Liverpool defenders to stop him. John Terry then set up a chance for Damien Duff to hit the ball in for Eidur Gudjohnsen but the Iceman couldn't quite connect with his diving header. While Liverpool were trying to move the ball up field quickly, Chelsea were content to try to slow things down and this tactic gradually appeared to frustrate the home side. On the hour mark, Didi The Drog's Ollocks Drogba replaced Gudjohnsen and his first touch on the ball resulted in an over-enthusiastic challenge from Gerrard. Although the Liverpool man then saw a shot go narrowly wide, his side were not making the inroads they had been making in the first half. In the 75th minute, Duff was rested and on came Joe Cole in his place. Almost immediately, the Liverpool goal came under pressure and their keeper Dudek was forced to come to the edge of his box to head the ball away from the path of The Drog's Ollocks after Lampard's ball in. With ten minutes left, Chelsea won a corner on the right-hand side. Swung in by Robben, Johnson rose to head the ball back from the far post into the path of Cole who made no mistake as he blasted it home from the edge of the box. Chelsea then replaced Robben with Mateja Kezman, the newcomer almost immediately setting up a chance for Lampard. Although they might have wilted, the home side came back at Chelsea, desperate to earn a point at least. Liverpool pressed forward. Johnson picked up a booking for a desperate challenge on Riise, the resulting free kick from Gerrard being hit over the bar. William Gallas then cleared away for the last time before the final whistle sounded and it was then that the celebrations began. Chelsea's Christmas and New Year period, a time that in previous seasons so often proved fruitless, had seen Jose Mourinho's side pick up maximum points.

Middlesbrough. H.W.2-0. Drogba 2

Att: 40,982

Ref: S Bennett. Date: 04.01.05

Chelsea: Cech, Ferreira, Terry, Gallas, Smertin (Johnson), Makelele, Lampard, Cole (Tiago), Duff, Robben, Drogba (Kezman). Non-playing subs: Cudicini, Gudjohnsen

Report: Chelsea started brightly against their opponents from Smogland, with Didi The Drog's Ollocks Drogba coming close with a header from an Arjen Robben cross as early as the fourth minute. After another incisive run from Damien Duff, his cross was nearly collected by Robben who, had he controlled it properly, would have been favourite to score. The Drog's Ollocks then had another go, Boro keeper Schwarzer saving with his legs. The breakthrough came in the 25th minute when The Drog's Ollocks received a ball from Lampard after the Englishman had linked up with Robben to provide an opening. Leaving Boro's Southgate standing, the Chelsea striker took the ball round the defender and make short work of slotting the ball home. Two minutes later, The Drog's Ollocks rose above everybody to head home from Lampard's free kick to double both his and Chelsea's total for the evening. Chelsea were rampant and nearly made it three when Schwarzer failed to hold a shot from Robben, but Duff just failed to convert the opportunity. In the 25th minute, Cole was booked for a rash challenge on Downing and then, some seven minutes later, Robben followed suit, picking up yet another caution as he felled Queudrue. Although Chelsea continued to dominate – a measure being the fact that Paulo Ferreira came close to scoring – the score remained 2-0 until half-time. Five minutes into the second half, Glen Johnson replaced Smertin before Cole, some six minutes later, drove his shot just wide of the target. Having messed up the resulting goal-kick by giving it straight to Duff, the Boro keeper was relieved when he watched the Irishman smash the ball against the bar. In the 62nd minute, Cole left the pitch to a standing ovation, taken off in favour of Tiago. While Chelsea were firmly in control, Middlesbrough worked hard in an effort to create chances. Cech was called into action when Downing's shot deflected off John Terry and caused the Chelsea goalkeeper to make a save with his legs. At the other end, Chelsea were looking for the killer third goal, but could not quite find it. With time running out, Chelsea thought they might have a chance to increase the lead when Duff was tripped as he made his way forward. The resulting free-kick from Robben was easily collected by the Boro keeper. With time running out, Chelsea supporters were given the chance of a flashback as Hasselbaink stepped up to blast a free-kick high over the goal and into the Matthew Harding End. As the rest of the evening's results filtered through, Chelsea supporters were soon celebrating the fact that, due to them dropping points against Manchester City, the Gooners – Chelsea's nearest league rivals – were now seven points behind.

Sp*rs. A.W.2-0. Lampard 2 (1 pen)

Att: 36,105

Ref: G Poll. Date: 15.01.05

Chelsea: Cech, Ferreira, Terry, Gallas, Johnson, Makelele, Lampard, Smertin (Jarosik), Robben, Duff (Cole), Drogba (Gudjohnsen). Non-playing subs: Cudicini, Bridge

Report: Chelsea went into this game on the back of a 29-game unbeaten run of league games against their bitterest enemy. Not only that, Chelsea captain John Terry would make his 200th appearance for The Blues. With confidence riding high, it was somewhat of a shock when Sp*rs had the first glimpse of goal after three minutes, but K*ane headed wide. Chelsea fought back and Damien Duff had a shot blocked. Fifteen minutes into the game, a long ball from Terry found Didi The Drog's Ollocks Drogba. With only the oncoming keeper to beat he lobbed the ball over the top, but could only watch on in vain as it bounced just clear of the far post. Sp*rs retaliated and Petr Cech made a great save, instinctively punching a 20-yard blast from D*foe clear of goal. Moments later, the Sp*rs forward looked like he was in again but a brilliant tackle by William Gallas stopped him in his tracks. In an end-to-end game, Glen Johnson was next up for Chelsea, taking the ball forward and laying off a great pass inside to Duff who turned and shot, but his effort was saved after a spectacular dive by R*binson. Chelsea were then denied a penalty when Arjen Robben was fouled in the box when chasing a long through ball from Terry. Three minutes later, Duff had his name taken for not withdrawing from a Sp*rs free kick quickly enough. Six minutes before half-time, Duff chased a long ball that appeared to be going out and managed to keep it in play and pass inside to Alexey Smertin who was running into the box. However, the Russian was brought down by C*rrick and the referee had no hesitation in pointing to the spot. Super Frank Lampard had no fear as he stepped up and made no mistake as he hit the ball home to give Chelsea the lead. Three minutes before the break, Johnson had his name taken but, as the whistle blew to signal the end of the half, it was the Chelsea players and supporters who were smiling. The home side came out for the second half eager to get back into the game, but although they huffed and puffed, the Chelsea defence and midfield remained resolute, while the long ball over the top to Didi The Drog's Ollocks Drogba was constantly stretching them at the back. However, Smertin was lucky when defending a rare home corner after he awkwardly sent the ball wide of Cech and just past his left hand post. At the other end, Robben was again denied a penalty when he was tripped inside the box when looking likely to score. With twenty minutes remaining, Smertin was withdrawn in favour of Jiri Jarosik and, six minutes later, Didi The Drog's Ollocks Drogba was replaced by Eidur Gudjohnsen. With Chelsea defending deep, Jose Mourinho made his final change with ten minutes to go, sending on Joe Cole in place of the work-weary Duff. With five minutes left, a disputed free-kick led to Terry receiving a booking for walking away with the ball, his actions also causing the dead ball to be moved ten yards closer to goal. As the wall lined up, Makelele was booked for tussling with a Sp*rs attacker. When the kick was eventually taken, it was well held by Cech. As the game moved into injury time, the Chelsea faithful were both nervous and excited. With seconds remaining, Gudjohnsen got around the back of the Sp*rs defence and took the ball along the goal line before cutting it back inside to Super Frank Lampard who made no mistake in smashing it home to give Chelsea a two-goal victory. 'You'll never beat the Chelsea.'

Portsmouth. H.W.3-0. Drogba 2, Robben

Att: 42,267

Ref; M Riley. Date: 22.01.05

Chelsea: Cech, Ferreira, Terry, Gallas, Bridge, Lampard, Makelele, Cole, Robben (Kezman), Drogba (Gudjohnsen), Duff (Tiago). Non-playing subs: Cudicini, Jarosik

Report: Although the visiting Pompey did well for the first few minutes or so, causing Chelsea two scares – one when Petr Cech missed a cross and the other when Super Frank Lampard lost the ball in Chelsea's half and Cech was called upon to save – once Jose Mourinho's side got into their rhythm there was only ever going to be one team in this contest. Arjen Robben and Damien Duff were causing major problems for Portsmouth and after 15 minutes it was Chelsea's Dutchman who created the breakthrough, engineering a dazzling run through the defence before putting the ball across to Didi The Drog's Ollocks Drogba who took the gift of a chance with glee. Six minutes later, it was Robben himself who found the net after another being put through by Super Frank Lampard. Although his first touch around the keeper looked as though it was going wide, Robben somehow managed to flick the ball in from the right to put Chelsea 2-0 up. With half an hour gone, another rare mistake from Super Frank Lampard left Terry short of the pass. Pompey's Yakubu beat Cech with a low shot but thankfully for Chelsea, the ball went just wide of the post. Eight minutes later, Robben won a free kick on the edge of the area. While Lampard and Duff stood ready, it was Didi The Drog's Ollocks Drogba who stepped up to hit a shot over the wall and below the crossbar to notch his second and give Chelsea a 3-0 lead. He was unlucky when, just before half-time, he was almost in for his hat-trick but was frustrated by a last-ditch tackle. The second period began with the home crowd expectant and the visitors desperate to keep the score down. Chelsea seemed content to play out the game by keeping the ball and creating clear-cut chances, and although Cech touched a shot over the bar, his main involvement for the remainder of the half was to collect and redistribute a backward pass or two. Duff and Robben combined to set up Didi The Drog's Ollocks Drogba, but he miss-hit his effort and when the ball came to Joe Cole he was unable to react with a firm enough shot. After being denied a claim for a penalty, Didi The Drog's Ollocks Drogba was replaced in the 65th minute by Eidur Gudjohnsen, with Tiago coming on for Duff in the 67th. With 15 minutes left, Robben departed to a hero's reception with Mateja Kezman given his chance. Although the Serbian striker came close with one effort and had a speculative shot saved, he again failed to hit the target. Nevertheless, the 3-0 score meant that Chelsea had now won seven consecutive Premiership games, each with a clean sheet.

Blackburn. A.W.1-0. Robben

Att: 23,414

Ref: U Rennie. Date: 02.02.05

Chelsea: Cech, Ferreira, Terry, Gallas, Bridge, Tiago, Makelele, Lampard, Duff, Gudjohnsen (Kezman), Robben (Cole (Jarosik)). Non-playing subs: Cudicini, Johnson

Report: Chelsea went into this game with the chance of going 11 points clear at the top of the league. They started the match looking like they really meant business and, after just five minutes, took the lead. Super Frank Lampard hit a long ball up to Eidur Gudjohnsen. His headed pass found Arjen Robben who took the ball around the defender and shot past Friedel in the Rovers goal. However, from the start it was clear that the home side were going out of their way to be physical and after just 11 minutes Chelsea suffered the consequences. Following another particularly heavy challenge for which the referee gave no foul, it was clear that Robben was badly injured. Although he tried to run the injury off, he was unable to continue and Jose Mourinho was forced to make a change early on. Joe Cole was sent on in place of the injured Dutchman who later learned his foot was broken in two places. Petr Cech had already beaten Peter Schmeichel's record of minutes gone in Premiership matches without conceding a goal and he looked determined to extend the feat with a couple of great saves that helped keep Chelsea ahead. Although The Blues were still marginally on top, the injury to Robben and the consequent shuffling of the team left Chelsea looking a little unsettled and, unusually for this season, somewhat under pressure. On the half-hour mark, Blackburn were awarded a penalty for what seemed like an innocuous challenge from Paulo Ferreira on Savage, the Welshman going down in the box, but the resulting kick from Dickov was expertly saved by Cech. However, the Rovers player followed up in an effort to get any rebound and injured Cech in the process. The Blackburn players were by now becoming reckless with every challenge and when Cole was hacked down, Rovers' Matteo was finally shown a yellow card. Moments later, Dickov again went in late on Cech and this caused several Chelsea players to spring to their goalkeeper's defence. The second half continued with more late and rash challenges and, although this current side is one that likes to play football, they proved against Blackburn that they will not be easily intimidated with John Terry and Super Frank Lampard being required to stand up for themselves and their team-mates. In the 57th minute, Terry found himself in trouble with the referee and had his name taken for responding to a Dickov challenge. Moments later, Duff was hacked down from behind, but again there was no sign of a card for the Rovers man. In the 78th minute, Cole was replaced by Jiri Jarosik and minute later Mateja Kezman got a chance, coming on for the very hard-working Gudjohnsen. Cech was again called upon to make an important save from a free-kick and, seconds before the final whistle, Kezman made his only contribution by having his name taken. A tough, hard match, but Chelsea proved that they can 'take it' when required as they maintain their lead at the top of the table.

Manchester City. H.D.0-0.
Att: 42,093
Ref: H Webb. Date: 06.02.05
Chelsea: Cech, Ferreira, Gallas, Terry, Bridge, Jarosik (Tiago), Lampard, Makelele, Duff, Gudjohnsen, Kezman (Cole). Non-playing subs: Cudicini, Johnson, Smertin
Report: Chelsea entertained Manchester City, the only team so far this season to have beaten The Blues in the Premiership, without the help of Arjen Robben who had broken two bones in his foot during the previous game at Blackburn. Chelsea started well but were up against a side that were playing 11 men behind the ball in an effort to gain a point at least from their trip to London. Mateja Kezman had the first opportunity early on as he ran to receive a ball on the edge of the City area but, after collecting it, he was easily brushed aside. With 23 minutes gone, Damien Duff was the first player on the pitch to have a shot at goal but his effort went high and wide. City came back at Chelsea almost straight away when the dangerous Wright-Phillips ran through The Blues defence but John Terry (Mr Dependable) was on hand to shepherd the ball clear. Just after the half-hour mark, Jiri Jarosik fed the ball through to Eidur

Gudjohnsen. He in turn passed it to Duff on the right who came inside and shot. His effort was half-saved by City keeper James, but when the ball came out to Kezman the Chelsea striker could only send the rebound wide. A minute later, and following a Chelsea corner, another chance to take the lead went begging as Jarosik rose above everybody and sent his header over the bar with the aid of a fist from James. Inspired by this spell of pressure, Chelsea seemed to step up a gear and Kezman again went close after being sent clear by Gudjohnsen, but the City keeper was in the way again. Moments later, Super Frank Lampard saw an effort saved by the busy James. While the front men were having no luck, William Gallas went forward in an effort to break the deadlock, his header from a corner cleared off the line by City defender Bosvelt. Chelsea were lucky when, in a rare attack by the visitors, Fowler missed a clear-cut chance, sending his header wide. Just before the break, Claude Makelele had his name taken for a needless trip on Fowler. Following the restart Kezman had another opportunity, James there again to act as the spoiler. Duff was then put through by Kezman, but he too was denied by James who pushed the ball away, just in front of the rapidly approaching Gudjohnsen. City then had two chances, the shots by Bosvelt and Wright-Phillips causing no danger to Petr Cech, both efforts going wide. In the 55th minute Tiago came on to replace Jarosik and seven minutes later Joe Cole was brought into the fray with Kezman making way. Gudjohnsen picked up a silly booking, kicking the ball away in frustration as the referee awarded City a free-kick. With time fast running out, Duff attempted to run through the defence himself and was only stopped when he was brought down on the edge of the box. Super Frank Lampard's free kick was stopped by the legs of James. With less than a minute to go Gudjohnsen thought he had won the game for Chelsea, but the ball was deflected over the bar. As the game went into stoppage time, John Terry headed a free-kick on to Super Frank Lampard, but James was there again to deny Chelsea the win and earn his side a valuable point.

Everton. A.W.1-0. Gudjohnsen
Att: 40,270
Ref: M Riley. Date: 12.02.05
Chelsea: Cech, Ferreira, Gallas, Terry, Bridge, Cole (Jarosik), Tiago (Carvalho), Lampard, Makelele, Duff (Johnson), Gudjohnsen. Non-playing subs: Cudicini, Smertin
Report: Chelsea arrived at Goodison with all the talk within the media speculating that their lead at the top of the Premiership would be reduced. However, after just eight minutes it was Everton who were on the back foot following a blatant and dangerous assault by Beattie on William Gallas. Chasing the long ball over the top, Gallas managed to get in front of Beattie and looked as though he was trying to see it out for a goal-kick. Beattie, in close pursuit, had other ideas and head-butted Chelsea's French defender on the back of his head not once, but twice, prompting referee Riley to produce an instant red card. The home support was less than happy and subsequently, for the remainder of the game, every time the ball went to Gallas, he was loudly booed. Following a lengthy delay while Gallas received treatment, Chelsea took the game to Everton, with Eidur Gudjohnsen putting in a low cross that both Damien Duff and Joe Cole just failed to meet. Following a Chelsea corner, the ten-man home side began to take the game to Chelsea and despite Everton being a man down, the game was evenly matched. Chelsea responded with Damien Duff going

close twice in quick succession, his efforts just clearing the crossbar. Tiago was next to have a go, his chip-cum-shot also just too high. Duff then put a ball across for Gudjohnsen, but his attempt at goal was saved by the legs of Martyn and went out for another corner. Either side of the half-hour mark, both Super Frank Lampard and Tiago went close with long-range shots, and the stalemate remained. Cole was sent flying by a rash challenge on the edge of the Everton box, the referee simply waving play on, but moments later they earned a free-kick when Everton's Cahill blocked a cross with his hand. Super Frank Lampard's shot was deflected away from its original path but the Everton keeper somehow managed to get across to it to keep the ball out. Following half-time, Chelsea went straight into attacking mode and three minutes in Gudjohnsen again came close, following a mazy run and cross in from Duff. Paulo Ferreira made a good run forward, cutting in and shooting across the face of the goal, the ball only just evading the far post. The 55th minute saw Duff combine with Super Frank Lampard, the England midfielder's effort causing the Everton keeper to make a fine save. By this time Chelsea were dominating the game and Cole went close again, hitting his shot just over the bar. Despite their pressure Chelsea didn't hit the net until the 69th minute. Ferreira's cross was met by Gallas who hit the ball on to the bar and Gudjohnsen was in the right place to knock home the rebound – it was nothing less than The Blues deserved. Following the goal, Jiri Jarosik was sent on in place of the hard-working Cole as Chelsea looked to consolidate their lead. In the 80th minute, with Chelsea defending, they conceded a free-kick. Not happy with the decision, John Terry threw the ball away and was booked for dissent. From the free-kick the home side created their best chance of the game so far, but Petr Cech was in the right place to hold a header from Carsley. With seconds of normal time remaining, Jarosik picked up a yellow card for arguing with the referee after he had awarded Everton a free-kick. In stoppage time, Jose Mourinho sent on Glen Johnson in place of Duff and Tiago was substituted by Ricardo Carvalho, who was making his comeback after sustaining a broken toe. As the final whistle went, both the Chelsea players and supporters celebrated a tenth consecutive Premiership clean sheet and an (albeit temporary) 12-point lead at the top of the table.

Norwich. A.W.3-1. Cole, Kezman, Carvalho

Att: 24,506

Ref: M Halsey. Date: 05.03.05

Chelsea: Cech, Johnson, Carvalho, Terry, Ferreira, Makelele, Lampard, Tiago (Gudjohnsen), Cole, Drogba (Kezman), Duff (Jarosik). Non-playing subs; Cudicini, Huth

Report: The home side had the first chance in this 5.15pm kick-off, winning an early corner, and moments later former Chelsea player Graham Stuart coasted past the defence to provide a dangerous ball into the area which, fortunately for Chelsea, Glen Johnson was there to clear. The eighth minute saw Super Frank Lampard send Damien Duff through and his chip over the advancing keeper was cleared away to safety by a Norwich defender. In the 22nd minute Joe Cole picked up a ball from Claude Makelele and turned towards the Norwich goal. Beating one defender and battling his way through a crunching tackle, Cole then reached the edge of the area before unleashing a wicked curling shot that flew into the net to give Chelsea the lead. For a time after the goal the referee began to lose control of the game and tempers flared. John Terry was injured as he attempted to head the ball away and was down receiving treatment for several minutes. Cole then pick up a booking some six minutes before the break for a tackle from behind on Huckerby. For a brief spell, the home side seemed to have got the better of things, but Chelsea recovered their composure and for the remainder of the half played football befitting a side at the top of the table. Although the second half began with Chelsea looking like they were in control, it appeared that they were content with the one-goal lead. In the 58th minute Makelele picked up a booking for tripping an opponent yet, minutes later, when Didi The Drog's Ollocks Drogba was fouled, the Norwich player walked away with just a telling off. In the 64th minute, the 'unthinkable' happened and, after ten previous Premiership games with a clean sheet, Petr Cech and Chelsea finally conceded a league goal when McKenzie headed into the net. In the 68th minute, Jose Mourinho changed things around, sending Mateja Kezman and Eidur Gudjohnsen on in place of Didi The Drog's Ollocks Drogba and Tiago. In the 71st minute, the substitution seemed to have proved worthwhile when Gudjohnsen pushed the ball forward to Super Frank Lampard who, in turn, passed sideways to Kezman who slotted home from two yards out. Following the goal, Duff was withdrawn in favour of Jiri Jarosik as Chelsea looked to consolidate their lead. Chelsea's third came after a corner following a sustained period of attack. Rising high above a static Norwich defence, Ricardo Carvalho headed home from Super Frank Lampard's corner to notch his first goal for the Blues. Eight points clear at the top of the league!

West Bromwich Albion. H.W.1-0. Drogba
Att: 41,713
Ref: N Barry. Date: 15.03.05
Chelsea: Cech, Ferreira, Terry, Huth, Gallas, Cole (Kezman), Makelele, Lampard, Duff (Smertin), Gudjohnsen (Jarosik), Drogba. Non-playing subs: Cudicini, Carvalho
Report: Following their win against Barcelona, it was back to domestic action for Chelsea and it was against a bottom-three side in the shape of West Brom. It was the perfect opportunity to extend the lead at the top of the Premiership to 11 points. After just one minute of the game, John Terry came close to opening the scoring but his header was taken away from the goal by team-mate Eidur Gudjohnsen. Minutes later Didi The Drog's Ollocks Drogba was fouled in the penalty box, but the referee denied the claim and play continued. Despite their lowly position, West Brom were intent on playing both attractive and attacking football and were taking the game to Chelsea. Despite their tactics, The Baggies conceded four corners in the first 20 minutes of the game and when they were defending their goal they had 11 men behind the ball. Meanwhile, at the other end, Didi The Drog's Ollocks Drogba frustrated the Chelsea support by missing two very good chances. Joe Cole provided him with the first, soon followed by Damien Duff, but he didn't seem to have his scoring boots on. However, he made amends in the 25th minute when he finally broke the deadlock. Super Frank Lampard slipped a ball down the flank to Duff who turned inside and pushed the ball across the box. Didi The Drog's Ollocks Drogba this time made no mistake, side-footing home from close range. Minutes later, the visitors had the chance to equalise but Campbell headed well wide, much to the relief of Robert Huth, whose mistake had left him clear. In the 31st minute Cole sent Didi The Drog's Ollocks Drogba through but, after taking the ball around the keeper, his touch let him down and he could only put the ball wide. The second half began with West Brom's Gera causing

229

Petr Cech to keep a careful eye on a ball that he sent just went wide of his post. While Chelsea had the chances in the first half to finish off the game, the second half saw them struggle to create any at all. Super Frank Lampard hit a shot just over the bar before Didi The Drog's Ollocks Drogba missed another great chance, putting the ball wide of both goal and keeper, after Claude Makelele and Super Frank Lampard combined well to give him an opening. With 20 minutes left, he had yet another clear opportunity but he got too much on his header and sent the ball wide from the edge of the six-yard box. Jiri Jarosik was sent on in place of Gudjohnsen in the 74th minute as Jose Mourinho sought to stiffen up the midfield in the face of ever-increasing breaks by The Baggies. In the 80th minute, Didi The Drog's Ollocks Drogba blasted over the top of the West Brom goal from close range to complete a miserable evening. With just four minutes remaining Mateja Kezman got his chance, going on in place of Cole while Alexey Smertin came on in place of Duff in the 90th minute. Although all three points were in the bag and Chelsea were once again 11 points clear at the top, it was a night when their goal difference should have been dramatically improved.

Crystal Palace. H.W.4-1. Lampard, Cole, Kezman 2
Att: 41,667
Ref: P Dowd. Date: 19.03.05
Chelsea: Cech, Ferreira, Terry, Carvalho, Johnson, Cole, Makelele, Lampard, Duff (Robben), Gudjohnsen (Kezman), Drogba (Tiago). Non-playing subs: Cudicini, Huth
Report: Following the game against West Brom, Chelsea again faced lowly opposition, this time in the shape of London neighbours Crystal Palace. Joe Cole was the first to test the resolve of the Palace defence, their keeper Kiraly dealing with his shot easily. At the other end, Petr Cech's goal came under threat from Riihilahti but his effort went wide. For the first twenty minutes or so, Chelsea, although looking confident, seemed to be struggling to make the final ball through count, just as they had done in their previous game. In the 20th minute however, Cole fed the ball through to Damien Duff who cut in and fired one at goal, and it was only the legs of the Palace keeper that saved the day. Chelsea finally took the lead in the 29th minute after a quality move. Taking the ball down the left flank, Paulo Ferreira found Cole. Turning on the ball, he held it up for a moment before laying it off for Super Frank Lampard who made no mistake with his well-struck shot that flew in from at least 25 yards. This was more like what the crowd wanted to see and when Didi The Drog's Ollocks Drogba was put through by Glen Johnson, many thought that the score would double but, although he did well to hold off the challenge, he could only direct his shot into the side of the net. Following this chance, Super Frank Lampard had a header and a shot go just wide of the target. As half-time approached, Palace won a corner. The ball came in from the right, Super Frank Lampard swung at it but totally mishit his clearance and, as the ball flew across the face of the Chelsea goal, Palace's Riihilahti fired home to level the score. Despite the best efforts of both The Drog's Ollocks and Ricardo Carvalho for Chelsea, and Johnson for Palace, all missed good chances and the teams went in at half-time with the score 1-1. Jose Mourinho made no changes during the break, but he certainly fired his side up as Chelsea looked sharper and hungrier than they had done in the first period. In the 54th minute, Chelsea regained the lead when Eidur Gudjohnsen, now in midfield, fed a quality ball to Cole, who made no mistake, slotting home from close range. Tiago made an entrance, replacing Didi The Drog's

Ollocks Drogba in the 63rd minute. In the 74th minute and to cheers of delight from the crowd, Arjen Robben made yet another comeback from injury, coming on in place of Duff and, three minutes later, Mateja Kezman made another substitute appearance, this time in place of Gudjohnsen. Within a minute of making his appearance, Kezman scored. Hitting a hopeful shot from the edge of the area, the ball squirmed through the arms and legs of the unfortunate Palace keeper to give Chelsea a two-goal advantage. Robben, Tiago and Kezman all came close, but in the final minute of added on time, Kezman made it 4-1, seizing on a rebound after Super Frank Lampard and Tiago both had efforts blocked. The win sent Chelsea 14 points clear at the top of the table.

Southampton. A.W.3-1. Lampard, Gudjohnsen 2

Att: 31,949

Ref: M Halsey. Date: 02.04.05

Chelsea: Cech, Johnson, Terry, Huth, Gallas, Cole (Tiago), Makelele, Lampard, Duff (Jarosik), Gudjohnsen, Kezman (Drogba). Non-playing subs: Cudicini, Carvalho

Report: Chelsea travelled to the South Coast to take on a Southampton side near the foot of the table and desperate for the points. Although the home team started brightly, winning a free-kick in a dangerous position and then a corner, Chelsea soon settled and began to play possession football. In the 22nd minute, Mateja Kezman was brought down some 25 yards from the Saints' goal. Super Frank Lampard stepped up to take the kick and blasted a trademark dead ball effort towards the goal. Unfortunately for Southampton, it hit the edge of their defensive wall and deflected into the goal to give Chelsea a 1-0 lead. Eleven minutes later, Saints' keeper Niemi did well to prevent an extraordinary own goal from a back pass. From the following corner, he was again called upon, this time saving well from a firm header by Robert Huth. In the 38th minute, Eidur Gudjohnsen scored with the simplest of touches, following a great run from Glen Johnson. Half-time saw Jose Mourinho replace Joe Cole with Tiago who slotted into midfield allowing Gudjohnsen to play up front. Although Chelsea were continuing to frustrate Southampton, the home side often looked dangerous on the break and the Chelsea defenders had to remain alert. Kezman was booked for a foul in the 61st minute and some three minutes later he repeated the feat. Moments after this, he was replaced by Didi The Drog's Ollocks Drogba. Southampton pulled one back in the 69th minute when Phillips touched the ball home following a low cross which the Chelsea defenders failed to clear. With Southampton looking like they might equalise, Jiri Jarosik replaced Damien Duff in order to bolster the midfield. Following the substitution, Gudjohnsen made a great run forward, but instead of passing to Didi The Drog's Ollocks Drogba, the Iceman shot direct at the keeper who saved well. Moments later, after good link-up play between Claude Makelele and Jarosik, Gudjohnsen received the ball and played a one-two off Didi The Drog's Ollocks Drogba before drawing the Saints' keeper off his line and pushing the ball past him into the net to score his second and Chelsea's third. With a minute remaining, Tiago had his name taken for a foul on the Southampton manager's son Jamie Redknapp. While the football was noteworthy, this game will be remembered by those who travelled for the incredible scenes at half-time when, in the concourse, there was a full-on, non-stop 15-minute rendition of Hello, Hello, We Are The Chelsea Boys.

Birmingham. H.D.1-1. Drogba
Att: 42,031
Ref: C Foy. Date: 09.04.05
Chelsea: Cech, Johnson (Jarosik), Huth, Terry, Gallas, Lampard, Smertin (Gudjohnsen), Cole, Duff, Tiago, Kezman (Drogba). Non-playing subs: Cudicini, Carvalho
Report: Although the Premiership had still to be won, Chelsea started the game as though it was a pre-season friendly. While they looked like they were in control, there was a distinct lack of urgency about their play. It might have been due to the fact that Claude Makelele was rested, thereby missing his first Premiership game since October. In the 20th minute Joe Cole was brought down on the way to goal, earning Chelsea a free-kick. Super Frank Lampard took it upon himself to have a shot, but his effort went straight to Birmingham keeper Taylor. Twelve minutes later, Cole was centre-stage again when he picked up the ball some 25 yards out, turned and sent a shot towards goal that beat the keeper but bounced agonisingly past the wrong side of the far post. Ex-Chelsea favourite and now Birmingham City star Mario Melchiot was having a great game, but uncharacteristically lost the ball to Tiago who crossed for Super Frank Lampard and, although the England midfielder stretched to reach the ball, he couldn't quite get to it and the chance was lost. Jose Mourinho changed things at half-time with Alexey Smertin and Mateja Kezman making way for Eidur Gudjohnsen and Didi The Drog's Ollocks Drogba respectively. The 47th minute saw Chelsea come close when they won a corner. As the ball was sent across, John Terry headed it on and Gudjohnsen attempted to flick it into the goal, but the ball went harmlessly over the bar and ended up on the roof of the net. The visitors nearly took the lead in the 49th minute when City's Carter volleyed the ball towards the Chelsea goal. Petr Cech could only manage to parry it and, as the ball came back out to Birmingham's Pandiani, it took an excellent last-ditch tackle from John Terry to prevent a goal. Six minutes later, at the other end, Gudjohnsen linked up with Damien Duff who put in a cross which Didi The Drog's Ollocks Drogba managed to get his head to, but his effort was too high. A minute later, Duff had an effort blocked and, as the ball came out, Super Frank Lampard's effort went wide of the target. In the 65th minute, Cole was booked for allegedly kicking the ball away after a free-kick was conceded. Pennant, taking the kick, floated the ball in and it appeared that Cech thought it was going to safety and let it go over his head. Unbeknown to him, City's Upson had got behind him and headed the ball back across the goal and Pandiani shot home via a deflection off Terry and the crossbar. Chelsea were now a goal down, seemingly in trouble, and in danger of losing their unbeaten home run. The frustration began to show as, straight from the restart, Chelsea lost the ball and Tiago was booked for an over-zealous tackle when attempting to win it back. Although they immediately stepped up their game, it looked as though they had left things too late and were never going to score. Cole was brought down while making a run towards goal but, when Didi The Drog's Ollocks Drogba took the ball, City keeper Taylor dealt with it easily. In the 69th minute, Jiri Jarosik was sent on in place of Glen Johnson in order to give height and strength to both the midfield and attack. With 15 minutes left, a Robert Huth free-kick from 30 yards was palmed over the bar as Chelsea grew desperate. With just eight minutes remaining, Terry went forward after winning the ball in midfield. He found Super Frank Lampard and, instead of shooting himself, he fed the ball to Didi The Drog's Ollocks Drogba in front of goal who made no mistake, slotting home past Taylor. In the remaining few minutes Birmingham survived a mini

onslaught with Gudjohnsen going close and a Didi The Drog's Ollocks Drogba claim for a penalty after he was brought down in the box. At the other end, a tackle from Terry denied Birmingham a last chance to grab a winner. There was clear relief from the home support when the referee finally blew the whistle for time. The draw means that Chelsea cannot now win the title against Fulham.

Arsenal. H.D.0-0.
Att: 41,621
Ref: S Bennett. Date: 20.04.05
Chelsea: Cech, Johnson, Terry, Carvalho, Gallas, Cole (Tiago), Lampard, Makelele, Duff (Kezman), Gudjohnsen (Jarosik), Drogba. Non-playing subs: Cudicini, Huth
Report: This was a game where Chelsea could really put one over their now arch-rivals the Goons by winning and pulling a further three points clear at the top of the table. Despite the incentive, Chelsea started somewhat tentatively and the visitors were, for the opening exchanges at least, playing the better football. Within the first three minutes, Pires strode forward to volley a shot against the bar. In the eighth minute, Super Frank Lampard made Lehmann stretch after he shot from the edge of the box. Almost immediately, but at the other end, John Terry blocked a shot from Bergkamp and Chelsea were somewhat lucky when the follow-up effort from Pires went wide. Although goalmouth action was quite rare, the battle in midfield was intriguing with Claude Makelele performing heroics for the Blues. Eidur Gudjohnsen came close with a header before Cech was again tested at the other end by yet another effort from Pires. On the half-hour mark, Makelele put Damien Duff through and he, in turn, sent it on to Didi The Drog's Ollocks Drogba on the right who shot and forced a good save from the Gooner keeper. Minutes later, he turned provider as his ball across the face of the goal was just missed by Cole and, when Gudjohnsen picked it up and sent it towards the goal, Pires was on the line to clear. With time running out in the first period, Didi The Drog's Ollocks Drogba gave Cole another chance but the Englishman could only put his shot over the bar. The second half began with Chelsea pressing and, as the tempo increased, Cole picked up a 52nd minute booking. Three minutes later Duff sent in a low cross, but Didi The Drog's Ollocks Drogba put his shot the wrong side of the post. With an hour gone, William Gallas crossed for Didi The Drog's Ollocks Drogba, and instead of shooting he dummied and let the ball run to Super Frank Lampard, but like all the previous Blues' efforts, he too put his shot wide of the target. After having a great game, Cole was taken off in favour of Tiago. Seven minutes later, Mateja Kezman replaced Duff and, in the last minute of normal time, Gudjohnsen came off in favour of Jiri Jarosik. In time added on, Chelsea were awarded a free-kick and the Chelsea faithful were hoping for a last-gasp winner but, instead of putting the ball across, Didi The Drog's Ollocks Drogba elected to go for glory and sent his effort over the bar. Not quite the result everyone had been hoping for, but it was another point closer to the Premiership title and Chelsea's unbeaten home record remained intact.

Fulham. H.W.3-1. Cole, Lampard, Gudjohnsen

Att: 42,081

Ref: A Wiley. Date: 23.04.05

Chelsea: Cech, Johnson, Carvalho, Terry, Huth (Jarosik), Makelele, Lampard, Cole (Robben), Duff, Drogba (Tiago), Gudjohnsen. Non-playing subs: Cudicini, Kezman

Report: While many Chelsea supporters were hoping that this would be the game in which Chelsea would clinch the Premiership title, following the midweek draw against the Goons it was still mathematically possible for the Blues to throw it away. Chelsea's first real opening came in the seventh minute when Damien Duff put the ball across to Didi The Drog's Ollocks Drogba, but the striker's header looped up and over the crossbar. With Duff and Eidur Gudjohnsen pushing up, it was only going to be a matter of time before Chelsea would take the lead. The goal came in the 17th minute when Didi The Drog's Ollocks Drogba stole the ball from Fulham's Volz on the edge of their penalty area and passed the ball to Joe Cole who picked it up with his back towards the goal. However, the young England star turned, pushed the ball past the oncoming defender and curled it beyond Fulham keeper Van der Sar and into the net. Within two minutes, Chelsea had a chance to double the lead when Duff again provided Didi The Drog's Ollocks Drogba with a chance, but although he turned well he could only place his shot the wrong side of the post. The same player then looked as though he might have won a free-kick after he was crudely tackled after Super Frank Lampard put him through, but the referee simply waved play on, while at the other end Fulham's McBride shot over the bar when Boa Morte put him in on goal. In the 40th minute, Didi The Drog's Ollocks Drogba sent a ball on to Duff, the Fulham keeper quickly coming off his line and denying the Chelsea winger his chance and collecting the ball safely. Retaining possession, the Cottagers went straight up the other end and, as Ricardo Carvalho failed to intercept a ball from Boa Morte, Collins John beat Petr Cech in a one-on-one. Moments later and buoyed on by the equaliser, the visitors nearly took the lead through Collins John after he had been put through on goal by Radzinski, but luckily for Chelsea his shot was well wide. While Chelsea momentarily looked at sixes and sevens, John Terry picked up a yellow card for a tackle on Volz and, as the half-time whistle blew, both the Chelsea side and the supporters breathed a collective sigh of relief. During the break, Jiri Jarosik came on in place of Robert Huth, while Arjen Robben made a welcome return from injury, replacing Chelsea's scorer Cole. With their first attack, Chelsea put the ball in the Fulham net through Eidur Gudjohnsen, but the referee disallowed the goal on the strength of the linesman's offside flag. Chelsea regained the advantage in the 63rd minute when Duff and Robben linked up on the left and the Dutchman put a ball through the defender's legs to set up Super Frank Lampard who made no mistake, hitting the ball into the Fulham net from 12 yards out, and notching Chelsea's 100th goal of the season. The 71st minute saw Didi The Drog's Ollocks Drogba withdrawn in favour of Tiago as Chelsea changed their shape yet again. In the 81st minute, Cech was called upon to tip the ball over the bar as Fulham searched for an equaliser, the shot coming in from Radzinski. However, with four minutes of normal time remaining Chelsea secured all three points, when Tiago picked up a loose ball and left the Fulham defence standing as he hit it through the middle to Gudjohnsen, who made no mistake, scoring his 15th of the season and Chelsea's third of the day. In the last minute Cech again showed why he is the best stopper in the Premiership, brilliantly turning away a deflected free-kick from Fulham's scorer. Not quite there yet, but a win the following week at Bolton would see Chelsea crowned Champions.

Bolton. A.W.2-0. Lampard 2
Att: 27,653
Ref: S Dunn. Date: 30.04.05
Chelsea: Cech, Terry, Carvalho, Gallas, Geremi, Tiago, Makelele (Smertin), Lampard, Jarosik, Gudjohnsen (Cole), Drogba (Huth). Non-playing subs: Cudicini, Kezman
Report: With a travelling support of over 4,000 and almost the entirety of the remaining West London population glued to television screens, Chelsea went to Bolton seeking their second Championship and first for 50 years. After a bright opening minute when Super Frank Lampard fired the opening shot of the game, record-breaking Blues keeper Petr Cech was forced into a couple of saves from Stelios and Speed. Claude Makelele received a booking in the fifth minute for jumping up in front of a Bolton throw-in, while John Terry was called into action to deny Diouf after he had broken past Ricardo Carvalho. With Bolton preferring a rather more physical approach, John Terry required medical attention as he collided with Davies. As the half-time whistle sounded Chelsea looked ready for the break and the home side left the field looking the stronger of the two teams. However, the second half was a totally different affair. Chelsea steamed into the attack from the start and began to peg Bolton back in their own half. In the 55th minute, Tiago volleyed just over as the game began to come to life. Five minutes later, Super Frank Lampard managed to control a flick-on from Didi Drogba and, turning into the box and inside the defender, the Englishman steered the ball home to give Chelsea the lead. Three minutes later, Carvalho missed a golden chance to score following a Super Frank Lampard free-kick into the box. Didi Drogba, after becoming involved with several Bolton players over the course of the second half, was taken off in the 65th minute, with Robert Huth coming on in his place. In the 68th minute, Cech was injured after colliding with a post following a miraculous save from a header by Davies. Fortunately, he recovered after receiving treatment. Geremi was fortunate that a misplaced header didn't give Bolton a goal and Davies saw a shot go just wide. With fourteen minutes left the ball came to Makelele on the right and just inside the Chelsea half. Turning, he swept it forward into the middle to Super Frank Lampard who was running on to it from Chelsea's half. With only Jaaskelainen in the Bolton goal to beat and with Carvalho supporting down the middle, Super Frank Lampard ran the ball around the outside of the outstretched keeper's arms and into the goal to score both his and Chelsea's second. With five minutes remaining Joe Cole came on in place of the gallant Eidur Gudjohnsen and was unlucky not to score. The dying moments saw Alexey Smertin replace Makelele and, as the clock ran down and the realisation that the title was Chelsea's sunk in, the celebrations began in earnest. Fifty years after their first League Championship and in their Centenary year, Chelsea were English League Champions.

Charlton Athletic. H.W.1-0. Makelele
Att: 42,065
Ref: M Riley. Date: 07.05.05
Chelsea: Cudicini (Pidgeley), Johnson (Jarosik), Terry, Carvalho, Gallas, Cole, Makelele, Lampard, Tiago (Forssell), Geremi, Gudjohnsen. Non-playing subs: Huth, Kezman
Report: Chelsea's celebratory game began with the air of a testimonial match with neither side looking committed to the tackle or even making any serious attempts to

go forward. The hangover from the mid-week Champions League defeat was still clouding the memories of many in the crowd and the rest seemed as though they were just waiting for the presentation of the Premiership trophy. In the fifth minute, a Super Frank Lampard corner was sent towards goal by Ricardo Carvalho but it was knocked away by a Charlton defender. Charlton then went on the attack and John Terry was well placed to clear the ball away after Carlo Cudicini, making his first league start of the season, had been beaten by Hughes. In the 24th minute, William Gallas beat his man and set Super Frank Lampard up with an excellent ball, but the Chelsea midfielder could only head the ball over the top of the bar. Charlton threatened again, with Fortune blazing a volley over the bar. A dull first half was lightened up by a piece of magic from Joey Cole, who struck a tremendous curling effort past Andersen, only for the Charlton keeper to get a fingertip to the ball and turn it against the bar. Just before the half-time whistle sounded, Joey Cole raced on to a pass from Tiago causing Charlton keeper Anderson to dive at his feet to save. Although he got down well, the ball deflected away from him and straight to Eidur Gudjohnsen, but it came back too quickly for him and he could only put the chance wide. The 52nd minute saw Glen Johnson cross for John Terry, but his header was just too high and grazed the wrong side of the crossbar. Two minutes later Chelsea had a fair claim for a penalty turned down after Tiago was sent tumbling by Charlton's Konchesky, the referee waiving away the appeals. Moments after, Cudicini was alert and showed his prowess when he dived full stretch to keep out a shot from Holland. In the 67th minute, Jose Mourinho made a double substitution, bring off Johnson and Tiago and replacing them with Jarosik and Forssell. Although Chelsea had stepped up a gear and were pressing hard, it seemed that nothing would go right for them. Cole had a couple of chances, but they came to nothing. Meanwhile, in the 82nd minute, Lenny Pidgeley replaced Cudicini in the Chelsea goal. Within moments, he was forced to get down low to scramble the ball away, the danger passing away much to the relief of all with Chelsea in their hearts. In the dying moments of the game, Super Frank Lampard burst through the middle and was heading straight for goal when he was tripped on the edge of the box. A generous referee obliged a hungry crowd and pointed to the spot. When Claude Makelele stepped forward at least half the crowd had the feeling that he would miss, and miss he did, the goalkeeper parrying well. Fortunately, he followed up and hit the rebound home to score his first for Chelsea and the only goal of the game. Once the match was over, the party began and the supporters were still in the stadium at least 90 minutes after the final whistle was blown. Before John Terry received the Premiership trophy, he poignantly presented 1950s Chelsea captain Roy Bentley with the 1955 Championship trophy in front of the Chelsea faithful, an honour he wasn't accorded when he originally led his side to the league title.

Manchester United. A.W.3-1. Tiago, Gudjohnsen, Cole
Att: 67,832
Ref: G Poll. Date: 10.05.05
Chelsea: Cudicini, Johnson (Jarosik), Carvalho, Huth, Gallas, Geremi, Tiago, Makelele, Lampard, Cole (Grant), Gudjohnsen (Morais). Non-playing subs: Cech, Forssell
Report: Chelsea were graciously accorded a 'guard of honour' by the home players as they entered the pitch, and went into this game with their heads held high as champions. However, it was Manchester United who had the first chance when

Ronaldo let fly with a long-range effort, Carlo Cudicini equal to the shot and turning it around the post. From the corner, Rooney's ball was touched in by van Nistelrooy despite claims from the Chelsea defence that it was offside. Referee Poll turned away the protests and the goal stood – 1-0 to United. Chelsea restarted and kept pressing and, in the 16th minute, their persistence paid off. Picking up the ball some 35 yards out, Tiago took it forward and hit a shot past a motionless Carroll in the United goal that went in off the right-hand post. The Chelsea support went into raptures as the home fans fell silent. The game was quite evenly matched with both sides trying to build chances and not to rush things. In the 34th minute, Ricardo Carvalho showed his class, intercepting van Nistelrooy before he had the chance to strike. Six minutes later, Eidur Gudjohnsen put Joe Cole through but his shot from 20 yards went the wrong side of the post. Just before the break, Rooney looked to have scored but Carvalho was on hand to clear. The second half began with Gudjohnsen putting Cole through and Carroll diving bravely to stop him, in the process injuring the Chelsea player. After receiving treatment, however, Cole played on. Moments later, he was in the thick of the action, passing to Johnson, the defender was unable to convert the chance. From this, the ball was sent up towards the Chelsea goal where van Nistelrooy was waiting to pounce. Once again, Cudicini was quick off the mark and, like his opposite number had done earlier, intercepted bravely by diving at the attacker's feet. In the 51st minute, Claude Makelele who had been involved with a couple of the United players, picked up a booking for dissent after William Gallas committed a foul. Rooney hit the ball just over the bar. A minute later, Chelsea had a free-kick in a similar position outside the United box. Robert Huth strode up and fired a cannon-like shot that hit a brave United wall, and the chance went by. Chelsea then had a let off when United's Fletcher smashed a shot off the bar with Cudicini well beaten. In the 60th minute, Tiago picked up the ball and put Gudjohnsen clean through on goal. As Carroll raced to meet him, the Iceman coolly chipped it over the advancing keeper to score his 16th goal of the season and send the Chelsea supporters wild with delight. Four minutes later, Super Frank Lampard received a booking for a foul. Gallas was unlucky when, after charging down a loose ball, it rebounded off him and just over the United bar. In the 72nd minute, Jiri Jarosik replaced Glen Johnson and, a minute later, Gallas became the third Chelsea player to be booked and, because he showed dissent, the kick was moved ten yards nearer to the Chelsea goal. When it was eventually taken, Scholes' effort was just wide. With eight minutes left, Super Frank Lampard stole the ball as United tried to bring it out and sent in a cross that Cole converted, albeit from a position that was suspiciously offside, but the goal stood. By the time Nuno Morais replaced Gudjohnsen to make his debut, the 'Manchester' section of the crowd had diminished by at least half. When the second Chelsea debutant of the evening, Anthony Grant, became a 90th minute replacement for Joe Cole, the home crowd was down to single figures. It was a brilliant display from Jose Mourinho's side and the Chelsea away support's best vocal performance of the season. In winning, Chelsea set a new Premiership record of winning 94 points and 29 games.

Newcastle United. A.D.1-1. Lampard (pen)
Att: 52,326
Ref: H Webb. Date: 15.05.05
Chelsea: Cudicini, Johnson, Carvalho, Huth, Geremi, Jarosik (Watt), Makelele, Tiago, Lampard, Cole (Morais), Gudjohnsen (Oliveira). Non-playing subs: Cech, Grant
Report: Chelsea were once again treated to a guard of honour at St James' Park and they were joined by former Blue Celestine Babayaro as they milked the generous applause of the Newcastle players and supporters. The match started slowly with a strange lack of atmosphere emanating from the home areas of the ground. Geordie hopes were raised in the 17th minute when Milner got past Carvalho to send in a cross for Shearer, but Geremi did well and cleared proficiently. Jiri Jarosik was the first Chelsea player to get a shot on target, his poor effort not coming until just after the half-hour mark. A minute later Newcastle counter-attacked and won a corner after Carlo Cudicini saved well from Milner's ball. From the corner a static defence could only watch helplessly as the ball came off Geremi and went in the net. Chelsea restarted and within a minute Eidur Gudjohnsen was brought down in the penalty box by Babayaro. Super Frank Lampard stepped up and, even though he seemed to lose his footing, smashed the ball home and the game was again level. It was now a question of whether Chelsea could keep the Newcastle score down to one. Four minutes before the break, Joe Cole was booked for playing on after the whistle was blown. The half ended, but not before Cudicini went to his right to stop a long-range drive from Shearer. The second half started with Chelsea on the back foot. Ambrose got down the Chelsea left and put the ball across, the Newcastle front men unable to connect. Robert Huth conceded a corner before Glen Johnson was beaten by his man and another United cross was sent in. Chelsea looked as though they might be rocking and momentarily lost their rhythm. In the 59th minute Tiago was booked for a foul, with Ricardo Carvalho following immediately after he prevented Newcastle taking a quick free-kick. Cudicini was again on hand to deny Milner and Kluivert. At the other end, Gudjohnsen forced Newcastle keeper Given into action as Chelsea looked to win all three points. Geremi picked up a booking 12 minutes from time, and six minutes later Gudjohnsen made way for Filipe Oliveira. With a minute left, Cole was replaced by Nuno Morais and, after failing to convert a chance to win the game, Jarosik made way for Steven Watt. As the whistle sounded for the end of the game, Chelsea celebrated reaching another milestone in achieving a Premiership record of having conceded a mere 15 goals all season.

We all followed the Chelsea... ON TO VICTORY